The Gourmet's
Guide to London

The Gourmet's Guide to London

ELAINE HALLGARTEN
AND
LINDA COLLISTER

photographs by Anthony Blake

VERMILION
LONDON

First published 1992 by Vermilion
an imprint of Ebury Press
Random Century House
20 Vauxhall Bridge Road
London SW1V 2SA

British Library Cataloguing in Publication Data

A catalogue record for this book is available from the British Library.

ISBN 0-09-177073-4

A Jill Norman Book

Filmset by SX Composing Ltd, Rayleigh, Essex
Printed and bound in Singapore by Kyodo Printing

Contents

ELAINE HALLGARTEN is the author of eight cookery books ranging in subject matter from cooking with alcohol to children's cookery. She has been a freelance contributor to magazines in Britain, the United States, Canada, Hong Kong and Israel, generally on food-related topics but also on travel and topics of general consumer interest. She is married to wine shipper, Peter Hallgarten, who, like her, enjoys good food and wine in the company of friends, interests which their three children share. Hobbies include travel, theatre and music.

LINDA COLLISTER trained as a cook at the Cordon Bleu cookery school before moving to the renowned Ecole de Cuisine La Varenne in Paris, where she gained the Grande Diplôme and was responsible for researching and testing recipes. Back in London, she spent six years as cookery editor at *Woman and Home* magazine before becoming a freelance cookery writer, contributing to magazines in Britain and the United States. She is a keen swimmer. Unlike Elaine, Linda is not a Londoner – she comes from East Anglia.

Introduction

How lucky we are to have had the opportunity to enjoy this wonderful taste of London – to sample so many different foods and *en passant* to meet so many interesting people. This was brought home to us when, in the course of one wet Monday, we explored the East End and had a lassi for elevenses and a quick bite of a spicy aubergine Thai dish for lunch. We followed this with a taste of pickled cucumber and a gefilte fish ball and rounded off the morning with a super apricot and banana crumble. Not, perhaps, everyone's idea of a fun day, but anything goes in the pursuit of good food.

In our quest we have explored as many highways and byways as possible, but we are only sorry we weren't able to follow through all the leads we had. In the end we were defeated by time and the space available. As we thought it was important to write with first-hand knowledge of all the shops and restaurants we describe, we have covered many miles and eaten much food, good and bad. What is sandwiched between these covers is a highly personal look at London's food. We hope it will be to your taste but *chacun à son goût*.

Our criteria for inclusion have been best of genre and best value for money. Also included are the most interesting examples of each category and obviously anything unique (which has sometimes defied categorisation).

We are, of course, aware that things change rapidly in the food world and inevitably some of the businesses mentioned will have changed hands, closed down or acquired a new chef by the time it takes the book to reach the shelves. However, we have done our best to make the book as accurate as possible. We would welcome any information about changes and also ideas for new entries for future editions.

Symbols have been avoided for the sake of simplicity, apart from the restaurants, where a rough guide to price is indicated, as are the credit cards which are accepted. We have included a by no means definitive guide to public transport. London is so huge we felt it would be practical to divide our directory into five sections: Central, North West, North East, South West and South East and we have categorised our entries in these areas – albeit somewhat arbitrarily in some cases. The Central section is that covered by Zone 1 of the underground.

We deplore those establishments run for the convenience of the staff rather than the patrons – for example, museum cafés which close at 4.30, thus preventing you from enjoying a cup of tea at teatime; and we abhor the British disease of suffering in silence instead of voicing a complaint. Cheap food is not always the bargain it seems, and it may be trite but it is true to say that you usually get what you pay for.

Writing this book has reinforced our belief that there is plenty of good food in London. You just have to know where to look. We hope this will help you to find it too.

Acknowledgments

We are blessed with many good friends who share our interest in food, and we would like to thank them for taking an enormous amount of trouble to furnish us with the many names and addresses which sent us on our fascinating journey. We are indebted to the following for their good taste and excellent advice: Lucille Barber, Maggie Black, Dorothy Brown, Derek Cooper, Rosemary Dale, Anna Del Conte, Roz Denny, Audrey Ellison, Sarah Jane Evans, Brigitte Friis, Aileen Hall, Lisa Hallgarten, Simon Hallgarten, Cecile Harris, Antoinette Hart, Helene Hodge, Anne Johnson, Gareth Jones, Celia Leigh, Keren Leigh, Gerard McCarten, Kathleen Miodownik, Sallie Morris, Jann Nielson, Penny Noble, Sarah Pierce, Arlene Rabin, Jessica Rabin, Sylvia Ring, Claudia Roden, Caroline Schuck, Hannah Singer, Tricia Sleigh, Cathy Smith, Marlena Spieler, Robert Stack, Carola Zentner.

❧ *Bakers and Pâtissiers* ❧

Although the British have long been renowned for their baking, the best cakes and pastries in London are to be found in continental establishments. French, Hungarian, Portuguese, Greek and Middle Eastern pâtissiers seem to have stolen a march on us. We do, however, have an *embarras de richesses*, for despite our dedicated and tireless research we have been hard put to nominate a favourite in this category because there are so many superlative pâtisseries. And these aren't just the shops at which to buy sweet and savoury baked goods, but many are much-loved places of refreshment which are invariably crowded not only with the archetypal tea-shop clientele but also with a new, appreciative generation of young customers.

Cake decorating is a particularly British art and we have discovered some fine craftswomen in this field who can turn sugar into 'such stuff as dreams are made on'.

The following entries from other sections may also be of interest for the bread and pastries they sell: Aziz Baba Deli Pastahanesi; Baily Lamartine; Bumblebee Natural Food Store; Monmouth Coffee House; Neal's Yard Dairy; Neal's Yard Wholefood Warehouse; Newens – the Original Maids of Honour Tearoom; Rippon Cheese Stores; Les Specialités St Quentin; Tom's; La Touraine; Wholefood.

Central

JANE ASHER PARTY CAKES

24 Cale Street, SW3
071 584 6177

Station South Kensington underground

You've seen the books about the cakes, now here they are for real – Jane Asher has opened a shop to give us the chance to let our wildest fantasies flourish in cake decoration. Whatever you want by way of a message ('Sod off, birthday boy' was ordered by one genteel Chelsea lady) or crazy shape (a Disney castle, all turreted and moated, complete with Cinderella and Prince Charming) is yours for the ordering. A team of pastry

Bus 14, 45a, 49, 219

Open Mon–Sat 0900–1800

chefs and decorators will face any challenge, it seems, and with Jane's sense of fun and imagination nothing is beyond their capabilities. Seasonal wedding cakes are a speciality – for summer a cascade of roses with bees and butterflies on a pale yellow base; autumn has a pale beige background to leaves, nuts and berries. Each cake comes signed by Jane Asher herself. If you want to bake your own cake but need a little help with decorations they will create just what you want – special figures, flowers or animals.

BAGATELLE BOUTIQUE

44 Harrington Road, SW7
071 581 1551

Station South Kensington underground

Bus 30, 74

Open Mon–Sat 0800–2000
Sun 0800–1500

We have an octogenarian friend who travels all the way from Hampstead to South Ken to buy pâtisserie here. It is chic as only a French shop can be and the Lenôtre-trained pâtissier fills the counters and window with utterly divine concoctions. There are tartes and gâteaux with bavarois, mousses, some topped with caramel – it's paradise on earth for lovers of fine pâtisserie; and breads to eat with cheese such as grenobloix aux noisettes, benoitton aux raisins. At four in the afternoon it is full of French mums and school-children from the near-by Lycée enjoying pains au chocolat, brioches or goûté – the teatime equivalent of marmite sandwiches for French kids. Savoury items and chocolates are made by a small company in Paris. They can cater your party: phone 081 453 1340 or 081 965 2002.

THE BEIGAL BAKE

159 Brick Lane, E1
071 729 0616

Station Aldgate East underground

Bus 8, 15, 25, 40, 67, 253

Open 24 hours a day, every day of the year, except during Passover

Whether you spell them beigels, bagels or bai-gels, they have lately found a new lease of life in the burgeoning bagel bakeries all over London. In the late nineteenth century Brick Lane was the centre of the newly arrived Jewish community, mainly from Eastern Europe, who brought with them this curious round roll with the hole in the middle which is first boiled and then baked. This gives it its distinctive texture. Today Brick Lane is home to more recent immigrants from the Indian sub-continent (hence the number of Indian restaurants, shops and mosques along the street), but this reminder of its Jewish past remains. An estimated seven million bagels leave the shop each year – no won-der, since it never closes and has queues of hungry customers all through the night. The three women working behind the counter stuff smoked salmon, chopped herring and cream cheese into the bagels like they are going out of fashion. Bagels are arguably the best in town, certainly the cheapest. Other items on sale include first-class rye and black bread, chocolate éclairs and 'mille feur' (*sic*). On Saturday nights an enterprising gent sells Sunday newspapers outside for the late-night punters.

CANNELLE

166 Fulham Road, SW10
071 370 5573

Station South Kensington underground

Bus 14

Open Mon–Thur 0830–1900
Fri–Sat 0830–1900
Sun 0900–1830

Pâtissier, traiteur, chocolatier *par élégance*, having trained with Paris's greatest, Gaston Lenôtre. The window has to be the best in London – a small glass box, like a top jeweller's, with a dish of jewel-like sweets wrapped in foil. Inside it is white and plain, with one vivid, dramatic vase of unusual blooms on the floor, then dull counters with exquisite pâtisserie. It really looks like a hat shop – certainly everything looks pretty enough to wear! There are honeys and preserves and petits fours, with a small range of quiches, cheeses, pâtés, canapés, terrines. Baskets of pains au chocolat, croissants, Danish pastries – all to eat in with tea, coffee (cappuccino), hot chocolate or to take out, along with filled baguettes and sandwiches.

Clarke's (see page 12)

CLARKE'S

122 Kensington Church Street, W8
071 229 2190

Station Notting Hill Gate underground

Bus 27, 28, 31, 52, 52a

Open Mon–Fri 0800–2000
Sat 0900–1600

MAISON BERTAUX

28 Greek Street, W1
071 437 6007

Station Leicester Square/ Tottenham Court Road underground

Bus 14, 24, 29, 176

Open Mon–Sat 0900–2030
Sun 0930–1300 and 1500–2030

MAISON BOUQUILLON

41 Moscow Road, W2
071 229 2107

Station Bayswater underground

Bus 7, 15, 27, 36

Open Mon–Sat 0830–2130
Sun 0830–2030

The huge baskets in the window are overflowing with bread from Sally Clarke's ovens – an offshoot of the restaurant next door. There are many unusual varieties, with sour dough, rye, raisin nut, baguettes – a treasure trove for lovers of fine bread. The shop stocks Clarke's own preserves, truffles and chocolates, biscuits, cakes and a good range of Neal's Yard Dairy's superb cheeses. There's also a selection of teas (Whittard's), coffee (Monmouth Street) and good oils and vinegars (including balsamic). You can sample the bakery items *in situ* with a cup of coffee, fresh English apple juice, or teas (herbal too).

Soho habitués will argue fervently over the merits of their favourite spot for coffee and pâtisserie – and the two names most mentioned are Valérie (page 14) and Bertaux. In the pursuit of fair play you should try both and make up your own mind. The original family no longer runs Bertaux, but the new proprietor, mindful of the traditions, strives to maintain the fine reputation. Aficionados praise the butter-made pastry at this old (1871) Soho landmark. The slightly chaotic air adds to the charm, whether you sit upstairs or down – or even outside in good weather. There are several almondy things, their best seller being an almond croissant, but all tastes can be satisfied, with a constant stream of freshly baked goods arriving from the kitchen behind the shop.

The products of this pâtisserie could be featured in an architectural magazine as well as a food journal, so grand are their fruit tarts and gâteaux. On a more modest scale are the marzipan frivolities and other small pastries – all made with finest ingredients, only butter pastry. Lessiters' ice cream is on sale. There's a Spanish as well as French slant, reflecting the two nationalities of the owners, and this is to be found in the small charcuterie cabinet, which offers sausages, cheeses, tortillas and serrano ham. Wedding cakes are made to order in all shapes and sizes and delivery is available on large orders. If you can't wait to eat these delights, they are available with a cup of coffee at Le Montmartre next door.

Also at 22 Vivian Avenue, NW4

MAISON SAGNE

105 Marylebone High Street, W1
071 935 6240

Station Baker Street/Bond Street underground

Bus 2a, 2b, 13, 18, 27, 30, 74, 113, 159

Open Mon–Fri 0900–1200 (coffee) 1200–1500 (lunch) 1500–1645 (tea) closes at 1700
Sat 0900–1300

A tea salon with wonderful murals, chandeliers and looking glasses (definitely not mirrors) – rather like visiting the rue Royale in Paris – whose owners have been making everything in their old-fashioned ovens on the premises since 1921. The continental touch is apparent not only in the elegant décor but also in the exquisite French pastries, the beautifully decorated cakes and the masses of marzipan (with seasonal shapes), chocolates, for which they are well known, petits fours and sweets. Brioches, croissants, old-fashioned cakes and excellent Danish pastries to eat in or take away. There's no minimum charge at lunch; the short menu offers omelettes and salads (highly recommended), vol-au-vents, pasta dishes, frankfurters and potato salad. Photos behind the counter bear witness to Sagne's popularity with visiting celebrities (it's close to the BBC). Service is very genteel. Telephone orders can be collected.

NEAL'S YARD BAKERY

6 Neal's Yard, WC2
071 836 5199

Station Covent Garden/ Leicester Square underground

Bus 14, 19, 22b, 24, 29, 38, 176

Open Mon–Fri 1030–1730
Sat 1030–1630
until 1900 during summer

There's a slight feeling of 70s hippies about this co-operative bakery cum café, with a shop downstairs and scrubbed pine tables aloft. The three women bakers start operations at midnight and their bread is all handmade with organic flour and purified water. This is one of the few places not to use sugar in the bread – which ranges through sunflower, three seeds, sour dough to cheese and herb. Everything is vegetarian, including the quiche, soup, beanburgers and the scones, biscuits and cakes, all of which can be taken away or taken upstairs (self-service), where tea and coffee, including barley cup and dandelion coffee, are served. It's slightly eccentric, but very pleasant.

PATISSERIE BLISS

428 St John Street, EC1
071 837 3720

Station Angel underground

Bus 4, 19, 30, 38, 43, 56, 73, 171, 214, 263a

Open Mon–Fri 0800–2000
Sat and Sun 0900–1800

What's in a name? This is surely the most aptly named place in town, for blissful it undoubtedly is. Those almond croissants, the brioches, the pain aux raisins, to say nothing of the lemon tart, cheesecakes and the particularly good carrot cake. The shop is small, but there are a few tables at the back for those who can't wait to sample the product. Cheese and herb bread, ciabatta and a country loaf are made with unbleached and untreated flours. Pork sausage and marmalade is just one of the unusal sandwich fillings. There are eleven different kinds of tea and cappuccino, espresso or filter coffee is served. Friendly staff.

PATISSERIE VALERIE

44 Old Compton Street, W1
071 437 3466

Station Leicester Square/
Tottenham Court Road
underground

Bus 14, 24, 29, 176

Open Mon–Fri 0800–2000
Sat 0800–1900
Sun 1000–1730

This establishment describes itself as a favourite hangout for starving artisans and journalists, but you need not be in either of these groups to enjoy the slightly bohemian feel of the place. The light snacks such as toasted sandwiches and savouries have to be a front for the real purpose of your visit – for the excellent coffee and mouth-watering pâtisserie – all baked on the premises. For breakfast you can choose from the 'morning goods' such as almond croissant or brioche. The fruit-laden tarts which sparkle like jewels in the window alongside the lavish gâteaux are perhaps more suited to morning coffee or afternoon tea – either there or at home.

Pâtisserie Valerie

PECHON

127 Queensway, W2
071 229 0746

Station Bayswater
underground

Bus 7, 15, 27, 36

Open Sun–Sat 0800–1900
including all Bank Holidays.
Closed Christmas and Easter

A busy shop (one of several in the family), which sells a large selection of breads made by traditional methods. The flavour and keeping qualities result from slow mixing and long fermentation and the sixty varieties include pain de campagne, pain brié, walnut bread and Auvergnat. Traditional French pâtisserie specialities include madeleines and Brittany sablés, Gugelhopf and large decorated gâteaux. Mondose chocolates are sold. Service is brusque (well, French, actually) both in the shop and the adjoining tea salon, which serves light snacks.

Also at 27 Kensington Church Street, W8, 071 937 9574
Pierre Pechon at 4 Chepstow Road, W2, 071 229 5289

North West

CARMELLI BAKERIES

128 Golders Green Road, NW11
081 455 3063

Station Golders Green
underground

Bus 83, 183

Open Mon–Wed 0700–2300
Thur 0700 through to Fri 0700
From sundown Sat evening through to Sun until 2300

This is north-west London's answer for the insomniac bagel eater (there are several for east Londoners too). The bagels are wonderful, and always fresh as they constantly roll off the production line (in full view). Buy them filled with smoked salmon for instant noshing. Pastries savoury and sweet, poppy-seed rolls, cholla and other breads are all good.

LE CONNAISSEUR

49 Charlbert Street, NW8
071 722 7070

Station St John's Wood
underground

Bus 13, 46, 82, 113

Open Mon–Fri 0800–1800
Sat 0800–1700
Sun 1000–1300

There are six pâtissiers hard at work in the basement of this small shop, baking magnificent *pièces montées* – like croquembouche – for special occasions. For ordinary everyday there are Sacher torte and Linzer torte and, perhaps surprisingly for a continental bakers, pecan pie. The bread is highly rated. Biscuits and chocolates – for Easter and Christmas – all made on the premises.

DANIEL'S BAGEL BAKERY

13 Hallswelle Parade,
Finchley Road, NW11
081 455 5826

Station Golders Green
underground

Bus 13, 26, 260

Open Mon–Wed 0700–2100
Thur 0700–2200
Fri 0700–1500

An American friend declares these to be the best bagels in London – which just goes to show the passions which this little round roll with a hole arouse, since others hotly proclaim those from Brick Lane, Carmelli, Ridley Road (see pages 10, 15, 20) to be the ultimate. *Chacun à son bagel* – we can only suggest you try them all and make up your own mind. Here Danny makes a selection of other pastries and cakes (all under the Beth Din), including 'morning goods' like scones, Danish pastries, pain au chocolat and cholla, platzels and so on.

DOMINIQUE'S

218 West End Lane, NW6
071 435 3703

Station West Hampstead
underground and BR

Bus 28, 159, C11

Open Sun–Sat 0900–1900

Everything French, everything homemade is Dominique's claim. The pâtisserie is inviting with lots of fruit tarts, gâteaux and good bread – sticks, rings, rolls and croissants sweet and plain. Light snacks are served throughout the day in the coffee shop, and the menu is changed daily.

FORREST THE BAKER

75 Uxbridge Road, W12
081 743 2675

Station Shepherd's Bush
underground

Bus 12, 207, 260

Open Mon–Sat 0700–1800

A very English bakery, with a marvellous smell of freshly baked bread from the ovens at the rear of the shop, it offers a tremendous selection – granary, French sticks, Greek daktyla, scofa bread, cottage loaves, bloomers. Everything you could want for an old-fashioned tea party – with tea loaves, scones, rock cakes, fancy cakes, cream doughnuts, jam tarts, sponge slices and cakes, custard tarts, mince slices, apple pies all there. Irresistible bread pudding, just like Granny made, will confirm that you are back in the nursery.

HENDON BAGEL BAKERY

55–7 Church Street, NW4
081 203 6919

Station Hendon Central
underground

Bus 143, 183

Open Mon–Thur 0800–2400
Fri 0800–1500
Sat open 1900–Sun 2400

A steaming vat at the back of the shop bears witness to the activities of this kosher bakery. Bagels are first boiled and then baked. There's a delicatessen attached (French kosher to be precise). The bakery produces a full range of Jewish-style baked goods – platzels, cholla, poppy-seed rolls and of course bagels, which you can buy filled with a variety of herrings, smoked salmon and other delicatessen items. The cakes look somewhat lurid. Like other bagel shops, they cater for starving somnambulists by staying open all night on Saturday.

LISBOA PATISSERIE

57 Golborne Road, W10
081 968 5242

Station Westbourne Park
underground and BR

Bus 7, 15, 28, 31, 52

Open Tues–Sun 0800–2000
(and Bank Holidays and
Christmas)

The local Portuguese community greatly appreciate this home from home, where they can enjoy fresh cream cakes, filled croissants, almond cakes and the yummiest custard tarts imaginable. There are tables, inside and out, which are always crowded, but it's well worth waiting to have a tea or coffee and sample the pastries, or a light meal of typically Portuguese dishes like prawn rissole or meat croquette. Aficionados will recognise pão de deus (God's bread) and at weekends they bake special Danish pastries with coconut and sugar.

LOUIS PATISSERIE HAMPSTEAD

32 Heath Street, NW3
071 435 9908

Station Hampstead
underground

Bus 46, 268

Open Sun–Sat 0900–1830
(tearoom 0930–1800)

The story goes that Louis came from Hungary in 1956 with other refugees to work in the mines here. When they arrived, the local work force went on strike and the government was obliged to compensate the outsiders. With his gratuity Louis started his pâtisserie business and Saturday morning coffee here is a regular date for many locals. The pâtissier and his creations remain Hungarian – dobos, pischinger, poppy seed and fresh cream cakes and breads, brioches, croissants and Danish pastries. If you need anything more, the bonus could be the chance to sit next to one of Hampstead's many famous residents. Very friendly service.

Also at 12 Harben Parade, Swiss Cottage, NW3 (no longer under the same ownership, but the pastries come from the Hampstead bakery). Morning coffee, afternoon tea and continental breakfasts all provide ample excuse for sampling their wares. Goulash soup is a staple on the menu, with salads, light snacks and ice creams. Cakes and pastries can be made to order.

MAISON BLANC

102 Holland Park Avenue,
W11
071 221 2494

Station Holland Park
underground

Bus 12, 94

Open Mon–Fri 0800–2000
Sat 0730–1930

Fans of this Oxford-based pâtisserie will be thrilled to find they can buy their toothsome delicacies in London. Everything is baked in the French way ('They have the touch,' the English manageress, married to the French pâtissier, assured us). The specialities are bonne femme, which is sugar pastry with apricots and crème légère, caramelised, and coquelin – a hazelnut, almond and chocolate sponge. The fruit tarts are ravishing. Recommended breads are seigle and paysan, though the croissants were surprisingly unexceptional. For parties there are petits fours salées, canapés and many other tasty possibilities.

MIMMA

414 Harrow Road, W9
071 266 4224

Bus 18, 28, 31, 36

Open Sun–Sat 0800–2000

OLYMPIC BAKERS PATISSERIE

281 Camden High Street, NW1
071 482 1649/267 3427

Station Camden Town underground

Bus 27, 134, 135, 214, C2

Open Mon–Sat 0830–1800
Sun 0900–1800
coffee lounge Sun–Sat 0930–1700

PRIMROSE PATISSERIE

136 Regent's Park Road, NW1
071 722 7848

Station Chalk Farm underground
Primrose Hill BR

Bus 31, 168

Open Tues–Sun 0900–1900

VICTORIA BAKERY

83 Barnet High Street, Barnet
081 449 0790

The next-door deli of the same name has been there for some time, but this corner continental pâtisserie/gelateria is a more recent attraction. In a somewhat bleak stretch of the Harrow Road it is very welcome. The pretty shop has a few tables and a counter full of tempting pâtisserie (including the lightest pastel de nata – custard tart). Everything is baked on the premises. They sell Marine Ices (see page 126) and you can sit and enjoy a good cup of espresso while sampling the work of the Portuguese pâtissier. You may have to queue for a seat, but persevere as it's all worth waiting for. They make special cakes to order.

Since this strip of Camden became an extension of near-by Camden Lock market, most of the old (and useful) shops have transmogrified into t-shirt and clothes emporia. Happily this indispensable Greek bakery stayed and gave itself a facelift, to include a small coffee lounge where you can enjoy the many delicacies which are on sale out front. These include wonderful honey and nut concoctions (some in miniature versions for cocktail parties), almond slices, flaounes, baklava, kadaifi and various filo pastries. Among the breads are daktyla and huge sesame loaves. There are savoury pastries and pies and the take-away counter has some filled rolls.

Polish pâtisserie may not generally be in the top league of this art form, but here it certainly wins all the prizes. This small, homely shop is invariably busy, for the locals have a nose for something really special. The fruit-packed apple strudel and wondrous cheese cake (even better than homemade) are much to be recommended, as are the Polish apple cake and many other enticing gâteaux. There are light snacks and salads, good coffee and tea – to eat in or take away. Marvellous breads complete the picture.

The old awning reads 'Choc bunnies and hot cross buns' above this busy shop run by the fifth generation of master bakers. There's nothing 'artificial' or bought in, they say. Beautifully decorated lattice-top Bakewell tarts, nutty almond rings, bun-loaf 'people', Chelsea and Bath buns, tiny custard tarts

Station High Barnet
underground + bus

Bus 34, 84a, 234, 263

Open Mon–Sat 0800–1700

heavily nutmegged, cinnamon puffs and at Easter homemade Easter eggs, bunnies and chocs, as promised outside. Cakes and bread (twenty different types) made from untreated, unbleached flour. Wholemeal bread made from 100 per cent stoneground (some organic). Wedding cakes to order.

North East

DUNN'S

6 The Broadway, Crouch End, N8
081 340 1614

Station Finsbury Park underground and BR + bus

Bus 14a, 41, W2, W7

Open Mon–Fri 0745–1730
Sat 0700–1730

For more than a century the same family of master bakers has plied its trade here, the London bloomer and cottage loaves a monument to tradition. The doughnuts, iced rolls and custard tarts are always hot favourites and croissants made an appearance thirty years ago, way ahead of more trendy bakers. There is a formidable display of fourteen wedding cakes in all shapes and sizes, which can be made to order.

NADELL PATISSERIE

Units 4 & 5, Angel House, White Lion Street, N1
071 833 2461

Station Angel underground

Bus 4, 19, 43, 153, 279

Open Mon–Fri 0900–1700

It is unlikely you have not tasted Michael Nadell's fine pâtisserie if you have eaten around town because his superlative wares are bought by many restaurateurs and caterers as well as discriminating party givers. He learnt his craft at Westminster Hotel school and is now passing on his knowledge to new generations who come to train with him in Islington. He started with three apprentices and now has fifty-three, who spend four months on each of nine sections, at the end of which they get a diploma. Private customers are welcome and they will make novelty cakes for any occasion. All you need to do is to phone for the brochure and then discuss your requirements. They can do a cake for up to 1,000 people, but more modest sizes are just as carefully considered. It is not only fancy cakes though – there are savoury and boulangerie items, and the mouth-watering list will tempt you to indulgent au chocolat, claire fontaine, vacherin, galette des poires caramel. You can put on inches just reading the brochure. Once ordered you can pick up when you like (on Friday for Saturday orders, but Sunday they are open for collection).

QUEEN OF TARTS

173 Priory Road, N8
081 340 1854

Station Hornsey BR + bus

Bus 144a, W2, W3

Open Mon–Sat 0830–1730
Sun 0800–1430

The picturesque fruit tarts are possibly the jewel in this Queen of Tarts' crown, but there are plenty of other riches among a large selection of savoury quiches, pies and pasties (many vegetarian) which are their best sellers, to cream cakes. On the whole the breads and cakes are English in style, in spite of the owner and all of the bakers being Moroccan. They are happy to produce traditional favourites – wholemeal scones, Viennese fingers, palmiers and some rather lurid-coloured small cakes.

RIDLEY HOT BAGEL BAKERY

13 Ridley Road, E8
071 241 1047

Station Dalston Kingsland BR

Bus 22a, 56, 67, 149

Open Sun–Sat 24 hours

Lurking with intent in the middle of the night might be a punishable offence, but when the intent is nothing more sinister than the purchase of a hot bagel, you can relax and enjoy yourself. This is just one of several London bagel bakeries where sleep walkers, shift workers and other night people can indulge their appetites for bagels and other, mainly Jewish-style, baked goods twenty-four hours a day, seven days a week. And believe it or not you are quite likely to find a queue at 2 a.m. Situated at the end of the not particularly pretty Ridley Road market, hot bagels are of course the speciality. Try them filled – great value – with smoked salmon, egg and onion mayonnaise or buy something from the deli counter to create your own nosh around the clock. There's a happy mix of different foods – Jamaican patties, Greek taramasalata, Indian samosas, Israeli felafels. No animal fats or fish oils are used in the baked products.

Yasar Halim

YASAR HALIM

495 Green Lanes, N4
081 340 8090

Station Manor House
underground
Haringey BR

Bus 29, 41, 141, 221

Open Mon 0800–2130
Tues–Sun 0800–2200

You might think you were in a street in Istanbul rather than Green Lanes, Haringey. There's a bustling crowd and an excited air on a Saturday at this wonderful Cypriot bakery, floor to ceiling with people and pastries. Alongside the staid British staples and American cheesecake you'll find pastirmali, lahmacun, plauna, skalthounia and trays of syrup-dripping sweetmeats. Everything you dream about (in baked goods at least) is there. Loads of different breads. They make cakes to order – multi-tiered wedding cakes a speciality. The adjoining shop (at 493) is a supermarket with vegetables, butchery and general groceries – but the bakery is what will make your journey worthwhile.

South West

ANNABEL

33 High Street, SW19
081 947 4326

Station Wimbledon
underground and BR

Bus 93

Open Sun–Sat 0900–1900

This is a *salon de thé* in the continental manner and the pâtisserie matches the style – very high class, very rich and very delicious. A selection of cakes, quiches, petits fours, baguettes, fancy breads and Belgian chocolates. Light meals are served.

CECIL'S BAKERY

143 Stockwell Road, SW9
071 737 6743

Station Stockwell
underground

Bus 2b, 45a, 196

Open Mon–Fri 0700–1730
Sat 0700–1700

Cecil is from Guyana and makes wonderful West Indian cakes complete with bride and groom atop – full of fruit and 'a lot of wine' the cheerful Jamaican lady explained. During the week there are ordinary English bread and cakes, but on Fridays and Saturdays there are Jamaican bread, which has a little sugar, just for flavour, and Guyanese bread, which has spice added to it. And there are West Indian cakes – cornmeal, carrot, ripe banana. Everything is baked on the premises.

CELEBRATION CAKES BY SUZELLE

10 Replingham Road,
Southfields, SW18
081 874 4616/8997

Station Southfields
underground

Bus 39

Open Mon–Fri 0900–1800
Sat 0900–1730

An ace of a place, only a long lob away from the All England Tennis Club. Susan Flatau, barrister turned pâtissière, took a City & Guilds Cake Design and Decoration course. She's rightly proud of her record for consistently winning Wandsworth's environmental health award for the cleanest food shop. Everything is made in the kitchens below by her team of young bakers. Wedding cakes are fabulous. Light meals, with a daily dish, soup, pasta, etc – or just coffee and pâtisserie, with scones and cream for tea. Wimbledon fortnight is hectic, with opening hours from 6 am 'until the traffic stops'.

DI LIETO

175 South Lambeth Road,
SW8
071 735 1997

Station Vauxhall/Stockwell
underground + bus

Bus 2a, 2b, 88, 155

Open Mon–Sat 0930–2000
Sun 1200–1700

Gino di Lieto has been baking bread in Lambeth for ten years, long before ciabatta and other Italian breads became trendy (and incidentally his ciabatta is much cheaper than most others around town). He makes English-style breads too, as well as some Italian pâtisserie – sfogliata (mille feuilles in English!) and fruit tarts. The shop is also a deli selling mostly Italian food – salamis, provolone, and so on, but the bakery is the thing to go for.

FLORIDIA PATISSERIE

224 Brixton Road, SW9
071 737 3371

Station Brixton underground
and BR

Bus 3, 59, 109, 159, 196

Open Mon–Sat 0900–1800
Sun 0900–1400

Just the place to go for your party pâtisserie – it specialises in *pièces montées* such as croquembouche, as well as pastries filled with pastry cream flavoured with liqueur, like cannolli. Given twenty-four hours' notice they can make anything you want, birthday, wedding or any special occasion cakes. The petits fours are made fresh every day and everything looks irresistible.

South East

J. F. AYRE

133 Evelina Road, Nunhead,
SE15
071 639 0648

Station Nunhead BR

Bus P12

Open Mon–Sat 0600–1730

Massive bakers in true British style – Vincent Ayre is a sixth-generation baker – and very proud of their bread. Ninety gallons of cream are used each week in cakes and pastries. They also make filled rolls, hot pasties and pies, plus, to order, wedding and birthday cakes. They do 'football' look-alikes – cakes decorated with white and dark chocolate for your son's treat. Everything is made on the premises (also handmade truffles). Go at weekends to see the business at its best.

Also at 114 Westmount Road, SE9, 081 850 1786

CELEBRATION CAKE CRAFT

86 Lee High Road, SE13
081 297 0798

Bus 21, 178

Open Mon–Tues, Thur–Sat
0930–1700
Wed 0945–1700

Everything for the home cake decorator and baker: tins and cake stands to hire; all decorations, ribbons, equipment, regal ice, silk flowers and everything to beautify your cake are for sale. If you haven't the skill to do it yourself, this firm will ice your cake – in royal, Australian or soft icing. They will also make the cake to your choice of sponge, Madeira, rich and light fruit cakes. They run classes in cake decoration, given by qualified adult education teachers.

H. HIRST & SON

227 Deptford High Street,
SE8
081 692 2053

Station Deptford BR

Bus 1, 188

Open Mon–Fri 0500–1730
Sat 0500–1500

For what would appear at first glance to be an ordinary baker's shop, there is a most inviting line of different breads, some of which are supplied to various places in the area (like the Maritime Museum). Choose from mixed grain, sunflower seed, organic wholemeal, cheese and onion, as well as a range of traditional breads. The weekend trade is quiet for fancy stuff, but during the week you can buy German plum cake, chocolate fudge and hazelnut slice, mixed fruit and oatmeal slice or paradise slice. Father and son bake in their brick ovens down the road in Lewisham, where they have another shop.

Also at 350, Lewisham High Street, SE13, 081 690 2297 (Mon–Fri 0700–1700, Sat 0700–1300)

Margaret

MARGARET'S

224 Camberwell Road, SE5
071 701 1940

Station Dulwich BR + bus

Bus 12, 35, 36, 68, 171

Open Mon–Sat 0900–1700

Truly beautiful, in fact exquisite, cakes – fruit and Madeira mostly – are all made by Margaret Akrong, who used to work for Selfridges and Harrods before she opened her shop. She will make your wedding, novelty and celebration cakes (both English and West Indian style) all to order (minimum ten days). She ices her cakes in the traditional way, with handmade sugar flowers. Good news for home bakers – Margaret will decorate your own cakes.

USE YOUR LOAF

9 Turnpin Lane, SE10
081 853 2018

Station Greenwich BR

Bus 18, 286

Open Sun–Sat 0600–1900
All-night service at weekends
Bank Holidays 1000–1700

In a small lane off the covered Greenwich Craft Market (which is open only on weekends), this little shop serves thousands of hungry tourists with hot pies, pasties, pizzas and sandwiches made to order. Their normal run-of-the-mill breads are supplemented at weekends with more exotic offerings – Turkestan, olive, garlic, onion and cheese loaves, which might appeal more than the somewhat lurid gooey cakes and stodgy buns.

Butchers

Because the demand for meat has fallen for ethical, price and quality reasons, the better butchers have had to meet the challenge to survive. Out of this situation have come the Q Guild of British Specialist High Grade Butchers and The Real Meat Company, to name only two. The Q Guild looks for meat that is naturally reared and fed from the ideal breed with proper husbandry used and is concerned that the animals are correctly slaughtered and butchered. The Real Meat Company is a name you will see in many places, since a growing number of butchers buy their supplies from this source. It was set up by Gillian Metherell and Richard Guy to provide meat from animals reared under humane conditions which have not been fed growth promoters, antibiotics or hormones. They have very strict standards both in their farming practices and in the shops they supply and they regularly check for hygiene, cleanliness and friendliness of staff.

Complain where necessary and don't hesitate to ask for advice or any special service. By being demanding you will help to raise standards.

The following entries from other sections may also be of interest as they also sell meat: B & M Seafoods; Boucherie Lamartine; Chinatown Fish and Meat Market; Fish and Fowl; A. A. King.

Central

R. ALLEN & CO

117 Mount Street, W1
071 499 5831

Station Bond Street
underground

Bus 6, 7, 8, 10, 12, 13, 15, 16, 16a, 25, 73, 88, 94

Open Mon–Thur 0400–1600
Fri 0400–1700 Sat 0500–1230

Mayfair residents are indeed fortunate to have two first-class butchers side by side. Allen's is a delightfully old-fashioned shop, with fur and feather hanging outside in great abundance in season. They supply and deliver to restaurants and, like their immediate neighbours (see Baily Lamartine, page 27), have impressive opening hours. Meat and game of the finest quality are sold here.

R. Allen & Co (see page 25)

ARTHUR'S

19 Bute Street, SW7
071 589 5731

Station South Kensington underground

Bus 14, 45a, 49, 219

Open Mon–Fri 0730–1800
Sat 0730–1700

'Arthur Butcher peut préparer toutes les coupes de viande à la Française' – which says it all. You can expect to hear a lot of French here, especially when school's out – school being the Lycée Française at the end of the road. French cuts of meat are, *naturellement*, available. Meat is hung 'to perfection' – four weeks minimum. Free-range pork from The Real Meat Company, along with some lamb and beef, and they have Aberdeen Angus. They will dress your orders for dinner parties, deliver free within a six-mile radius, have account facilities – and converse in French. What more could you want? They also have game and corn-fed chickens and will obtain fish for you from Charles (see below) to whom, like sausages, they are linked.

Also Charles, 46 Elizabeth Street, SW1, 071 730 3321

R. ASBY LIMITED

32 Leadenhall Market, EC3
071 626 3871

Station Aldgate underground,
Fenchurch Street BR

Bus 5, 15, 25, 40, 42, 67,
78, 100, 253, X15

Open Mon–Fri 0400–1600

Y ou could say this is a Great British butcher, with
Scotch beef, Welsh lamb and English pork.
Established for over forty years, this is a traditional
style firm – it does everything and its jolly staff are only
too willing to advise. The Christmas turkeys are dry
plucked and properly hung and there are hams and
gammons for the holiday season. The homemade
sausages are highly recommended; bacon is cut to
order. Delivery in the City.

BAILY LAMARTINE

116 Mount Street, W1
071 499 1833

Station Bond Street
underground

Bus 6, 7, 8, 10, 12, 13, 15,
16a, 25, 73, 88, 94

Open Mon–Fri 0400–1600

E stablished in 1720 this butcher's is now part of the
Roux empire, linked to the Boucherie Lamartine
(see pages 115–16) whence the selection of pâtisserie
hails. Poilâne bread arrives twice a week. There's also a
small area for choice fresh vegetables, but meat and
poultry of the highest standards are what the shop is
really all about. Handsome black-feathered turkeys can
be ordered for Thanksgiving and Christmas. They will
deliver almost anywhere in London and outlying areas
and insomniacs will be happy to know they can buy a
lamb chop from four in the morning onwards.

BIGGLES

66 Marylebone Lane, W1
071 224 5937

Station Bond Street
underground

Bus 6, 7, 8, 10, 12, 13, 15,
16a, 25, 73, 88, 94

Open Mon–Fri 0930–1830
Sat 0930–1630

T his charming shop offers a range of traditional,
continental and exotic gourmet sausages freshly
made each day by a 'sausage craftsman'. Using only the
best natural ingredients – no artificial additives or
mechanically recovered meat – the sausages are between 85 per cent and 95 per cent pure meat. The range
includes traditional English (Cumberland, Yorkshire,
Manchester), Welsh leek, Toulouse, bratwurst,
Greek, orange, wild boar to name but a few from the
extensive list. Each day four varieties are available
cooked for take-away in a roll with condiments, and
make a very substantial snack. An interesting collection of pickles and preserves is also on sale. The proprietor (who is also the master sausage maker) is very
enthusiastic and delighted to find recipes for sausages,
however obscure.

CURNICK

170 Fulham Road, SW10
071 370 1191

Station South Kensington
underground + bus

A basket in the entrance contains a sample of the
feed the Old Springfield Farm breed eat – the
steers (hormone-free Angus cattle from their own farm
in Colgate near Crawley) graze on organic pastureland
and eat a mix of grains and seeds. Truly beautiful display of meats in window – fair prices for such quality

Bus 14, 31, 45a, C3

Open Mon–Thur 0800–1730
Sat 0800–1300

in the middle of such an expensive area. This is a very busy, if not very elegant, traditional butcher's – in business for 150 years. Old-fashioned meat, correctly hung, exquisitely butchered and carefully prepared for the oven. Game in season and a huge selection of cuts/joints, with sides of beef dangling from hooks. The staff are most helpful and will do anything within reason for you. See oxtail as you didn't think it still existed and chicken with feet on and the best rib of beef in town.

LIDGATE

110 Holland Park Avenue,
W11
071 727 8243

Station Holland Park underground

Bus 12, 94

Open Mon–Fri 0700–1800
Sat 0700–1700

Established in 1850 and still family run, here you feel you are in a real butcher's shop, festooned with awards from Smithfield and other competitions for butchers and charcuteries. David Lidgate is founding chairman of Q Guild butchers, who aim to raise standards. Farmers grow animals specifically for Lidgate's, whose policy is to buy the best organic meat without compromising on quality. Wonderful sausages include homemade bratwurst, Toulouse, Cumberland pork and many more. Mild-cure, low-salt bacons from Dorset Farm and lots of prepared meat – marinated in spices, good salamis and Parma ham, pressed English

ox tongue and home-cooked roast beef are among the many excellent meats. French escargots with garlic butter, magret of duck. Also quiches, pâtés, pork and game pies, all made on the premises. A vast selection of British farmhouse raw milk cheeses and from France etorki (ewes' milk from the Basque country). Free-range eggs by Martin Pitt, and Derek Kelly's turkeys come with a guarantee of perfection – no growth promoters or antibiotics used.

SIMPLY SAUSAGES

Hart's Corner, 341 Central Markets, Farringdon Street, EC4
071 329 3227

Station Farringdon underground and BR

Bus 55, 63, 221, 259

Open Mon–Wed, Fri 0800–'late'
Thur 0800–2000
Sat 0800–1330

'Sophisticated sausages' you could call Martin Heap's creations, which he modestly considers 'gastronomically speaking the most critically prepared' sausages to be had in London. He and his team, perched on the corner of Smithfield market, are constantly inventing new varieties, such as spicy pork with wild mushrooms for Hallowe'en, but you can regularly find beef and Guinness or duck and orange, various game sausages – venison liver with wild rabbit is a good seller – and dozens more. They are all handmade, which is why they come out all shapes and sizes and they use no artificial additives and only natural skins. They prepare stuffings for your Christmas bird, with a suggestion that you could make rather special sausage rolls from, say, the pork, prune and cognac stuffing. The shop is very busy so telephone ordering is a good idea.

SLATER & COOKE & BISNEY JONES

68 Brewer Street, W1
071 437 2026

Station Piccadilly Circus underground

Bus 3, 6, 9, 13, 14, 15, 19, 22, 38, 53, 88, 94

Open Mon–Thur 0730–1700
Fri 0730–1730
Sat 0730–1430

This shop seems at odds with the surrounding district – perhaps too modern looking, too clinical and unusually large for a Soho food shop. Prices are remarkably good given the area, and there's a great selection. A wide range of poultry – roasters, free-range chickens, guinea fowl, smoked turkey, Barbary ducks (very large ones), poussins, wood pigeon. The staff can provide just about anything you want, cut in any way you desire. Plenty of cooked meats, pâtés and sausages. They deliver in central London and a bit beyond.

WHOLEFOOD BUTCHERS

31 Paddington Street, W1
071 486 1390

This firm sells meat that conforms to Soil Association organic standards regarding stock rearing, feeding and management. All chemicals and hormone treatment are banned. There are guinea fowl, mallard, wood pigeon and venison in season, as well as goose

Station Baker Street
underground

Bus 2a, 2b, 13, 18, 27, 30,
74, 113, 159

Open Tues–Fri 0830–1800
Sat 0830–1300

eggs. Organic veal, which has suckled and grazed with its dam on organic pasture, is occasionally available. There's a range of cooked meats, faggots, black pudding, homemade pork pies and Cornish pasties and homemade sausages which are 98 per cent meat. Organic lamb and beef (mostly from Aberdeen) and range-reared pork and poultry: the chickens come with label of origin and with details of rearing and feeding. This is a traditional butcher's; highly skilled, knowledgeable, selling old-fashioned cuts and bits and pieces such as trotters, oxtail, gizzards and chicken hearts.

North West

GRAHAMS BUTCHERS

134 East End Road, N2
081 883 6187

Station East Finchley
underground + bus

Bus 143

Open Tues–Fri 0830–1730
Sat 0830–1600

Mr Mien, and his sister, Ann, have been supplying top-quality meat to the East Finchley gentry for twenty-five years and consider themselves to be traditional butchers with a modern slant. The shop lacks the gloss and glitter of other places, but the expertise and care are what matter and you will find plenty of them here. They sell Welsh premium lamb and certified Aberdeen Angus (only a handful of London butchers sell it; though many sell Aberdeen Angus beef it is not as rigorously controlled as the Certified AA). At barbecue time there are homemade sausages, marinated steaks and South African specialities such as lamb sosaties, boerreworst, droegworst (a dried sausage) and biltong, all aimed at the ex-pat South Africans in the area. In winter there are homemade pies – steak and kidney and chicken and mushroom.

QUATRO BELLA

170 Portobello Road, W11
071 221 8360

Station Ladbroke Grove
underground

Bus 15, 52, 52a

Open Mon–Thur, Sat 0800–
1800
Fri 0800–1830

Long-standing customers of the popular Bifulco's in St John's Wood were mortified when the shop closed recently. They cheered up greatly when four of the employees set up in Portobello Road doing all the same meat, poultry and sausages and the impressive range of readymade items like beef olives, lamb or chicken kebabs, kievs, stuffed peppers, and so on. They have game in season, quail all year round. They will get anything you want and prepare it whatever way you ask and they will deliver as far as Stanmore and Totteridge to the north – the south is unknown territory, but they'll try.

THE REAL MEAT COMPANY

3a Nugent Terrace, NW8
071 286 3124

Station St John's Wood/Maida
Vale underground

Bus 46, 159

Open Mon–Sat 0830–1700

Although bearing the name The Real Meat Company, this St John's Wood shop is a franchise owned by B&M Seafoods (see page 73) and so has fish as well as meat. The meat counter has homemade sausage, bacon which they cut in the shop, poultry (which has been allowed genuine access to pasture) and lamb, beef and pigs all produced by this caring company.

RICHARDSON BUTCHERS

88 Northfield Avenue, W13
081 567 1064

Station Northfields
underground

Bus E2, E3

Open Mon–Thur 0800–1730
Fri 0700–1800
Sat 0800–1600

This is a busy and very jolly shop, with friendly staff. Diplomas up and down the walls attest to Mr Richardson's expertise in his field, and as he is a member of the Q Guild you can be sure of the best quality here. He does a few ready-to-cook items like lamb rosettes, meatballs and kebabs, chicken or pork stir fry and Italian-style lambs' liver (cut into small pieces and marinaded with herbs and spices). A square sausage (Lorne, from Scotland), low-fat pork sausages and his Gold Award sausage are all made here, as are the cooked meats, pressed brisket, hams, haggis, and so on. Great-value bags of chicken or veal bones for soup and stock. Local deliveries and freezer orders.

SLOPERS POND FARM

Cockfosters Road, Hadley
Wood, Herts
081 441 3006

Open Thur–Fri 1230–1800
Sat 0900–1800

Everything sold here is produced on the farm, including venison, duck, pigeon, rabbit, partridge, hare and pheasant. Beef is free from hormones and antibiotics. The farm is just opposite Plumridge Farm, where Gedi cheese (see page 39) is produced – make it a day out in the country.

J. A. STEELE

8 Flask Walk, NW3
071 435 3587

Station Hampstead
underground

Bus 46, 268

Open Mon–Thur 0730–1730
Fri–Sat 0700–1730

Flask Walk, a pretty part of old Hampstead Village, is an appropriate setting for this butcher (established for over thirty years). They make ten different sausages including all meat (no rusk) and organic, and sell award-winning sausages made by the local firm, Corrigan's. When we visited, the osso bucco looked good and there were wonderful braising steak, Barbary duck breasts, French poulet fermier as well as English birds and game in season (free-range English and French and corn-fed). Some meat is from The Real Meat Company, including bacon, which comes in whole sides. Lots of offal. 'If we haven't got it, we'll get it,' is their motto.

R. TREVOR

110 Pitshanger Lane, W5
081 997 1922

Bus E7

Open Mon, Wed, Sat 0630–1300
Tues, Thur, Fri 0630–1200
and 1400–1800

Mr Trevor is a charming, if somewhat eccentric gentleman – eccentric only in that there is absolutely no meat on show in his spanking clean shop, with butcher's blocks that look brand new (but are many years old). Everything is scrubbed clean - 'All you need is elbow grease.' In the window are immaculate, but empty trays. Mr Trevor doesn't display any meat because he feels it is his job to know exactly what his customers want. This a real old-fashioned family business. Meat is properly hung. Scotch beef, Dutch veal, Devon lamb, free-range poultry are all waiting in the wings for Mr Trevor to make up your order.

North East

JAMES ELLIOTT

96 Essex Road, N1
071 226 3658

Station Essex Road BR

Bus 38, 56, 73, 171a

Open Mon–Sat 0730–1730

A real family-run business with lots of elderly (ninety-year-old) customers who have always shopped here. Well-hung beef and nothing frozen. They give 'proper' service and don't charge for boning out joints or chickens if that's what you want. Fresh farm cheeses are bought straight from the farm – Cashel Blue, Yarg, unpasteurised Lancashire – lots of lovely unusual handmade cheeses, plus Neal's Yard yoghurt, crème fraîche and fromage frais. Homemade preserves – fig jam, chilli pickle, lime curd. You can see sides of beef being dismembered behind the counter.

FRANK GODFREY LIMITED

7 Highbury Park, N5
071 226 2425

Station Highbury and Islington underground and BR

Bus 19, 236

Open Mon–Fri 0900–1800
Sat 0900–1700

'If we can't get it, nobody can,' proclaims Jeremy Godfrey, who is the fourth generation in this family business, and one of the few people in London certified to sell Aberdeen Angus (which will have been hung for fourteen days). Records are kept of how much is sold and who sells it, in order to maintain a tight control on this beef. They are also members of the exclusive Q Guild. They have been selling free-range pork, from Piccard's Farm, for many years – long before it became fashionable – simply because it is better. They will order free-range bacon, venison or roe, red, sika or fallow deer for you and game, including wild boar. The cabinets are full of interesting cuts and ready-to-cook items like marinated steaks and kebabs.

South West

H. J. GRIMES LIMITED

77 High Street,
Wimbledon, SW19
081 946 4347

Station Wimbledon
underground and BR

Bus 93

Open Mon–Fri 0800–1700
Sat 0800–1530

'High Class Butchers and Boucherie' is what this firm calls itself. It specialises in continental cuts – noisettes, rôti de veau, carré d'agneau, and so on – but has plenty of British produce too, with Gressingham duck and a big variety of game. They make their own sausages and prepare kebabs for barbecuing. Fresh fish from Billingsgate is at the back of the shop, with undyed haddock, salmon and trout direct from Scotland.

Over the road (at 13 High Street, 081 946 5485) there is another H. J. Grimes shop, selling meat from Natural Farms, where the animals are reared without the use of routine drugs and under a strict welfare code.

Also H. J. Grimes, 19a Leopold Road, SW19, 081 946 5834

JEFFERIES

42 Coombe Road, Norbiton,
Kingston
081 546 0453

Station Norbiton BR

Bus K2, K3

Open Mon–Tues 0700–1600
Wed 0700–1300
Thur 0700–1700
Fri 0600–1800
Sat 0600–1600

This is a family butcher's, selling certified Aberdeen Angus beef, all the fancy butchery like crowns of lamb and noisettes and also catering for the considerable Korean and Japanese community in the area. There's a whole counter just for organic meat – pork, lamb, beef and their homemade sausages – all of which are kept entirely separate from the ordinary meat. Ham and other meats are cooked on the premises and are particularly popular at Christmas time. They deliver locally and will go all over London for large enough orders.

RANDALLS

113 Wandsworth Bridge
Road, SW6
071 736 3426

Station Fulham Broadway
underground + bus

Bus 28, 295

Open Mon–Fri 0730–1800
Sat 0630–1500

Free-range, additive-free and organic meat, Scotch grass-fed beef, French duck breasts and a window full of interesting prepared meats and poultry make this a very inviting butcher's. There are marinated chicken, cubed pork in marinade, a selection of prize-winning sausages (all made in the shop), kebabs and Hawaiian chicken for barbecuing. Cold meats are cooked fresh daily.

J. SEAL

7 Barnes High Street, SW13
081 876 5118

Station Barnes Bridge BR

Bus 9

Open Mon–Tues, Thur–Fri
0630–1730
Wed 0630–1300
Sat 0630–1600

This traditional butcher is bang up to date, offering Aberdeen additive-free beef, free-range organic lamb and eggs from Martin Pitt. Cold meats, pâtés and shepherd's pie are prepared daily for the deli counter. More exotic offerings are haggis and wild boar (from Australia). And something really useful – you can buy good knives here.

South East

DRING'S

22 Royal Hill, Greenwich,
SE10
081 858 4032

Station Greenwich BR

Bus 18, 286

Open Mon–Wed, Fri–Sat
0730–1700
Thur 0730–1300

This is one of three shops in a small parade all selling good quality food (see also The Cheese Board and Food Parcels, pages 40–1 and 122). The Messrs Dring are from a long line of butchers and take great pride in their skills. Their well-hung Scotch beef (preferably on the bone) is a speciality and they report a growing interest in their free-range poultry. They make their own Cumberland sausages. No frozen meat is sold here.

B. KINGSTON

33 Dulwich Village, SE21
081 693 2952

Station North Dulwich BR

Bus 37, P4

Open Tues–Sat 0730–1700

Friendly butcher's/fishmonger's with basic choice. He makes his own fishcakes and sausages and cooks his own hams. Good calf's liver and bacon, fresh poultry. It's best to go towards the end of the week if you can. He will do any butchering, filleting and preparation to customers' specifications. Parking outside.

O'HAGANS
$AUSAGE SHOP

192 Trafalgar Road, SE10
081 858 2833

Station Maze Hill BR

Bus 177, 180, 286

Open Mon 0800–1600
Tues–Thur 0830–1730
Fri 0830–1730
Sat 0800–1800

'Monosodium glutamate is banned from our shop' is proudly proclaimed, along with assurances that all their sausages are made from selected meat cuts with no artificial additives, no colorants, no 'rubbish'. Choose from up to fifty varieties (plus sausages for your pet) of the three tons a week they make using many exotic recipes and ingredients. O'Hagans' Special is based on an early Victorian recipe; Cajun is hot spicy pork, beef-n-Guinness, Farmer's (boerreworst from a Cape Malay recipe) and so on. All the sausages are made fresh every day, with any unsold going into the freezer. Follow their excellent advice to bake the sausages without pricking them. For orders over £30 they will deliver anywhere in London – worth sharing an order with friends and freezing any unused; these sausages make wonderful party food.

G. C. SPARKES

24 Old Dover Road, SE3
081 858 7672

Station Westcombe Park BR

Bus 108, 286

Open Tues–Fri 0830–1730
Sat 0830–1630

Mr Sparkes (third-generation butcher) tells us he's a step ahead of many others as the first UK meat retailer with the Demeter Symbol. This refers to the method of rearing the meat he sells – which he describes as like 'homoeopathic farming'. The farmers concerned stick to the principles of Rudolf Steiner, using the rhythms of the earth. Bio-dynamics in farming is big in Germany and the Low Countries and Mr Sparkes is obviously an enthusiast. Ninety per cent of his meat carries the Soil Association symbol. The shop is also a delicatessen, with traditional cured bacon from Maynard Davis, and sells a huge range of cheeses ('no plastic'), makes its own pasta and has all the trendy breads.

Cheesemongers

There's no question that the remarkable renaissance of desirable British farmhouse cheeses in London has come about through the inspiration of one man, Randolph Hodgson of Neal's Yard Dairy. Anyone who is serious about cheese has to visit his shop; we guarantee that you will be impressed.

Londoners are fortunate to have some cheesemongers of considerable stature, with a small but growing band of retailers who are passionate about the cheese they sell. And now the cleverer supermarkets too have begun to realise that customers want to have a choice between plastic-wrapped factory-made mousetrap and a prizewinning farmhouse truckle cut to order. If only more restaurants would follow suit then we really could smile as we say 'cheese'.

The following entries from other sections may also be of interest for their excellent selection of cheeses: Bushwacker Wholefoods; Clarke's; Cornucopia Health Food; James Elliott; C. Lidgate; Neal's Yard Wholefood Warehouse; John Nicholson; G. C. Sparkes.

Central

INTERNATIONAL CHEESE CENTRE

22 Strutton Ground, SW1
071 233 0962

Station Victoria underground and BR

Bus 11, 24, 29, 76, 88

Open Mon–Fri 0900–1830
Sat 0930–1730

This is a larger version of the original shop in Goodge Street – with an equally impressive range of over 450 cheeses. They have the individual truckles of Chewton Cheddar, and all the now familiar up-and-coming British and Irish cheeses as well as the old favourites. Like their sister shop, they carry a huge number of good quality preserves and pickles, oils, vinegars, mustards and wafer biscuits to go with the cheese. They have some unusual English fruit wines and a choice of Australian, French and other grape wines. Local delivery (as far as the City).

Also 21 Goodge Street, W1, 071 631 4191 – open Mon–Fri 0800–1830 (Thur 1930), Sat 0900–1830

JEROBOAMS

51 Elizabeth Street, SW1
071 823 5623
fax 071 495 3314

Station Victoria underground
and BR

Bus 11, 16, 24, 25, 29, 76,
82, 135, 239

Open Mon–Fri 0900–1830
Sat 0900–1400

Juliet Harbutt, the New Zealand proprietor, considers herself 'a little bossy'; she likes her customers to go away with something they have tried and enjoyed. An extension of this is the Cheese Club, which offers a monthly selection of four different cheeses with a fact sheet. As a Maître Fromager she cares for all the cheeses (the best farmhouse cheeses from Britain and France) in the cellars below the shop from which they supply many hotels and restaurants in and out of town. You can also buy wine accessories, a few choice oils, Cipriani pasta, nuts, crackers, ham and salami. As the name implies, they are known for wines as much as cheeses, importers for Georges Vesselle's range of champagnes and Bouzy rouge, Pierre André's Burgundy and several New Zealand wines (Redwood Valley and Cloudy Bay). Each month they introduce a few new wines and offer a 10 per cent discount on a mixed case. Free local delivery for twelve or more bottles. Tutored tastings for wine or cheese can be arranged for eight or more people.

Also at 24 Bute Street, SW7, 071 225 2232

Randolph Hodgson of Neal's Yard Dairy (see page 38)

NEAL'S YARD DAIRY

9 Neal's Yard, WC2
071 379 7646

Station Covent Garden
underground

Bus 1, 4, 6, 9, 11, 13, 15, 77,
168, 171, 176

Open Mon–Sat 0930–1730
Thur and Fri 0930–1800

PAXTON & WHITFIELD

93 Jermyn Street, SW1
071 930 0259

Station Piccadilly Circus/
Green Park underground

Bus 3, 6, 9, 13, 14, 15, 19,
22, 38, 53, 88, 94

Open Mon–Fri 0900–1800
Sat 0900–1600

RIPPON CHEESE STORES

26 Upper Tachbrook Street,
SW1
071 931 0628
fax 071 828 2368

Station Victoria underground
and BR

Bus 2, 11, 16, 24, 25, 29,
76, 82, 135, 239

Randolph Hodgson, the saviour of British raw-milk farmhouse cheeses, has around fifty cheeses on his list, with about thirty in stock at any one time. It all depends on what is available at the time of year. He is not only an *affineur* but also a cheese-maker himself, and has an encyclopaedic knowledge of his stock. The tiny shop is filled, floor to ceiling, with everything you could wish to taste that can be made from cow's, sheep's or goat's milk. Look out for Montgomery's unpasteurised Cheddar, Kirkham's Lancashire (it can't be bettered) or Ann Wigmore's Spenwood – a hard sheep's milk cheese with a lovely matured taste, a bit like young parmesan. There are too unpasteurised butter, crème fraîche, yoghurt, cream and fromage frais – all British, except for a selection of fine Irish cheeses. Plus breads from Sally Clarke's (see page 12).

Best known for its wonderful cheeses, this old favourite firm, by Royal Appointment, also has the best hams on the bone in London, plus double-smoked Wiltshire bacon, cold meat pies, thirteen salamis, pâtés, condiments, a small range of bread and an ample range of coffees. But to the matter of cheese – truckles of Cheddar by the shelf full and over 250 types of French, English, Irish, Welsh, Scottish, Dutch, Swiss, German, Italian, Norwegian, Spanish, Austrian . . . have we left out your favourite country? What more could you want – and all in perfect nick. They will deliver to account customers and they run a Cheese Club ('like a club with no subscription') which, for a monthly fee, gives you three different cheeses and an information sheet. You can order a month at a time: it makes an original gift.

Philip Rippon had been a cheese wholesaler for some years before opening his retail shop, which he aims to make the best in Europe. He has over 150 varieties of cheeses from more than twelve countries. In the main body of the shop he is able to keep his hard cheeses at the correct temperature, while the inner room houses the blues, goat's and soft cheeses which need to be in a cooler atmosphere. While he has Keen's extra mature Cheddar and others, he also stocks good block Cheddar for customers who may not want to spend farmhouse cheese prices yet still want something better than the offerings in the local convenience store. A few crackers

Open Mon–Fri 0800–1900
Sat 0900–1600

and some good bread are sold and there's a small bar where you can have a plate of cheeses with salad, or one of a number of cheese-related dishes including soup.

North West

CHEESES

13 Fortis Green Road, N10
081 444 9141

Bus 43, 107, 234

Open Mon–Thur, Sat 0930–1800
Fri 0930–1830

Bryan Mansfield may well be the only ex-policeman running a cheese shop. His well-informed manageress, Mala, can tell you whatever you need to know about the impressive array of cheeses from all over Europe. Some of the British cheeses come from one of the few *affineurs* in this country, James Aldridge. A Kentish cheese, tornegus, is cured in wine and covered in herbs. Isle of Avalon is a semi-soft cheese which Aldridge washes in brine and then cures. The excellent Montgomery's eighteen-month unpasteurised Cheddar and the Colton Basset Stilton (alas no longer unpasteurised) are among the popular English cheeses, and he likes to offer seasonal cheeses when they are at their best, like French goat's cheeses from spring to late September. There's a weekly delivery from Jacques Hennart in France. As well as cheese there are English sheep's milk yoghurts and ricotta, olive oils, biscuits, a few chutneys, a natty Swiss cheese grater for table use and a pretty collection of decorative old cheese dishes.

GEDI ENTERPRISES LIMITED

Plumridge Farm, Stagg Hill, Barnet
081 449 0695
fax 081 449 1528

Open Sun–Sat 1100–1800

Just on London's northern fringes, a mere forty minutes from Piccadilly Circus, it's a pleasant jaunt (by car, right off the Cockfosters Road just past White Lodge Hotel) to see and buy surely the only cheeses made in a London suburb and see the 500 goats kept in large barns on straw. The fourteen different cheeses (all vegetarian) are French style, made with Israeli technique, from British goats (white zanen and black Anglo-Nubian breeds) and come in two basic varieties -- fresh and mature. They are delicious and well made, consistently winning prizes (even beating French chèvres) at international contests.

South West

THE REAL CHEESE SHOP

96a High Street, Wimbledon Village, SW19
081 947 0564

This airy and uncluttered shop is pungent smelling from the fine array of British farmhouse cheeses, all in excellent condition. A cheese of the month is featured and the stock changes with the seasons, so you

Station Wimbledon
underground and BR

Bus 93

Open Tues–Sat 0900–1700
(closed 1300–1400 Tues–
Thur)

will always have the best choice of what is available. You can taste before you buy and there is a guarantee: 'If you are ever dissatisfied, return the cheese and we will refund the price or replace it.' They also advise on how to keep and serve cheese. There are a few accessories like Orkney Isles water biscuits and oat cakes.

Also at 62 Barnes High Street, SW13, 081 878 6676

LA SIENNE

54 Coombe Road, Norbiton,
Kingston
081 546 3767

Station Norbiton BR

Bus K2, K3

Open Mon–Tues, Thur–Sat
0900–1730
Wed 0900–1300

Kenyan-born Rasik Chauhan has the singular distinction of being the only Asian member of the Guilde des Fromagers. He frequently judges cheeses at French fairs and his excellent selection of cheeses from all around the world in his shop proves his dedication and expertise. He claims his Roquefort is the best you can get. In season he has Vacherin Mont d'Or and you'll always find something unusual among the cheeses. In spite of the Italian name, this is certainly not an Italian deli – in fact it isn't, according to Mr Chauhan, a deli at all, but rather a speciality food shop. So there's caviar rather than cornflakes, truffles but no tomatoes, fresh foie gras de canard. Free-range eggs are from Martin Pitt.

South East

THE CHEESE BOARD

Michael Jones has a wonderful collection of old cheese dishes which he displays around his shop. Otherwise everything on sale is edible, but all related to cheese in some way – from the excellent pickled onions (his grandmother's recipe) and Kalamata olives in oil, orange and cardamom, to the biscuits and bread.

Station Greenwich BR

Bus 18, 286

Open Mon–Wed, Fri 0930–1700
Thur 0930–1300
Sat 0900–1700

This includes the omnipresent ciabatta (cheaper here than in other shops) and locally made onion and olive breads. But the cheeses are the shop's *raison d'être* and they are well chosen from British farmhouses to French favourites. Around Christmas you can buy baby truckles of Cheddar, Cheshire and others which make lovely gifts. A small range of oils, vinegars and wines, including champagne from Alain Thienot and some port, completes the picture.

Delicatessens

What makes a delicatessen different from any other food shop? Our interpretation is that although you can buy staples like bread, pasta and rice, it is the 'delicacies' that truly make a delicatessen. Certainly salamis, cold, cured and smoked meats are *de rigueur* along with cheeses and specialities of the proprietor's provenance . . . and invariably olives.

Delicatessens are mostly family owned and in spite of the fact that the word is German, the vast majority in London are Italian run. Just about every type of delicatessen food can be found – Spanish and Portuguese, Greek and Turkish, Polish and Jewish and, we were relieved to find, even English.

The following entries from other sections may also be of interest for their range of delicatessen: Di Lieto; A. A. King; C. Lidgate; Paxton & Whitfield; Seymour Brothers; G. C. Sparkes.

Central

I. CAMISA & SON

61 Old Compton Street, W1
071 437 7610

Station Tottenham Court Road/Leicester Square/Piccadilly Circus underground

Bus 14, 24, 29, 176

Open Mon–Sat 0900–1800

Whatever the Italian for *embarras de richesses* is, Soho has that in its delicatessens. Like its near neighbours, this one is an old favourite. It is very traditional – not so much of the new styles. 'No red pasta,' Signor Camisa told us, but they have been making fresh pasta for twenty-five years – long before it became trendy. Quality and seasonal things – like fresh truffles – and they also have white truffle olive oil. Freshly baked focaccia and other breads, cooked sauces like wild mushroom, hare, pesto in season. And they are ready and willing to impart information on products and cooking.

CIACCIO

5 Warwick Way, SW1
071 828 1342

Station Victoria underground
and BR

Bus 2, 11, 16, 24, 25, 29,
76, 82, 135, 239

Open Mon–Fri 0930–1900
Sat 0930–1700

Asmall shop with odds and ends of Italian deli, but fresh pasta is the main attraction. Their spinach ravioli are very popular and spaghetti, tagliatelle, ravioli, tortellini are all made regularly in front of you by the young Italian staff. Accompanying sauces of mushroom cream, green or red pesto and tomato are also homemade. Fresh parmesan, olives, seafood salad, various pickled vegetables including mushrooms, oils, vinegars and biscuits. Good cappuccino and espresso can be taken out.

FRATELLI CAMISA

1a Berwick Street, W1
071 437 7120
fax 071 287 1953

Station Tottenham Court
Road/Piccadilly Circus
underground

Bus 7, 8, 9, 13, 14, 15, 25,
36

Open Mon–Wed, Fri–Sat
0900–1800
Thur 0900–1400

It is somewhat confusing that there are so many Camisas around town. This is, so they say, the original Camisa family shop, with another shop in Charlotte Street. All things Italian are to be bought here, including their homemade pasta. Italian sausages are delivered several times a week, with a peppery variety from Calabria. Balsamic vinegar – aged for three to six years (which is young by *tradizionale balsamico* standards) and a huge choice in olive oils will give your salads that Italian flavour. The small selection of wines includes one made by a cousin of the family in Italy.

Also at 53 Charlotte Street, W1, 071 255 1240

G. GAZZANO & SON LIMITED

167–9 Farringdon Road, EC1
071 837 1586

Station Farringdon
underground and BR

Bus 55, 63, 221, 259

Open Tues–Thur, Sat 0800–
1730
Fri 0800–1800
Sun 1030–1400

There has been a Gazzano shop on this site since 1901 and the family is still at the helm – the fourth generation (with occasional help from the fifth). When asked how he accounted for the fact that there were so many good Italian delis in London, Signor Gazzano said convincingly, 'There's only one food in the world to eat!' The enticing smells and sight of Parma hams hanging from the ceiling, the 104 shapes of dried pasta in the original cabinets, the exceptional selection of salamis and sausages – you know you are in the hands of experts here. Some of their fresh pasta comes from Italy – as do almost all the basic groceries, wines, cheeses. Although there are few residents in the area, old customers come at the weekends to shop and talk, and during the week people from the local office community can drop in to find something tasty for lunch.

LE GOURMET GASCON

3 Hillgate Street, W8
071 221 4131
fax 071 221 1995

Station Notting Hill Gate
underground

Bus 12, 27, 28, 31, 52, 52a,
94

Open Mon–Sat 1000–1800

This wood-lined shop imports the best food and wines from Gascony – tins of rillettes d'oie, foie gras, pâtés (lièvre and sanglier), haricots aux saucisses, lovely rich soups, huge tins of confits of all sorts. Jars of mustards and cornichons, bottles of flavoured vinegars and walnut oils – and wet walnuts wrapped in clear cellophane and tied with ribbons – all bring back the tastes and smells of Gascony. Naturally there are wines of Madiran and Gascony, and Pousse Rapière, an orangey armagnac liqueur from St Puy to mix with sparkling wine to make a lethal cocktail. Cider and Calvados represent Normandy along with French Pré-sident butter and a small selection of cheese and charcu-terie. The French pâtisserie comes from Wembley.

LINA STORES

18 Brewer Street, W1
071 437 6482

Station Piccadilly Circus/
Leicester Square underground

Bus 3, 6, 9, 13, 14, 15, 19,
22, 38, 53, 88, 94

Open Mon–Wed, Fri–Sat
0700–1730
Thur 0700–1300

Everyone thinks of Lina Stores when you mention Soho and Italian food. It has always been family owned but the current incumbents, the charming Filippis, have only been there fifteen or so years. They continue the tradition of good Italian supplies with their freshly made pasta (pumpkin tortelloni is a speciality), which they also supply to restaurants. Though they don't do much in take-away, they will make a huge tray of pasta to order and Papa Filippi is happy to suggest ways of using their products – try balsamic vinegar on eggs and bacon, for instance! They go for quality and you can buy all your Italian ingredients here, including holiday souvenirs like panforte, cantuccini and panettone.

LUIGI'S DELICATESSEN

347 Fulham Road, SW10
071 352 7739

Station South Kensington
underground + bus

Bus 14

Open Mon–Fri 0930–2200
Sat 0900–1900

London is well endowed with Italian delis, but Fulham is especially fortunate to have Luigi's, where the eponymous proprietor has a great enthusiasm for good food and wine (see also Luigi's Euroteca, pages 59–60). His full to overflowing shop has over 350 wines, forty different oils and a whole section of dried pasta, to say nothing of fresh. This is the place to find white truffles in season if you have access to a second mortgage. On a more modest level a mushroom sauce, with some dried and fresh porcini, or char-grilled vegetables, Carpegna prosciutto (which is over two years old, sweet cured and contains no preservatives) and sensational steamed garlic are just a few of the splendid ready-to-eat foods Luigi sells. And with the instant pudding to end all – a glass bowl containing tiramisu – your guests will be impressed!

Lina Stores

L. TERRONI & SONS

138–40 Clerkenwell Road, EC1
071 837 1712

Station Farringdon underground and BR

Bus 55, 63, 221, 259

Open Mon–Wed, Fri 0900–1745
Thur 0900–1300
Sat 0900–1530
Sun 1030–1400

The firm of L. Terroni has been in business in the Clerkenwell Road since 1878 and has the considerable distinction of being the oldest Italian delicatessen in England. Now run by the Annessa family who hail from sunny Bedford, the spacious shop buzzes with Italian clientele, most especially on Sunday morning since it is next door to the Italian church. ('We can hear the Mass from here,' Donato Annessa told us.) In fact that is the busiest time, and great for absorbing local colour. The Annessas are prime importers of much of what they sell, as well as being wholesalers. One of their specialities is whole suckling pig. They have a fine selection of oils – a first cold pressing of oil from Lucca and oil in flasks from ½ litre to 5 litre size. All the Christmas and Easter cakes and chocolates, a variety of cooked and smoked hams, bresaola, San Daniele and Parma, packets of mixed pre-sliced salamis, tripe in tins. The Italians are getting into lazy ways too – packs of ready-to-cook rice all prepared to make risotto. Good bread comes fresh daily from Bedford.

North West

AUSTRIAN SAUSAGE CENTRE

10a Belmont Street, NW1
071 267 3601/5412
fax 071 482 4965

Station Chalk Farm
underground
Primrose Hill BR

Bus 31, 168

Open Mon–Fri 0800–1700
Sat 0800–1300

Tucked away behind Chalk Farm Road this hard-to-find manufacturer/wholesaler/retailer is definitely worth the detour for its vast variety of traditional Polish sausages – all with unpronounceable names, like zywiecka and wiejska. The shop is really more of a warehouse, spotlessly clean and staffed by pleasant people who can help you with descriptions of the different products. Much of the stock is made on the premises, but some is imported, along with jars of pickles, jams and sauerkraut. Avoid the more ordinary English products and go for the continental meats, which are more interesting and better quality. Fresh Austrian rye bread and Polish cakes are also available.

PHILIP BARRETTA

78 High Road, N2
081 444 2932

Station East Finchley
underground

Bus 17, 102, 143, 263

Open Mon–Fri 0900–1900
Sat 0900–1800
Sun 1000–1300

Philip Barretta is East Finchley born, of Neopolitan parents who are in the catering trade. So both Italy and food are in his blood, hence his dedication to his business, which he developed from an already well-established deli run by Osio and Gioberti. They taught him well and he acknowledges their influence. He uses only the best suppliers for his Italian meats and salamis, which mostly come from the area round Cremona and Modena. He is one of the only people in Britain to hand-bone and hand-tie his Parma hams, which gives a rounder shape, a sweeter taste and a softer texture. The parmesan, which Barretta claims is the best available, is matured in copper vats. He sells it by the slice or freshly grated if you prefer. 'None of that sawdust that passes for parmesan in packets,' he says.

BELSIZE VILLAGE DELICATESSEN

39 Belsize Lane, NW3
071 794 4258

Station Swiss Cottage/Belsize
Park underground

Bus 46, 268

Open Mon–Sat 0800–1900

Ken and Marie formerly owned this shop (having moved from their original premises off Finchley Road), but have now retired to the south of France after a lifetime of providing Polish deli to the appreciative patrons of British West Hampstead. The popular new owners (ex Rosslyn Deli, see page 51) are keeping the Polish/French emphasis with a wealth of ingredients, including ground poppy seeds for Eastern European cooking, plus herring, salami and cooked meats and sausages from France, Italy, Poland and Hungary. The cheese counter is well stocked and they have a chef (on the premises) producing the many ready-to-serve dishes.

MR CHRISTIAN'S

11 **Elgin Crescent, W11**
071 229 0501
fax 071 221 1995

Station Ladbroke Grove
underground

Bus 15, 52

Open Mon–Fri 0900–1900
Sat 0900–1800
Sun 0900–1400

Portobello Road on a Saturday is where it all happens and Mr Christian's attracts the hungry hordes by putting up a stall from which to sell their ready-made, all cooked on the premises, food, together with cups of steaming coffee and soup. Inside is pretty busy too, all the week long, with take-away food, 120 cheeses from all over Europe and a huge choice of breads. Sausages are from O'Hagans (see page 34) and they have own-label chocolates and preserves. Their

Outside Mr Christian's

Christmas puddings have real threepenny pieces in them – a great work of detection on the part of the Australian proprietor, Gregg Scott. Organic, Californian and Australian wines.

THE DELICATESSEN SHOP

23 South End Road, NW3
071 435 7315

Station Hampstead Heath BR

Bus 24, 46, 168

Open Mon–Fri 0930–1900
Sat 0900–1800

John Cavaciuti was the first Maître Fromager in Britain and also one of the first to have a pasta machine installed in his shop. Sandra Cavaciuti is now in charge and sensibly does not try to compete with supermarkets. She buys the best she can find whether in fine olive oils or unusual cheeses, like Eminencia, a Spanish goat's cheese, or Mona Lisa, a fresh pecorino from Tuscany. The pasta is, of course, fresh every day. Their speciality is tortelloni and there are homemade sauces. Sandra insists the basil for her pesto should come from Genoa and the pesto rosso is a wonderful variation of that classic sauce, using sun-dried tomatoes and olives. Filled brioches and classy sausage rolls, frittate and quiches are all excellent.

A. ELLINAS

146 Ballards Lane, N3
081 346 0904

Station Finchley Central
underground

Bus 13, 26, 260

Open Mon–Thur 0900–1900
Fri and Sat 0900–2000

Greek deli with fresh dill, coriander and other Cypriot greengrocery. Tarama paste (as opposed to cod's roe which is more generally used for taramasalata), Greek coffee beans, oodles of olives, kolokasi, sausages, big jars of vine leaves vacuum packed (not in brine). Greek cheese and wonderful pastries like kourapiedes, melomakarounda and even Cypriot chewing gum for homesick expats. Talk to them if you want Greek party food.

FABRIZI

289 Regents Park Road, N3
081 349 9422

Station Finchley Central
underground

Bus 13, 26, 82, 260

Open Mon–Sat 0900–1800
Sun 0900–1330

Several generations of Finchley residents have come to appreciate Italian food through the Fabrizi family, whose long, narrow shop has changed little over the years. What has changed is the presence of the machines which provide the shop with fresh pasta and delicious ice cream (including bombes and cassatas). There is, too, an unbelievably huge selection of dried pasta – you could certainly find anything you want. Signor Fabrizi is especially proud of his salumeria – the Parma ham, coppa and other salamis, many made by Veroni. Homemade gnocchi, marinated artichokes, nine different types of olives (all prepared on the premises, sometimes four or five times a day) and tiramisu are all in the capable hands of Signora Fabrizi. In keeping with the 'all Italian' stock are the coffee, bread and the best of Italian wines (Barolo and Chianti being top sellers).

R. GARCIA & SONS

248–56 Portobello Road, W11
071 221 6119

Station Ladbroke Grove underground

Bus 15, 52

Open Mon–Wed, Fri–Sat 0900–1800
Thur 0900–1330

AU GOURMET GREC

124 Northfields Avenue, W13
081 579 2722

Station Northfields underground

Bus E2, E3

Open Mon–Fri 0900–1800
Wed 0900–1330
Sat 0900–1730

JOE & MARY

70 Pitshanger Lane, W5
081 997 2885

Bus E7

Open Mon–Thur 0900–1800
Fri–Sat 0900–1930
Sun 1000–1400

If you are searching for _recherché_ Galician specialities like unto (cured lard) or tocino (fresh lard) this is the place for you. Chorizos, serrano ham, morcilla, codillos de jamon – all those wonderful Spanish delicacies can be bought here. At Christmas they carry a huge selection of sweetmeats like polverones and torron and year round there will be Spanish cheeses – six varieties of Manchego, cabra, Mahon, tierno. Best Spanish olives, and tins of sardines, calamares, mejillones, bacalao.

Vengelis Gougoulis is the Greek proprietor of this excellent deli but, with a Polish wife and many Polish customers, you mustn't be surprised to find pierogi and zywiecka next to the pastourma and loukanika. And since Ealing is such an incredibly international area, with Yugoslavs, Hungarians, Czechs, Vangelis tries to cater to this polyglot clientele and considers this to be a fully continental deli. He imports speciality goods from Poland, including sweets, wild cranberry relish and very good horseradish. From Greece there are honey, best feta, kadaifi. Among his readymade foods are uska (to garnish your bortsch), a variety of salads (Greek of course), marinated olives. There are Parma ham and Parmigiano Reggiano, borek, schmaltz (matjes) herrings, a big range of pickled cucumbers and sauerkraut in jars.

Everything in this shop, according to Joe, is the best you will find anywhere and certainly there are some exquisite nuts (especially fine pistachios), beautiful Iranian biscuits, sweetmeats made of saffron, honey and pistachios and lavash bread. Smoked white fish (whole) and Caspian Sea caviar will tempt homesick Iranians, as will the charming offerings for special Iranian holidays like the basket made up for the Spring Festival, consisting of traditional foods – garlic, somak, wheat and essence of wheat, incense, special dates and coloured eggs. The dried fruits, including unusual miniature figs, are excellent. They make much of their pizzas – select your own topping and take it home to bake. If you need gum arabic for your sweet making, this is the place to find it, and many other Iranian and Armenian specialities too.

LISBOA DELICATESSEN

54 Golborne Road, W10
081 969 1052

Station Westbourne Park
underground and BR

Bus 15, 52

Open Mon–Sat 0930–1930
Sun 1000–1300

The largest fresh chestnuts you'll ever see are to be found here around the festivals of St Martin and All Saints' Day when, traditionally, the new wine is tasted in Portugal (and Golborne Road). Paio and torresmos, choriço, cozido – all Portuguese sausage specialities are here, alongside the expected sardines, anchovies and other canned fish, indeed any Portuguese ingredient you might need. A good selection of wines and ports. Enormous pieces of salt cod can be cut to size and there are other salted bits and pieces of pork – trotters, tails, belly and ribs, which the proprietor prepares himself.

PARADE DELICATESSEN

8 Central Buildings, The
Broadway, W5
081 567 9066

Station Ealing Broadway
underground and BR

Bus 65, 297, E1, E8

Open Mon–Fri 0915–1830
Wed 0915–1300
Sat 0915–1700

Serving the large Polish community in Ealing, here you might well think yourself in Warsaw not West London. Most of the customers speak Polish as do the staff, and the food is predominantly Polish. Traditional cakes for special holidays come from Poland, others from local bakeries – as does the excellent rye bread. Cabanos sausages hang from a rail to dry. There's a well-stocked cabinet full of Polish and German sausages and pots of pork fat with crackling. Pork in aspic, tripe Polish style, bigos and packets of soups – everything you need to give you a taste of Poland.

PLATTERS

10 Hallswelle Parade,
Finchley Road, NW11
081 455 7345

Station Golders Green
underground

Bus 13, 26, 260

Open Mon–Sat 0830–1730
Sun 0830–1400

A lively, fresh and tempting Jewish-style (but not kosher) delicatessen, where huge platters of cold cuts, cocktail sandwiches and other good food are the specialities. Their smoked salmon is freshly carved by two gentlemen who between them notch up 160 years – a dying art it would seem as much smoked salmon comes prepacked. Everything is cooked on the premises and the chilled counter bulges with all the tasty items good Jewish mothers used to make but don't have time for any more – chopped liver, chopped herring, gefilte fish, ten different kinds of herring, salt beef and fifteen different salads, plus salmon en croûte. A lochshen pudding (noodles, raisins, eggs – all low calories of course), apple strudel and cheesecake provide the desserts in this traditional food line up. Staff are friendly, they deliver locally.

Also at 83–5 Allitsen Road, NW8, 071 722 5352

ROBINSON (BARNET) LIMITED

182 High Street, Barnet
081 449 0828

Station High Barnet
underground + bus

Bus 34, 84, 234, 263

Open Mon–Sat 0830–1730

Tiny but good, old-fashioned English deli. Bacon sliced from sides, home-cooked hams and cold joints of stuffed pork, plus Parma ham and a variety of sausages, including chorizo. They sell every sort of Tiptree jam made (sixty in all). A good cheese counter and lots of old-fashioned favourites like cheese wafers in tins from Holland, Bath Olivers, relishes and stem ginger in honey.

ROSSLYN HILL DELICATESSEN

56 Rosslyn Hill, NW3
071 794 9210

Station Hampstead
underground

Bus 46, 268

Open Tues–Sat 0900–1900
Sun 0900–1700

Smart Hampstead deli chock-a-block full of 'designer food' with fancy labels (at fancy prices) from all over the world. Long famous for their smoked salmon and homemade croissants, they also make an extensive (and good) range of homemade ready meals – prawn creole, stroganoff, sauté de veau à la moutarde. Squid-ink pasta, wild mushroom pasta, lots of bread. The pâtisserie is exquisite and there's a huge cheese and cold meat/deli counter.

LA SALUMERIA

59a-61 Abbey Road, NW8
071 624 2857

Station South Hampstead BR

Bus 31, 159

Open Mon–Fri 0900–1900
Sat 0900–1800

Although this is an Italian deli (according to the card), Franco the proprietor prefers to call it a rosticceria, which describes it rather more precisely (for the *cognoscenti* that is). The ready-prepared foods are certainly his main interest with a basic menu of ratatouille, lasagne, melanzane parmigiana, chicken cacciatore, pizzas, pollo sorpresa – all made from top-quality ingredients. There is, too, a menu which is changed daily, with such delights as celery and seafood salad, polpettone, mozzarella in carozza – *tutto fatt'in casa*.

North East

AZIZ BABA DELI PASTAHANESI

47 Newington Green, N16
071 226 5381

Station Canonbury BR + bus

Bus 73, 141, 171a, 236

Open Sun–Sat 0830–2100

Everything is made on the premises and looks and tastes fresh. The excellent breads and pastries are Turkish – with sweet tahini bread, olive bread or round borek stuffed with cheese and spinach. The salads include Middle Eastern favourites with aubergines, hummus, taramasalata, stuffed vegetables and other dishes with which you could impress your family and friends. There are a few tables and benches if you want to eat there and then.

THE COOLER

67 Stoke Newington Church Street, N16
071 275 7266

Station Stoke Newington BR

Bus 67, 73, 76

Open Mon–Sat 0900–2100
Sun 1000–1500

GALLO NERO

45 Newington Green Road, N1
071 226 2002

Station Canonbury BR

Bus 236

Open Mon–Sat 0830–1830

OLGA STORES

30 Penton Street, N1
071 837 5467

Station Angel underground

Bus 153

Open Mon–Sat 0900–2000
Sun 0900–1400

A great enthusiast for fine British produce, Marcus Zäuner aims to provide good, interesting food at 'not Mickey Mouse prices'. He's exceedingly proud of his Devon-made sausages, ten varieties of which sell like hot cakes. The pies (also from Devon) look gorgeous. Ham and bacon from Dunmow and cheeses from all the best farmhouse cheesemakers. Off the beaten track wines, Whittard's teas, a courtyard café for snacks and local staff who care about what they sell.

The Mori family achieved a certain fame some years ago when they appeared on television treading grapes in darkest north London to make the annual cuvée (from grapes which Signor Mori buys from the London fruit markets). Sadly they have become mechanised, so one more bit of local folklore bites the dust. They do sell a full range of quality wines here, though the vino della casa is not their own home brew. This is a fresh and friendly shop, with Mama behind the counter and her son very capably in charge. The seasons are marked in Italian style with the appearance of colomba at Easter and panettone at Christmas. They cook their own gammon with no additives or preservatives and the meat counter also has bresaola, punta d'anca, Parma and San Daniele hams. Homemade lasagne is regularly available and the occasional dish of polpettine or other specialities from Signora Mori. Cheeses, mainly Italian, with the delicious torta basilico, and inevitably plenty of olive oils and lovely olives.

Also at 75 Stoke Newington High Street, N16, 071 254 9770

Though this does not proclaim itself an Italian delicatessen, that is what it appears to be, although it is run by Aida from the Philippines, who is full of good advice should you need help to find your way around this well-stocked shop. They have fresh basil all year to make their own pesto (and to sell with the mozzarella di bufala), plus various homemade sauces, spreads and purées. Plenty of dried pasta, an extensive selection of salamis, sausages, San Daniele ham and general Italian groceries, rice, polenta. Pizza bases are waiting for you to choose the topping, fresh lasagne is brought in piping hot every day. Good breads, Italian coffee. Everything you might want – but the prices are high.

J. ROGG

137 Cannon Street Road, E1
071 488 3368

Station Shadwell underground

Bus 5, 15, 40, D3

Open Mon–Fri 0900–1700
Sun 0700–1430

Barry Rogg is among the last of a dying breed in this once predominantly Jewish part of London. His true Jewish deli is crammed with barrels of pickled cucumbers, smoked salmon, bagels and sandwiches to take away. Chopped herrings, chopped liver, gefilte fish, schmaltz herring – you name it, Barry has it. 'There are no health foods here,' he says. From the kitchen at the back he brings a piece of freshly made matzo latke for you to taste (you shouldn't go hungry).

Barry Rogg

South West

BURCHELL'S OF OLD ISLEWORTH

Lawrence Parade, Lower Square, Old Isleworth, Middlesex
081 569 9278

Station Isleworth BR

Bus 37, 267

Open Mon–Fri 0800–1630
Sat 0930–1430

Set in the new square near the bridge and close to the river, this brand-new shop sells a good range of delicatessen staples (and Taylor's coffees and teas) plus a really good selection of homemade goodies – unusual salads that taste wonderful, lots of cakes. Sandwiches can be made to order. Plenty of cheese, salamis, etc. They also are good outside caterers for large and small occasions and very friendly and helpful to boot.

DELICATESSEN PIACENZA

2 Brixton Road, SW9
071 735 2121

Station Oval underground

Bus 3, 59, 109, 159, 196

Open Sun–Sat 0900–1830

In spite of a grave case of Italian deli fatigue, we still found this one a joy and agreed with the recommendation from a local friend, who shops there regularly. She particularly likes the speck, which is thinly sliced and tastes as good as the best Parma ham, and the pasta, made *alla casa*, especially the Sicilian ravioli (with ricotta, orange and saffron), pesto ravioli and the homemade pesto and pizza. Signora Coda marinates olives for her focaccia, which, with bruschetta and other delicacies, she makes to order. Cans of venus clams, five litres of olive oil, wines, coffees, pandolce Genovese and lots of hard-to-find Italian foods are crammed into this shop.

EMORY ST MARCUS

1 Rockingham Close (off Priory Lane), Roehampton, SW15
081 878 1898

Station East Putney underground + bus

Bus 33, 37

Open Sun–Sat 0800–1800

This has to be one of the most bizarre shops in London in the most eccentrically sited position in the middle of a housing estate. Not the place you would expect to find so much exotica, it must be the mecca of all homesick South Africans yearning for their national food – biltong. From the ceiling hang stalactites of this curious delicacy – very much an acquired taste but if you love it, this is the place for you. They sell it standard, with little fat, and lean, with no fat, and they can also offer beef jerky, Malaysian spiced beef, wild game, smoked venison and a host of different meats and sausages from all over the world. Other South African products, like mieles in tins and wines by the case, are there.

Emory St Marcus

FRATELLI

57 Park Road, Kingston, Surrey
081 549 8021

Station Norbiton BR

Bus 371

Open Mon–Thur 0830–1800
Sat 0830–1700

DA GIULIANO

45 Broadway, SW19
081 543 7366

Station Wimbledon underground and BR

Bus 57, 93, 155, 352

Open Mon–Fri 0900–1930
Sat 0900–1830

SALUMERIA ESTENSE

837 Fulham Road, SW6
071 731 7643

Station Parson's Green underground

Bus 14

Open Mon–Fri 1000–1945
Sat 1000–1800

If the name doesn't assure you this is an Italian delicatessen, the smell certainly will. All the ready-prepared food is made on the premises and you'll find everything you need to make your own Italian specialities – with San Daniele prosciutto, speck and porchetta, pancetta and mozzarella di bufala, antipasto in oil and of course fresh pasta. Arborio rice for your authentic risotto is sold loose. Since they prefer to deal with small producers, expect to see items which you may not find elsewhere.

Giuliano prefers his shop to be known as *specialità Italiana* rather than a deli – but whatever it is, it's a light and airy place full of great smells and wonderful food. Mostly Italian products, of course, with plenty of very good ready-made snacks – supplì, bruschetta, mozzarella in carrozza – all of which can be heated in the shop and packed up to take back to the office. The lasagne is a popular lunchtime dish, as are the bulging sandwiches, made to order. A particularly good range of Italian breads – Toscana wheel, casareccio, rosette, maltagliati rolls and the ubiquitous ciabatta. The usual Italian grocery items, lots of dried pasta and a fair choice of salamis of many different types. Ice-cream specialities like stregatini, bombetta, tartufo. Altogether a very pleasing and happy shop.

The sounds, sights and above all the smells of Italy greet you in this very friendly, family-run shop. The pesto is, according to Signor Gorini, 'supposed to be the best' and you can see if he's right by buying the fresh pasta to go with it which Signora makes and dries by hand in the shop. As well as all the usual Italian favourites there are a number of rarer goods – like bottled tomatoes in brine from Calabria (very good flavour and practical as you use what you need), delicious honey from Badia a Coltibuono, posh packs of pasta, unfiltered oils, wonderful panforte. There's always a basket full of reasonable wines. Plenty of homemade terrines, lasagne, osso bucco, crespolini and fresh salads. They make up baskets of food for presents – just take in the basket and leave them to it.

SHEEN CUISINE DELICATESSEN

32 Sheen Lane, SW14
081 876 7616

Station Mortlake BR

Bus 33, 37

Open Mon–Fri 0930–1900
Sat 0900–1630

Homemade cakes and tarts, pâtés and salads and a freezer full of ready-to-heat meals make this a useful shop. There's a great selection of cheeses, some tempting mutton pies and brioches filled with mushrooms and herbs; baguettes and baps are filled to order – all good stuff for their lunchtime trade. On the shelves are classy Italian products, preserves, and come Christmas their orange pastry, mincemeat, puddings and pies do a rapid disappearing act. Go next door for homemade chocolates.

VIVIAN'S

2 Worple Way, Richmond, Surrey
081 940 3600

Station Richmond underground and BR

Bus 27, R69

Open Mon–Fri 0830–1930
Sat 0800–1800
Sun 0800–1130

Behind the charming shop front (ex Chez Max in Kew), Vivian is selling everything delicious you can think of. He has a huge range (over 130) of serious cheeses with a strong emphasis on British and French farm cheeses, although some Spanish ones are in stock. 'No commercial or factory rubbish. I've tried everything I sell.' This includes top-quality rice by weight, whole spices, Valrhona chocolate, Philippe Dadé's baked goods and fresh baguettes delivered twice daily. Exotic coffees by mail order only – phone for details.

South East

PAUL'S

62 Camberwell Church Street, SE5
071 703 0156

Station Dulwich BR + bus

Bus 12, 36, 36b

Open Mon–Sat 1000–1900

Tiny Greek food shop (not smart but good stuff). Olives marinating in a variety of mixes, good vegetables and herbs, pastas, fruits, chillies and peppers. Huge trays of syrupy cakes and pastries. Greek breads. Free-range eggs.

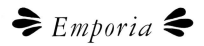

Emporia

The common link between the shops in this section is that they are all basically grocers from the mundane to the magnificent, whether in Green Lanes, Haringey, or Brompton Road, Knightsbridge. We have included the leading branches of the better supermarkets, which today rival some of the more ritzy establishments in providing top-quality food from around the world. Food halls in department stores and smaller shops which sell food that can't be neatly pigeon-holed into delicatessens or our other sections are likely to be found here.

Although listed under 'A Good Cuppa', W. Martyn also deserves a mention in this section for his wide-ranging stock of general food – not just the coffee for which he is noted.

Central

FORTNUM & MASON

181 Piccadilly, W1
071 734 8040

Station Piccadilly Circus underground

Bus 3, 6, 9, 13, 15, 19, 22, 38, 53, 88, 94

Open Mon–Fri – Shop 0930–1800
Patio restaurant 0930–1730
Fountain restaurant 0930–2300
St James's restaurant 0930–1720

A London landmark, Fortnum's food hall has been selling high-class groceries since 1707 and still has a few tailcoated assistants. There's an incredible range of own-blend teas and coffees – the Royal blend tea is drunk by countless foreign visitors. Chocolates to drool over and a small but select fruit and veg corner. Caviar and foie gras to your heart's desire. Lots of presentation packs, ideal for gifts for overseas friends, a large deli counter mainly catering to English tastes – gala pies, solid quiches, sliced hams, smoked salmon and a catholic selection of cheeses. Grand wedding cakes and splendid pastries. As well as their famous hampers (which they will deliver to account customers), they do very good individual picnic boxes. A pricey cook shop in the basement. Of the three restaurants, the Patio and Fountain (now lacking character since its face lift) serve old-fashioned delicacies like buck rarebit, from breakfast onwards. The latter is open for after theatre meals. The St James's restaurant serves from breakfast, has a pianist at teatime, and substantial high teas. The *à la carte* lunch includes classics like roast beef and chicken pie.

THE GREEN VALLEY

36 Upper Berkeley Street, W1
071 402 7385

Station Marble Arch underground

Bus 2a, 2b, 6, 7, 8, 10, 12, 15, 36, 73, 88, 137

Open Mon–Sat 0930–2200
Sun 0930–2000
Closed Sundays from end Sept to 30 June

A Lebanese grocer stocking ingredients for all the Middle Eastern recipes – rosewater, orange blossom water, syrups of rose, jallab, tamarind. A huge range of nuts, spices, rice, olives – all sold loose as well as fruit and vegetables. There's a meat and deli counter with some made-up dishes. And a window filled with trays and trays of pastries so beloved in the Middle East, with nuts, honey and all good things. Coffee pots and hubble-bubble pipes too!

HARRODS

Knightsbridge, SW1
071 730 1234

Station Knightsbridge underground

Bus 9, 14, 22, C1

Open Mon, Thur, Fri, Sat
0900–1800
Tues 0930–1800
Wed 0900–2000

With coachloads of tourists passing through every day, Harrods could be regarded as a theme park as well as an emporium. It covers 4½ acres. The fish counter is a must for camera-clicking visitors with around fifty varieties of wet fish on show. If you like facts and figures as well as food, you can choose from 130 types of bread, 163 whiskies, and almost 600 different cheeses. The most expensive wine is a jeroboam of Château Lafite-Rothschild 1945 for £8,500, the cheapest is Harrods' own hock at £3.15. You can have anything exported or delivered nationwide or mailed – for a price. One New York customer ordered six bread rolls worth 30p. Another, a Texan gourmet, regularly sends for Loch Fyne kippers. The traiteur offers ready-prepared food from many nations – Thai, French, Indian – whatever is *à la mode*. Fresh pasta, salads – a tremendous selection of everything. And don't forget to look at the beautiful mosaics on the walls and ceilings of the food halls. A supermarket downstairs provides staples.

See also Harrods restaurants, pages 148–9.

Game and poultry counter at Harrods

LOON FUNG SUPERMARKET

42 Gerrard Street, W1
071 437 7332

Station Leicester Square/
Piccadilly Circus underground

Bus 3, 6, 9, 13, 15, 19, 22, 38, 53, 88, 94

Open Sun–Sat 1000–2030

LUIGI'S EUROTECA CENTRE

359–61 Fulham Road, SW6
071 351 7825

Station South Kensington
underground + bus

Bus 14

A plaque on this most Chinese of establishments tells us that John Dryden lived here in the seventeenth century. In Chinatown supermarkets selling everything are two a penny. This one is our choice, but have a look at the others too. Here you will certainly find everything you're looking for, from frozen dim sum, shark's fin, fresh meat (including pig's trotters), chickens and won ton skins. It helps if you can read Chinese but someone may be able to assist (don't bank on it though). Plenty of fresh vegetables and exotic fruit, canned and bottled sauces of all sorts. The adjoining shop has utensils, crockery, vases and other indispensable items.

If the word 'gourmet' had not been so over-exposed one would be tempted to say this is the ultimate gourmet shop. Luigi, proprietor of a near-by delicatessen (see page 44) and fishmonger Jim Moran have come together to provide high-class one-stop shopping. Each section is run by an expert. The Butchteca is in the capable hands of an ex-Lidgate (see page 28) manager, whose counter is filled with many interesting cuts and items ready prepared — loin of pork stuffed with prunes and apricots, kebabs, own-make sausages,

Open Mon–Fri 0800–2000
Sat 0800–1800

noisettes of Barbary duck, meat bones for stock are just a few of the many temptations. The Fishteca has a resident fishmonger, who sells exotic fish, wonderful clams and other crustaceans, caviar, lobster, bouillabaisse and sauces for you to transport home to make an awesome dinner party. In the Paninoteca, run by Franca Zucconi, are ciabatta sandwiches, espresso coffee, and anything you choose to eat here or take away can be heated. Outside is the Frutteca – with a beautiful display of fruits and vegetables. And Signor Luigi pops in from down the road to keep a tender eye on the operation.

MARKS & SPENCER

458 Oxford Street, W1
071 935 7954

Station Marble Arch/Bond Street underground

Bus 2a, 7, 10, 13, 30, 74, 88, 113, 137, 159

Open Mon–Wed 0900–1900
Thur, Fri 0900–2000
Sat 0900–1830

This M&S London store has their flagship food section. With up to 70,000 customers a week, it's streets ahead in takings compared to the rest (the average 'spend' is said to be £8). Food manager Paul McManus told us that they describe themselves as a 'speciality and top-up store' with 2,300 different lines. You can buy a complete ready-made meal – Italian, Indian, Chinese, Thai, vegetarian and British for a single person or for a whole banquet. Pitta bread is the fastest selling bread line – perhaps reflecting their cosmopolitan customers. There's expensive fish, a range of fresh meals for children, take-away sandwiches and salads and speciality fruit and vegetables. The recipe dishes may be pricey but loyal shoppers say it's cheaper to heat up an M&S aromatic crispy duck (Peking style) than buy one at a Chinese take-away.

See also Marks & Spencer Sandwich Bar, Moorgate, EC2, page 133.

MATAHARI

102 Westbourne Grove, W2
071 221 7468
fax 071 373 3861

Station Bayswater underground

Bus 15, 28, 31

Open Sun–Thur 1000–1900
Fri–Sat 1000–2000 and all holidays

A general south-east Asian supermarket, one of three in London, you will undoubtedly find whatever specialities you need for most of the cuisines of the area. They have ingredients for Chinese cooking and a smaller selection of Japanese food. There's a section for utensils, a small but useful range of cookery books and some interesting frozen food. As in many of the shops of this genre, there are lots of treasures if you have the patience to look for them.

Also at 30 Shrubbery Road, SW16, 081 769 2129
328 Balham High Road, SW17, 081 767 3107

PARTRIDGES

132–4 Sloane Street, SW1
071 730 0651

Station Sloane Square
underground

Bus 11, 19, 22, 137, C1

Open Sun–Sat 0830–2100

O h, that all grocers were so nice – a lovely old-fashioned shop – self-service in the main, plus deli, pastry and bread counters. There's fresh fruit and vegetables and wines too. It is clean and well laid out, with helpful service and not too large, not too small. Coffee, beans or ground, and mundane as well as hard-to-find items. Classy but not snobbish.

SAFEWAY

Cherry Walk Shopping
Centre, Whitecross Street,
EC1
071 638 5262

Station Barbican underground

Bus 4, 279a

Open Mon–Thur and Sat
0800–2000
Fri 0800–2100

S afeway has broken new ground with the sale of organic fruit, vegetables, wine, grocery and meat in supermarkets, at reasonable prices too. Maison Blanc pâtisserie (see page 17) is available in five stores. Their city concept stores (Chelsea, East Sheen, Edgware Road and Kensington as well as Barbican) are designed for those who live and/or work in central London. Each has a very good organic range and distinctly upmarket selection of exotics and other foods, plus all the staples one would expect at a supermarket. The Barbican has recently had a £1 million refurbishment.

Also at 35–7 King's Road, SW3, 071 730 9151 (excellent for wine, no car park)
20 Ealing Broadway Centre, W5, 081 840 3502 (larger – almost as big as a superstore)
284–8 Upper Richmond Road West, East Sheen, SW14, 081 876 8222
159–69 Edgware Road, W2, 071 723 1946 (good car parking, excellent wine selection, cosmopolitan selection of food)
150–8 Kensington High Street, W8, 071 937 4345 (the most upmarket, though quite small, of all stores. Safeway's chairman shops here)
114–16 Shepherd's Bush Centre, W12, 081 743 5744 (car park plus £5 million new extension)

J. SAINSBURY

West London Air Terminal,
Cromwell Road, SW7
071 373 8313

Station South Kensington
underground

Bus 14, 30, 45a, 49, 74, 219,
C1

T his is one of Sainsbury's larger stores and like those listed below it offers a tremendous service to customers, including parking and help for disabled, public toilets, trolleys which fit on the front of wheelchairs, a delicatessen counter, bakery with French range, comprehensive ranges of exotic fruit and vegetables and of wines and spirits. Sainsbury's fresh-fish counters offer a wide choice. Added to these and other extras is the company's commitment

Open Mon–Wed 0900–2100
Thur–Fri 0900–2200
Sat 0830–2000

to good prices and good quality.

Large stores also at 2 Canal Way, Ladbroke Grove, W10, 081 960 4324
62 Wandsworth Road, SW8, 071 622 9426
480 Streatham High Road, SW16, 081 764 0435 – this store is housed in a listed building.
Check on opening times, which vary from store to store.

SELFRIDGES

400 Oxford Street, W1
071 629 1234
fax 071 493 0568

Station Bond Street/Marble Arch underground

Bus 2a, 7, 10, 13, 30, 74, 88, 113, 137, 159

Open Mon–Wed, Fri–Sat 0830–1800
Thur 0830–2000

This used to be the Cinderella of food halls but after a much-needed rethink and refit, it is now a pleasure to shop there. The greengrocery has an extensive range of organic produce and prepared salads. The bakery has a selection of foreign breads and Arab sweetmeats. Readymade 'ethnic' food is a big seller and there is a changing menu of Indian, Italian, Middle Eastern, Thai specialities (from a top restaurant), sushi and Mexican food, plus a kosher section. Salmon is specially smoked for Selfridges. Unusual fresh fish, salmon poached to order. Among the take-away are gourmet sandwiches and fish and chips (freshly fried). The butcher will prepare anything you want. He usually has venison, kid and goat. Exotic grocery includes 200 lines from Fauchon, teas, coffees and food gifts galore. It's just a local supermarket for many so you can find everyday things too. Delivery in their normal area and shopping carried to their car park. Look at the wine department for a great selection – with a section for old, rare wines.

TAWANA ORIENTAL SUPERMARKET

18–20 Chepstow Road, W2
071 221 6316

Station Bayswater underground

Bus 15, 28, 31

Open Every day including Christmas and holidays 0930–2030

These two adjoining shops are bursting with all types of Thai and south-east Asian foodstuffs, fresh, frozen and canned. Fruit, vegetables and herbs are flown in twice a week so you can expect to find all manner of exotic ingredients. The ample utensils section includes tiffin containers and steamers as well as giant mortars and pestles. In the freezer cabinets reside soft-shell crabs, shrimps, squid and other fish and such useful stand-bys as coconut milk. This place is a treasure trove and the proprietors are happy to help if you aren't sure what is what.

Also at 179 Wandsworth High Street, SW18, 081 874 7742

VINIRON

119 Drummond Street,
NW1
071 387 8653

Station Euston Square/Euston
underground and BR

Bus 10, 14, 18, 24, 27, 29,
30, 73, 134, 135

Open Sun–Sat 0900–2130

A spice supermarket is a fair description of this shop, which must have one of the most comprehensive selections of spices in London. There's a whole wall of Patak products and packs and tins of spices of all sorts; rarely seen are cardamom seeds and powder in addition to the whole pods. The shop is well kept and everything well displayed. Buy your chappati flour or rice in 10 kilo sacks; large packs of nuts are extremely well priced. There is some cooking equipment and all the usual Indian groceries – plus Cadbury's fruit and nut bars. Outside is a selection of Indian fruit and vegetables – definitely superior to any other in this street of Asian shops. Weird and wonderful bitter gourds, tindoori, dudi, baby aubergines and green mangoes - and in season the superb Alfonso mangoes are sold here. The staff are always charming and happy to explain what is what.

North West

ADAMOU

126 Chiswick High Road,
W4
081 994 0752

Station Turnham Green
underground

Bus 27, 237, 267

Open Mon–Sat 0830–1900
Sun 0930–1330 half day Bank
Holidays (closed Christmas
Day)

Here is another United Nations of a shop, with produce and products from just about everywhere, though Greek and Cypriot are the mainstay. Lots of Greek olive oils and olives – the lovely coriander and lemon variety and fresh unpickled ones too as well as pickles, sausages, wine. Lebanese wholemeal cracked wheat, Indian sauces, spices and nuts, Italian cakes, couscous, matzos – a wonderful mixture. The outside greengrocery has outstanding fresh produce.

CHARLIE'S WEST AFRICAN FOOD SHOP

56–8 Esmond Road, NW6
071 624 6559

Station Queen's Park
underground and BR

Bus 36, 187

Open Mon–Thur 0915–1745
Fri–Sat 0915–1800
Sun 1000–1200

A bazaar selection of great piles of foods and goods mainly from Nigeria, Ghana, Sierra Leone. You'll find smoked and dried fish, smoked goat meat, salted cow's feet and pig's feet, cuttlefish and cornmeal. Avocados the size of melons, spices and leaves and fresh produce, breads and cakes are just a few more of the items Charlie has for sale. There's also a wonderful selection of videos, music (records and tapes), magazines, books and cosmetics from West Africa. The staff are generous with help and advice.

FUDGO

184 Ealing Road, Wembley
081 902 4820

Station Alperton underground

Bus 79, 83, 297

Open Sun–Sat 0930–1830

MOON FOODS

183 Shepherd's Bush
Market, W12
081 749 1412

Station Shepherd's Bush/
Goldhawk Road underground

Bus 94, 237

Open Mon–Sat 0900–1800
closed public holidays

PANZER
DELICATESSEN
LIMITED

15 Circus Road, NW8
071 722 8162

Station St John's Wood
underground

Bus 13, 46, 82, 113

Open Mon–Fri 0800–1900
Sat 0800–1800
Sun 0800–1400

Another cash-and-carry type of place with lots of tins of Indian vegetables ready to cook, jars of pickles, bags of rice, etc. But the interesting feature here is the tremendous range of flours for preparing so many different dishes – each one requiring a special type of flour – iddly, juwar, doosa and so on. Much of the flour is freshly milled at the back of the shop – just as it might still be in the sub-continent. They also grind spices.

This is a cash and carry cum supermarket – open to all and a great place for bulk buys, therefore good value, for lentils, yellow split peas and the like. For serious rice eaters there are 10 kilo sacks of basmati and other types. It's really international – from Saxa salt to Buitoni macaroni, south-east Asian food, Middle Eastern (tabbouleh and felafel mix), Greek, Chinese (noodles, dried silver fish and anchovies), Indian (chapattis, ground spices, ghee in tins), Jamaican buns and breads. Plus any spice you could imagine, a wide range of oils and, in with the exotica, the mundane – corned beef, crisps and sponge-cake mix. And if you ever wanted to know where to find Constitution bitters – here it is.

It's hard to know where to start in this tightly packed shop. It is a supermarket carrying ordinary everyday items and innumerable delicacies and specialities. An American friend comes from miles away for packs and tins of North American products. Many luxury lines, from caviar to fine French preserves, Cipriani pasta, chocolates from Ackerman and Charbonnel et Walker (see pages 125, 123–4). Häagen-Dazs and New England ices nestle in the freezer. They carry many kosher lines and the deli counter is well stocked with chopped herring, gefilte fish and other Jewish favourites, including hot salt beef and foods from Greece and the Middle East. The bakery has a surprising number of unusual breads. The outside greengrocery is quite exceptional with species you may not see anywhere else and many miniature vegetables.

TESCO STORES LIMITED

Coppetts Centre, North
Circular Road, N12
081 368 1244

Bus 134, 234

Open Mon–Thur 0930–2000
Fri 0930–2100
Sat 0800–2000

This is one of Tesco's larger stores with free car parking, fresh-fish counter, in-store bakery and a coffee shop, to name but a few of the wonders this supermarket chain now provides. In recent years there's been a total change throughout Tesco's with health, nutrition and food education taking a major role. They have been pioneers in the area of organic produce. All the major stores have good ranges of wines and spirits and selected stores have fresh oysters from Loch Fyne.

Also at Brent Park, Great Central Way, Neasden, NW10, 081 459 6591, where in addition they cater for the large local Indian community with interesting specialities. Smaller stores throughout London.

V.B. & SONS

218 Ealing Road, Wembley
081 902 8579/903 7507

Station Alperton underground

Bus 79, 83, 297

Open Mon–Sat 0900–1830

Indian housewives like to buy their groceries in large quantities and this is just the place to go, in the middle of Ealing Road, which could be Bombay, with the sari shops and teeming hordes jostling on the pavements. It's impossible to list all the things you can find – simply everything you could ever need to make Indian food, from sacks of Basmati rice to spices in such huge packs it would need a lifetime to use them . . . but our friend Mrs Patel buys supplies for just a year at a time. Plastic bins full of wonderful pickles and chutneys, gram flour (from Leicester), pressed rice, pistachios salted and plain, shelled and unshelled. Nuts are particularly good buys, but everything is well priced so go with an empty car boot.

WAITROSE

191 Finchley Road, NW3
071 624 0453

Station Finchley Road
underground
Finchley Road and Frognal BR

Bus 13, 82, 113, C11, C12

Open Mon–Wed 0900–2000
Thur–Fri 0830–2000
Sat 0830–1730

This is Waitrose's flagship and thus one of the largest and best stocked branches. It caters for a quite demanding local clientele and the helpful staff are adept at solving problems. On Thursday, Friday and Saturday the fresh-fish counter has a selection of exotic fish (parrot, shark and swordfish and others from far-flung seas) in addition to the more mundane varieties. They also have a useful loan service if you need a fish kettle. The cheese counter carries an interesting range of British farmhouse cheeses, the bakery tempts with freshly baked bread and pâtisserie. The greengrocery often has unusual items and many organic fruits and vegetables. The wine department has a good selection especially in the middle price range.

There's a coffee/snack shop at the side of the shop with food to eat in or take away.

Branches throughout London. Specially recommended at Brent Cross for fresh fish and often hare, pheasant, guinea fowl, etc and excellent cheese counter. King's Road – 'it's consistent'. Sheen for vegetables, fruit and better than average fish.

WING YIP

395 Edgware Road, NW2
081 450 0422
fax 081 452 1478

Open Mon–Sat 0930–1900
Sun 1030–1900
Closed only on Christmas and
Boxing Days

A huge Chinese cash and carry located on an industrial estate (at the corner of Humber Road and Edgware Road) – this is somewhere to go with a car with a large boot. Massive stocks of everything Chinese and most oriental ingredients you might fancy. There's a Japanese corner, with very pretty lacquer and other bowls (inexpensive too) and a limited selection of food. Freezers full of steamed dumplings, prawns in all sizes, Cherry Valley Peking duck (a favourite of Chinese restaurateurs), duck's tongues, feet and other parts. Most things available in case lots or singly – no problem about buying domestic quantities. Utensils, Indian spices, fruit and vegetables, yards of shelves of jars. And all very well priced.

YOSHINO

15 Monkville Parade,
Finchley Road, NW11
081 209 0966

Station Golders Green/
Finchley Central underground

Bus 13, 26, 260

Open Mon–Fri 1000–1800
Sat and Sun 1000–1900 and
most Bank Holidays

For the adventurous, the knowledgeable and preferably the Japanese speaker, this is a fascinating shop with all things Japanese. It goes without saying that the fish is of the freshest, and expertly prepared (with a team working from 4 a.m. every morning), whether for eating raw or cooking. The choice is tremendous, with octopus, cuttle fish, tuna, salted salmon, fish cut for sushi and sashimi, cod's roe plain and with spice. The meat is lean and beautifully butchered.

Yoshino

There are just a few prepared dishes. The shelves and freezers are full of Japanese products – certainly indispensable to the *cognoscenti* – take a Japanese-speaking friend if you don't know the language, though there is a manager who can be pressed into translating if necessary. This firm has a travelling grocery shop which ventures all the way to Scotland to supply food to far-flung expats. Also related to the Japan Centre (see page 150).

North East

CAMLIK

13 Green Lanes, N16
071 226 5925

Station Canonbury BR

Bus 73, 141, 171, 236

Open Sun–Sat 0900–2000

Describing itself as an English and continental grocers, this well-stocked shop has a good cross-section of food – with a heavy tilt towards Turkish/Cypriot goods. Outside is a greengrocery section which has some unusual produce, much of it from Cyprus: gomëc (a green vegetable similar to spinach), sivri and carliston, varieties of chillies, white courgettes, spring onions thicker than baby leeks. Inside everything is delightfully higgledy-piggledy with Turkish sausages suspended under brooms, tahini next to pot noodles and pickled peppers, bottled pickled vine leaves. Natural strained yoghurt in 2 kilo containers at a fraction of supermarket prices. Sheep's yoghurt from Cyprus in earthenware pots. Pepper sauce, tripe, soup and apricot compôte. Fresh quinces, halva so rich and so reasonable! Loose dried figs and apricots, olives and feta in oil-drum-sized tins. Delicious pickled aubergines, gorgeous Turkish delight, kadaifi pastry . . . and on and on.

TURKISH FOOD CENTRE

89 Ridley Road, E8
071 254 6754
fax 071 249 4872

Station Dalston Kingsland BR

Bus 22a, 56, 67, 149

Open Mon–Sat 0800–1900

A modern supermarket, lacking perhaps the grandeur of the Grand Bazaar, but offering everything you need for Turkish cooking – much in wholesale packs if required. Groceries (including that apple tea you loved in Istanbul), good fresh fruit and vegetables, olives, pickles and peppers, halva and fresh meat, strained yoghurt (in 5 kilo containers).

Also at 332 Walworth Road, SE17, 071 703 9765 (open Mon–Sat 0900–2100, Sun 1000–1600)

South West

A & C CO

3 Atlantic Road, SW9
081 733 3766

Station Brixton underground
and BR

Bus 2b, 3a, 12, 45, 59, 109,
133, 159, 250

Open Mon–Sat 0800–2000

Previously Cypriot owned but now under a Portuguese proprietor, you can find the best of both countries here. Rich-flavoured Cypriot and Portuguese olive oils, Greek breads, marinated olives, nuts of all sorts. They make their own mayonnaise, taramasalata and hummus and have fresh vine leaves and many other Mediterranean herbs and fresh produce on the pavement. Everything is very clean and tidy and a contrast to the chaotic market a few steps away.

DEEPAK CASH & CARRY GROCERS

953 Garratt Lane, SW17
081 767 7819

Station Tooting Broadway
underground

Bus 44, 77, 220

Open Mon–Sat 0900–1900
Sun 1000–1530

Mainly Asian food in wholesale packs, this massive store is a good place to know in the area, with keen prices. There are boring British standards as well as the more exotic spices, lentils, rows of pickles, and everything for Indian cooking, including equipment. Catering packs of paper goods, an off-licence and greengrocery.

A. A. KING

30–4 New King's Road,
SW6
071 736 4004

Station Parsons Green
underground

Bus 22

Open Mon–Fri 0700–1730
Sat 0700–1700

Mr King's empire embraces three shops which together can provide almost all the food any self-respecting cook could possibly want. His first shop was a butcher's and when the one next door became available he turned it into a fish shop. Next door is a deli, baker's and confectioner's. In between he also sells fruit and vegetables. He considers the shops to be upmarket in everything, 'If you want anything classy we have it.' They have their own kitchens and bakery and offer to cook any type of bread you want. Such a claim has given rise to some interesting challenges. As traiteur Mr King provides pâtés, roulades, mousses, soups; if you take in your own dishes he'll fill them as you wish. Over eighty cheeses are in the deli. The fishmonger's deals in the top end – Dover soles, New Zealand mussels, whatever is best in the market. The butcher's is more like a French butcher with plenty of prepared cuts. As if all the retail activity were not enough for this energetic monarch, he runs a catering company too.

Butchers 071 736 4004
Delicatessen and catering 071 731 7355
Fishmonger's and greengrocer's 071 736 2826

ROBINSON'S

50–1 3rd Avenue, Granville
Arcade, Coldharbour Lane,
SW9
071 733 2405

Station Brixton underground
and BR

Bus 2, 2b, 3a, 45, 59, 109,
133, 159

Open Mon–Sat 0700–1830

All you need for Afro-Caribbean cookery is likely to be tucked into this small corner of Granville Arcade. There are greengroceries and general groceries, salt and smoked fish, salted pig's trotters, pounded yam, white cornmeal, canned breadfruit and ackees, fresh fu fu and ogi and plenty of West Indian breads. Various other shops in the arcade have interesting if not immediately recognisable edibles. There are a number of fishmongers selling ordinary and extraordinary fish. Otto's at number 23 is an old Lambeth fish curer's.

TALAD THAI

320 Upper Richmond Road,
SW15
081 789 8084

Station Putney BR

Bus 37, 74

Open Mon–Sat 0900–2000
Sun 1000–1900

Everything for Thai cooking – and the books to tell you how. Plenty of fresh ingredients: tamarind, sliced and shredded fresh bamboo shoots for curry and soup, lemon grass, tiny white aubergines. And shelves of packets and canned foods. Thai sweetmeats and charming service make this a pleasant and fascinating stop.

South East

EUNICE TROPICAL FOOD SHOP

133 Deptford High Street,
SE8
081 469 3095

Station Deptford BR

Bus 1, 188

Open Mon–Sat 0900–1800

A smiling Eunice is in charge of her bazaar, which contains everything that local West Africans seek for their cooking pots. If you don't know much about this cuisine, you will find some very strange-looking items such as smoked bush meat, cowskins for stew and masses of smoked fish. There are different varieties – snapper, herring, cutfish – all imported from West Africa and used for gravies or soups. Bottles of home-made sauces, some looking very fiery like sheto with shrimps, peppers, onion and tomatoes, and kenkey – corn dumplings, made by Eunice or her family. Nestling amongst the boxes of fruit and vegetables you might see other exotica – such as the most enormous fresh snails, all the way from West Africa (fortunately by air, not under their own steam).

⇒ *Fishmongers* ⇐

Contrary to what we are led to believe, wet-fish shops are by no means sinking without trace, as the weekend queues outside Steve Hatt's in Islington confirm.

As the fish around our own coasts becomes depleted we are being introduced to exotic species from far-flung shores and our choice is ever widening. Consequently shopping for fish has become a great adventure and entrepreneurial fishmongers have risen to meet the challenge.

All the fishmongers we have met not only sell fish, they are happy both to give advice and to take the pain out of preparation which, as well as filleting and scaling, often includes selling sauces and stocks. The better supermarkets (pages 61, 65) now recognise this growing interest and are installing or improving existing wet-fish counters.

The following entries from other sections may also be of interest for good fresh fish: Arthur's; Faulkner's; The Fresh Fish Company; H. J. Grimes Limited; A. A. King; B. Kingston; Pat Piggott; The Real Meat Company; Yoshino.

Central

ABERDEEN SEA PRODUCTS LIMITED

Unit 4, Toulmin Street, SE1
071 407 0247

Station Borough underground

Bus 133, P3

Open Mon–Fri 0800–1730
Sat 0900–1300

This could win the prize for the best (and most modest) fish place in town. Mainly wholesale, they supply Harrods, the Savoy, etc, at crack of dawn, but are also very welcoming to retail customers. They sell the finest quality at amazing prices (20 per cent less than supermarkets, they claim). They'll poach a whole salmon for you, boil a lobster, or sell it live if you prefer. Fresh langoustines and oysters, frozen soft-shell crabs and plenty more – all kept under absolutely ideal conditions since the proprietors hold basic food hygiene certificates so know what's what. They also can give you recipes and will deliver locally or further afield for big orders. A super find.

ASHDOWN LIMITED

23 Leadenhall Market, EC3
071 626 0178/1949

Station Aldgate underground
Fenchurch Street BR

Bus 5, 15, 25, 40, 42, 67,
78, 100, 253, X15

Open Mon–Fri 0530–1530

BLAGDEN FISHMONGERS

65 Paddington Street, W1
071 935 8321

Station Baker Street
underground

Bus 2a, 2b, 13, 18, 27, 30,
74, 113, 159

'We do everything that is available in the market,' which can mean squid from the Falklands or lobsters from Scotland, which are kept in their own tanks and cooked on the premises. There is, indeed, everything, from herrings upwards, with oysters, mussels, tiger prawns, dressed crab, Finnan haddies, smoked fish, including tuna, swordfish and marlin. Busy City folk can have their fish delivered to their offices.

This old-fashioned, long-established fishmonger deals in game and poultry too. In season expect to find partridge, grouse, wild duck, guinea fowl, pigeon, pheasant, snipe and plover. Venison can be ordered. Smoked magret de canard is always in stock, as will be a selection of smoked fish – eel, salmon, trout, mackerel, finnan haddock and smoked roe. Loch Fyne kippers. Mussels from Aberdeen, oysters, Devon scallops, squid, and potted shrimps are regularly to be found and they will get anything to order (including

Blagden fishmongers

Open Mon 0730–1700
Tues–Fri 0730–1730
Sat 0730–1300

wild boar). They cook their own lobster and crabs. Turkey and geese for Christmas come from Norfolk and capons (large chicks officially). Delivery is free over a wide area of London, and as if all this was not enough, John Blagden has plenty of printed recipes and advice to give away at the cash desk, including a cheerful monthly newsletter detailing the seasonal specialities.

CHALMERS & GRAY

67 Notting Hill Gate, W11
071 221 6177
fax 071 221 1995

Station Notting Hill Gate underground

Bus 12, 27, 28, 31, 52

Open Mon–Sat 0800–1800

Daily deliveries in west and central London and provision of attractive recipes on cards make this fishmonger, game and poultryman a user-friendly place. There's haggis all year, game in season and plenty more of interest. The shop is well designed and modern, the service helpful – no problem with filleting or trimming to order. Particularly good range of seafood – oysters, cockles, mussels, scallops. Crabs come from Devon and Cornwall and, like the lobsters, are cooked on the premises. They supply the dining rooms of many large City banks and financial institutions. Free-range poultry, including geese.

CHINATOWN FISH AND MEAT MARKET

14 Newport Place, WC2
071 437 0712

Station Leicester Square/ Piccadilly Circus underground

Bus 14, 24, 29, 176

Open Sun–Sat 1030–1900

In the heart of Chinatown, open seven days a week, this is the place to go for more exotic and interesting fish than your local fishmonger may have on offer. The two large tanks contain huge carp and eel and the slabs have a wonderful array – emperor bream or sea bream, bass, fresh king prawns, grouper, clams, oysters and fresh scallops and many others. The friendly young staff are eager to please and are likely to offer a bargain such as conger head for soup if you show interest in the unusual. A freezer contains odds and ends of meat, but the fresh fish is the real attraction.

H. S. LINWOOD & SONS LIMITED

67 Leadenhall Market, EC3
071 929 0554

Station Aldgate underground
Fenchurch Street BR

Bus 5, 15, 25, 40, 42, 67, 78, 100, 253, X15

Open Mon–Fri 0630–1500

There has been a market around this area since the fourteenth century, but the current buildings date from the 1880s, when this high-class fish shop was established. They have an excellent display of good-looking fresh fish – with lobsters, fresh king prawns, queen scallops, fresh crabs and massive tuna fish, squid, Cornish skate. Smoked salmon comes from the Queen's fish supplier, Sproston's (see page 78). There is, too, somewhat unnervingly, a large tank of ornamental exotic fish. They deliver in London.

RICHARD'S

21 Brewer Street, W1
071 437 1358

Station Piccadilly Circus/
Leicester Square underground

Bus 3, 6, 9, 13, 14, 15, 19,
22, 38, 53, 88, 94

Open Tues–Thur 0800–1700
Fri 0800–1730
Sat 0800–1500

There was great gloom when this old-established Soho fishmonger closed down recently – the end of an era. Then they re-appeared several shops further down the road and though the spanking new premises lack the old-fashioned charm of the original shop, regulars are pleased to see them back. Wild Scotch smoked salmon has always been a mainstay of their trade, sliced as required, not prepacked. Prices are very competitive – Dover soles were selling for considerably less here than from a stall in Berwick Street. Wild salmon and sea trout, fresh English squid (as opposed to frozen foreign) and fresh tuna and swordfish are all likely to be on the list when in season. They cook crabs and lobsters on the premises and have undyed smoked haddock and cod's roe. The staff are friendly and helpful and it's comforting to know Soho's old reliable fishmonger is still in business.

North West

B & M SEAFOODS

258 Kentish Town Road,
NW5
071 485 0346

Station Kentish Town
underground and BR

Bus 214, C2, C11

Open Tues–Sat 0730–1830

In a perhaps curious reversal of trends, this fishmonger is now a butcher as well – with supplies from The Real Meat Company. They make seventeen varieties of really meaty sausage – 'no rubbish' we were assured – and have freshly cut bacon. On the fish side they have daily deliveries from Devon, including squid, bags of live mussels, conger, mullet, whiting, plenty of 'mainstream' fish, but not a lot of the exotic and unusual. All of which proves a fish shop doesn't have to be glam to be good.

See also The Real Meat Company, 3a Nugent Terrace, NW8

BROWN'S

37–9 Charlbert Street, NW8
071 722 8237

Station St John's Wood
underground

Bus 13, 46, 82, 113

Open Tues–Fri 0830–1730
Sat 0830–1530

There's a tremendous choice of fish in this well-staffed shop, which has won the Seafood Industry Award for best fishmonger. It would be difficult not to find something interesting and perhaps novel to try. They make up fish kebabs with salmon, monkfish, tuna, mackerel, and prepare sushi. There are fresh squid, fresh peeled prawns, Scottish langoustines, baby hakes. They have deliveries from France including Normandy and Brittany oysters and direct from the English coast, with sea bass from Cornwall. Lobster and crabs are boiled in the shop. Local delivery as far as the West End and once a week all the way to Totteridge.

J. A. CORNEY LIMITED

9 Hallswelle Parade,
Finchley Road, NW11
081 455 9588

Station Golders Green
underground + bus

Bus 13, 26, 260

Open Tues–Thur 0730–1700
Fri 0730–1600
Sat–Sun 0730–1300

Like its rival down the road (Stoller's, see page 76), Corney's offers Jewish specialities like minced fish and gefilte fish balls, but it is not licensed as kosher and therefore opens on Saturdays. Expect to queue at weekends as it is a popular place to buy keenly priced good-quality fish – salmon especially. Helpful staff will always find bones for your fish soup.

COVENT GARDEN FISHMONGERS

37 Turnham Green Terrace,
W4
081 995 9273

Station Turnham Green
underground

Bus 27, 237, 267

Open Tues–Sat 0730–1730

Phil Diamond was a taxi driver for many years before his love of fish drove him into the business. His enthusiasm is catching and the fine display in his window reflects this. You don't have to ask for your fish to be filleted, it's always available that way. You are likely to see plenty of exotic fish – bourgeois and parrot, job jaune and job gris, green-lip mussels – as well as home-grown turbot, mullet, kippers from Loch Fyne and the Isle of Man, oysters and plenty of smoked fish. Barbary duck breasts, mallard and pheasant are usually in stock

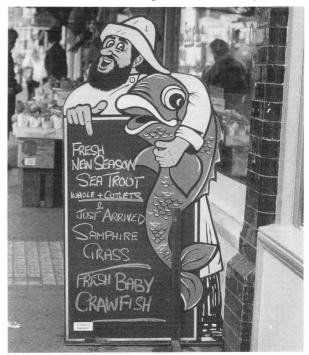

Covent Garden fishmongers

as are jars of French fish soup. Phil is putting his considerable knowledge to good use and writing a book about his favourite subject.

FISH AND FOWL

145 Highgate Road, NW5
071 284 4184

Station Kentish Town
underground
Gospel Oak BR

Bus 214, C2, C11

Open Tues–Sat 0930–1730

As the name suggests, this enterprising shop deals in fish and fowl and a lot more besides. The owners started by supplying top restaurants and now combine that with their retail outlet, where you can find oils and vinegars, dried wild mushrooms or fish soup in jars. There's always a good selection of fresh fish, which arrives from Cornwall daily, plus frozen large prawns, etc. French duck breasts, smoked and unsmoked, are a useful item for the freezer, as are other French game and poultry. You'll find a range of interesting sausages, including venison. With an eye to keeping customers happy, they offer advice on cooking (being professional chefs themselves) and provide recipes on request.

JOHN NICHOLSON

46 Devonshire Road, W4
081 994 0809

Station Turnham Green
underground

Bus 27, 237, 267

Open Mon–Fri 0800–1800
Sat 0800–1700

The delightful John Nicholson's aim in life is to give his customers pain-free fishmongery, to which end the walls of his shop are plastered with signs like 'for a stylish evening of minimalist chic with sashimi on octagonal black plates, set the scene with your fishmonger'. Classy stuff indeed. As a fifth-generation fishmonger (by way of a law degree) he obviously has a feel for fish and how to present it. Undyed smoked haddock, made to his grandfather's recipe, the best of the day's deliveries from Cornwall and Scotland and plenty of useful extras for home cooks like sauces (just add cream) and dill mustard for his gravadlax. Since Chiswick is short of good cheese he has jumped into the gap. His chiller cabinets have giant prawns, boned chicken and lamb parcels stuffed with apricot, honey and ginger. An exciting shop, an enthusiastic proprietor.

SCOTT'S

94 High Road, N2
081 444 7606

Station East Finchley
underground

Bus 17, 102, 143, 236

Open Tues–Thur 0830–1730
Fri 0830–1800
Sat 0830–1700

The invariable queues attest to the long-standing popularity of this splendid fishmonger's, where only fresh fish is sold (except for frozen prawns). It's kept on beds of ice which help to maintain the freshness – better than refrigeration which dries out fish, according to Albert Scott. Quality reigns and most interesting is the home-cured fish for which they are well known. Albert is proud of this side of his business, carried out in the traditional smokehole behind the shop. Large sides of salmon, undyed Finnan haddock and cod's roe are regularly smoked. Colchester oysters and clams, seaweeds and chopped fish, exotics like snappers and bourgeois, good advice and friendly service add up to the sort of fishmonger we all wish we had round the corner.

SAM STOLLER & SON

28 Temple Fortune Parade, NW11
081 458 1429

Station Golders Green underground + bus

Bus 13, 26, 260

Open Sun 0800–1300
Mon 0800–1400
Tues–Thur 0700–1700
Fri 0700–1430

Fresh deliveries on a Sunday would be a good reason to visit Sam Stoller, but another could be that you'll find the best-priced salmon (farmed or wild) anywhere in town. This fishmonger only sells kosher fish – but there's a wide enough choice, including ready minced fish and smoked fish.

Also at 8 Stamford Hill, N16 081 806 2101

North East

STEVE HATT

88 Essex Road, N1
071 226 3963

Station Angel underground/ Essex Road BR

Bus 38, 56, 73, 171a

Open Tues–Sat 0730–1700
Thur 0730–1300

Steve's great-grandfather started this business at the turn of the century and personal service is still one of its features. The staff cherish their long-term relationship with their customers and the long queues, especially at the weekends, confirm this. There's not much you can't get here if it is available, either from France, Newlyn market in Cornwall or Brixham, as well as fish from far-flung seas like swordfish from Florida, halibut from Iceland. Best farmed salmon from Shetland at very good prices, superb Rossmore oysters, whole turbot from Devon – whatever is best Steve is bound to have. The traditional smokeholes are in use every day to smoke salmon, trout, mackerel, haddock, cod and roe. Crabs are freshly cooked. Each weekend they have fresh Scotch saddles of venison. Customers make good use of the answerphone at Hatt's, calling in with their requirements so that they can be sure of getting exactly what they want before it goes on to the slabs.

South West

ALEXANDER & KNIGHT

18 Barnes High Street, SW13
081 876 1297

Barnes High Street has just about every shop you could want including this excellent fishmonger, who will deliver and do special orders, and even sells fish kettles. At weekends you can buy Loch Fyne and Manx kippers. They sell tiny smoked haddock, undyed

Station Barnes Bridge BR

Bus 9

Open Mon–Tues, Thur–Sat
0800–1700
Wed 0800–1300

THE CATCH

760 Fulham Road, SW6
071 736 1523

Station Putney Bridge
underground

Bus 22

Open Tues–Fri 0830–1730
Sat 0830–1700

and off the bone, Loch Etive mussels, Beluga and Sevruga caviar, bass, halibut, scallops and their own homemade salmon fishcakes.

Two very discriminating shoppers told us not to miss this Catch. Much of the first-rate fish here comes direct from Cornwall – the monkfish, squid, brill and mackerel. The salmon comes mainly from the Shetlands, via Billingsgate. If they don't have a species it is probably because it is not at its best so not worth buying. 'There's no point in having plaice for the sake of it if there's too much roe in it,' they will tell you. Advice on what to buy is worth taking. As well as the fresh fish there's a good stock of different types of prawns in the freezer.

Jarvis & Sons Limited

JARVIS & SONS LIMITED

56 Coombe Road, Norbiton,
Kingston

A very popular fishmonger with people coming some distance for its excellent quality and range of fish and game. It is always heartening to see Japanese in a fish shop since they will only buy the freshest; Jarvis's have many Japanese customers – indeed they stock fish

081 547 3664
(answerphone 081 546 2888)
fax 081 943 0470

Station Norbiton BR

Bus K2, K3

Open Tues 0830–1700
Wed 0830–1300
Thur 0830–1700
Fri 0800–1700
Sat 0800–1600
Good Friday and Easter
Saturday open half day

from Japanese waters like samma, and will fillet fish specially for sushi, etc. It is normal to find sea urchins, fresh squid and cuttlefish, large and small clams, fresh cockles, fresh king prawns, tuna and swordfish. They smoke their own salmon, haddock and bloaters. Venison (at a bargain price for stewing), smoked quail, fresh guinea fowl are amongst the game.

L. S. MASH

11 Atlantic Road, SW9
071 274 6423

Station Brixton underground
and BR

Bus 2b, 3a, 12, 45, 59, 109,
133, 159

Open Mon–Sat 0730–1800

Underneath the arches there's a lovely show of fish all scaled and gutted and looking very appealing. Plenty of choice here, with squid, red snapper, herring, salt fish, smoked fish. They'll get anything to order.

W. F. SPROSTON

17–19 Claylands Place, SW8
071 735 3331

Station Oval underground

Bus 3, 36, 59, 95, 109, 133

Open Mon–Fri 0930–1200
Sat 0800–1030

From these tiny premises, down a little alley behind the Oval, some of the top restaurants in the city are supplied, as are the Queen and Queen Mother. Answerphone for orders – they go home early in order to be at the market long before dawn.

❧ *A Good Cuppa* ❧

The tea and coffee houses of eighteenth-century London were where everything happened – where the business and the gossip of the town was enthusiastically carried on. Nowadays relatively few tea and coffee shops offer the chance to sit and while away the hours over newspapers and chess boards. None the less we feel we should be very proud of today's tea and coffee merchants – many long established – who provide the citizens of the capital with a breadth of choice and quality which would be hard to find anywhere else in the world.

Apart from the shops which only sell the wherewithal to make tea and coffee at home, there are still some where you can sample before you buy and we have noted these, along with cafés which excel in providing a good cuppa and appropriate accompaniments. And the only good thing about the concourses of the mainline stations is the Costa coffee shops, where you can buy the beans and have an excellent cappuccino.

Afternoon tea is one of the great glories of British life and rightly a perennial favourite with tourists. All the major hotels offer a traditional, if pricey, set tea and our favourites include Brown's (Albermarle Street), the Ritz (Piccadilly), the Waldorf (Aldwych), the Inn on the Park (Hamilton Place), the Langham Hotel (Portland Place), the Lanesborough (Hyde Park Corner) and Claridge's (Brook Street). On a sartorial note, be prepared to be turned away if 'improperly' dressed.

The following entries from other sections may also be of interest for their coffee: Bodum Shop; Clarke's; The Coffee Gallery; Richard Hart; The Narrow Gauge (Shop).

Central

ALGERIAN COFFEE STORES

52 Old Compton Street, W1
071 437 2480
fax 071 437 5470

Station Piccadilly Circus/
Leicester Square underground

Bus 14, 24, 29, 176

Open Mon–Sat 0900–1900

Established in 1887 by an Algerian family, the shop is now in Italian hands but has changed very little over the years, as the old photos witness. A welcoming smell greets you – you can sip a cup of coffee while you choose from their amazing selection, including house specials of Lebanese with cardamoms or Arabic with spices. There is a formidable array of teas (138 varieties), plus tins and coffee makers, tea bricks and many marvellous sweetmeats (chocolate-covered figs specially recommended). They post worldwide and deliver in the W1 area.

Algerian Coffee Stores

ANGELUCCI COFFEE MERCHANTS

23b Frith Street, W1
071 437 5889

This is just a sliver of a shop, but it is much loved by devoted customers of long standing. The business has been in the family since 1929. The coffee is freshly roasted three times a week, 'which is the secret of good coffee', Mr Angelucci says. Most popular is Mokital, which is their own blend. A few packs of Italian dried

Station Tottenham Court
Road/Leicester Square
underground

Bus 7, 8, 10, 14, 19, 22b,
55, 73, 134, 176

Open Mon–Wed, Fri–Sat
0900–1700
Thur 0900–1300

AROMA

1a Dean Street, W1
071 287 1633
fax 071 287 1714

Station Tottenham Court
Road underground

Bus 7, 8, 10, 14, 19, 22b,
25, 29, 38, 73, 134

Open Mon–Fri 0730–2030
Sat 0900–1900

BAR ITALIA

22 Frith Street, W1
071 437 4520

Station Tottenham Court
Road/Leicester Square
underground

Bus 14, 24, 29, 176

Open 24 hours a day, 7 days a
week

BETJEMAN &
BARTON

43 Elizabeth Street, SW1
071 730 5086

Station Victoria underground
and BR

Bus 11, 239, C1

goods – arborio rice, pasta, and so on – sit upon the shelves. They are there more as a service to customers than as a gesture to commerce.

Oxford Street and environs are not, sadly, noted for much except an excess of dirt and general tat, but this fresh and modern designer coffee bar is in a different class. The feeling is of a very *à la mode* Italian café. The owner, Michael Zur-Szpiro, has sought out good sources for his supplies of excellent bread and pâtisserie; for his two dishes of the day which can be eaten hot or cold, one of which is always vegetarian; for unusual vegetarian sandwiches like mangetout and broccoli with mushrooms, pine kernels and sesame dressing. Coffee is espresso (strong) or ristretto (stronger) or cappuccino, café au lait or café crème. Packets of tea, coffee and Swiss chocolate and the colourful plates which are used in the shop are all on sale. Whether you stop just for a coffee and croissant on your way to the office, or longer for lunch, this is definitely a step in the right direction. They will fax their up-to-date menu and deliver in the area.

A Soho institution, almost like a time warp of the 1950s, this was one of London's first coffee bars and is still going strong. They obviously don't feel the need to modernise – down to the black and white TV at the back of the shop. You are guaranteed authentic, and some say 'the best', espresso in town, with some fairly solid-looking cakes, Italian ices and filled rolls. Like the Windmill Theatre, they never close ('Well, maybe one hour between 0600 and 0700').

If you think that the be all and end all of tea buying is a pack of eighty tea bags at your local supermarket, do look in at this splendid shop, which is known for its high-quality teas and also for its unusual ceramic teapots. It imports pure teas, which are often from a named garden, much in the same way as you would choose a wine from a particular vineyard. And such magnificent names – bombagalla fannings (fannings

Open Mon–Fri 1000–1730
Sat 1000–1400

means finely cut tea) or Pouchkine (which is very aromatic, like an Earl Grey with orange and grapefruit oils as well as bergamot). For the real connoisseur there are a dozen Darjeelings, the grandest of which will cost you more than £30 a quarter. All the teas come in pretty caddies as well as packets and can be mailed for you. A few very good coffees are available, and at Christmas they sell biscuits, chocolates and cakes.

Also at Chelsea Garden Market, Chelsea Harbour, SW10, 071 823 3273, where you can have a tea tasting of any of their many teas.

BUTLERS TEA & COFFEE COMPANY

26 Rupert Street, W1
071 734 5821

Station Piccadilly Circus underground

Bus 3, 6, 9, 13, 14, 15, 19, 22, 38, 53, 88, 94

Open Mon–Fri 0845–2000
Sat 1000–2100
Sun 1200–2200

How wonderful to find a pretty and peaceful spot to have a good cup of coffee only a few steps away from the grot and noise of Piccadilly Circus. The shop is on the corner of the historically interesting site of Rupert Court, which has been restored. As well as freshly roasted coffee and an impressive selection of tea, they sell some fun mugs, teapots and a few gadgets. No cooked food (except reheated snacks) but a few cakes and a choice of coffee or tea or a wondrous mocha – chocolate and coffee served in a large cup with a minuscule macaroon.

H. R. HIGGINS (COFFEE-MAN) LIMITED

79 Duke Street, W1
071 629 3913

Station Bond Street underground

Bus 6, 7, 8, 10, 12, 13, 15, 16, 25, 73, 88, 94

Open Mon–Wed 0845–1730
Thur–Fri 0845–1800
Sat 1000–1700

The gentle Miss Audrey Higgins, daughter of the coffee-man himself, is the perfect person to tell you about this most wonderful commodity – and where better than sitting over a cup of the delicious liquid in the downstairs tasting area of the shop. Since they moved from their original premises in South Molton Street, they have, alas, had to forgo roasting beans on the premises, but nothing much else has altered the charm of this firm. Now joined by the third generation (Tony's son, David) they continue to offer the very finest coffees, and now teas too. They keep their eyes open and buy interesting small parcels of top grade – which is something only a small family business can do. They sell coffee makers, especially espresso machines, and have a flourishing mail-order business. They can arrange tasting sessions for small groups and Miss Audrey and Mr Tony are available to talk on coffee – a subject they know and love.

MARKUS COFFEE COMPANY

13 Connaught Street, W2
071 723 4020

Station Marble Arch
underground

Bus 6, 7, 8, 15, 16, 30, 36,
36b, 73, 74, 82, 88

Open Mon–Fri 0830–1730
Sat 0830–1300

Serious coffee drinkers will certainly agree with Markus that to be enjoyed at its best coffee should always be freshly roasted and ground. They deliver in and around central London and guarantee the beans will have been roasted within the past twenty-four hours. Near-by residents have the pleasure of enjoying the wonderful aroma which floats across Connaught Square when the daily ritual is performed. There are twenty-six different coffees and they blend to suit all tastes and occasions. Their specialities are their own blend called Regent & Negresco and a dark roast decaffeinated (steam processed), both of which are good enough to please the most discriminating. They also sell a range of teas and a number of different sugars and carry a stock of coffee makers for both domestic and commercial use.

MONMOUTH COFFEE HOUSE

27 Monmouth Street, WC2
071 836 5272
071 379 4337 (credit card orders)
fax 071 240 2442

Station Tottenham Court
Road/Leicester Square/Covent
Garden underground

Bus 14, 19, 22b, 24, 29, 38,
176

Open Mon–Fri 0930–1830
Sat 0930–1800
Sun 1100–1700

The coffee talk here is serious – a small tasting area is reserved for sampling and they like to promote the idea of tasting before you buy. But you can also pay and sit down to enjoy a cup of the black stuff and read the papers. Croissants and pastries are sometimes available and they sell bread from Sally Clarke. A descriptive list is available and they will deliver in central London (free for orders of over £30) as well as posting throughout the UK. They select the finest unblended Arabica coffees and roast six days a week, so it is all as fresh as can be. Each coffee is roasted dark or medium and among the more unusual varieties are two from Papua New Guinea, one organic. You can buy in bulk and save.

THE TEA HOUSE

15a Neal Street, WC2
071 240 7539

Station Covent Garden
underground

Bus 1, 4, 6, 9, 11, 13, 15, 77,
168, 171, 176

Open Mon–Sat 1100–1900
Sun 1100–1800

All you ever wanted to know about tea but were afraid to ask. Wonderful aromas fill the air – specially if they are packing their whole-fruit teas. This is such a pretty and fascinating shop stocking absolutely everything imaginable connected with tea, with eighty different varieties of 'real' tea and many herb and fruit teas. There are eighty tea bricks looking like giant dominoes, made of compressed tea, and a host of small gadgetry – infusers, fortune-telling cups, kettle protectors, handles for pots. There are a few select jams and honeys and caddies, cosies and mugs. And upstairs, pots and pots of pots with a wall of pigeon holes holding sixty-one, with more on shelves. They come in the wildest possible shapes – a polo mint, a camel, the Red Baron, country cottages – you name it. The book selection has some esoteric numbers – *The Urasenke Tradition of Tea* (didn't you always yearn to know about that?), *The Japanese Tea Ceremony* and guides to afternoon tea in and out of the capital.

TWININGS

216 Strand, WC2
071 353 3511

Station Aldwych/Temple underground

Bus 1, 4, 6, 9, 11, 13, 15, 68, 168, 171, 176

Open Mon–Fri 0930–1700

In 1706, when the City coffee houses were beginning to move to Westminster, Thomas Twining opened Tom's Coffee House at this address in the Strand. The family firm has been selling its wares (now coffee takes a bit of a back seat to teas) there ever since. In addition to the long narrow shop, which stocks all the huge variety of teas made by this well-known company, at the back is a very interesting little museum devoted to the history of Twinings. There are family portraits, documents

Sam Twining

relating to early business matters, pictures of the old horse-drawn vans that used to deliver tea and coffee and general tea memorabilia. Don't miss it if you are in the shop buying your quarter pound of Gunpowder, best Darjeeling, or Russian Caravan — just a few of the vast range of fine teas, herbal infusions and fruit teas. There are other tea-related items — tea towels, caddies, gift packs, and a few marmalades and preserves, biscuits and chocolates.

WHITTARD OF CHELSEA

Whiteleys, Queensway, W2
071 243 0350

Station Bayswater underground

Bus 7, 15, 27, 36

Open Mon–Thur, Sat 1000–2030
Fri 1000–2130
Sun 1100–1800

One of several shops of this old-established Chelsea company dealing in fine-quality teas and coffees, this particular branch is really for those who regard shopping as a spectator sport. It is a good place to find tea- or coffee-related gifts such as tea strainers, infusers, collectors' teapots and a deal of esoteric equipment for brewing the beverages. Needless to say they also have innumerable blends of tea and coffee for all tastes. In addition there are conserves, pickles, cakes, biscuits and hand-painted pottery cups, mugs, etc. Perhaps its most appealing *raison d'être* is that it is in one of London's most attractive shopping centres.

Also at 81 Fulham Road, SW3, 071 589 4261
73 Northcote Road, SW11, 071 924 1888
5 Artillery Row, SW1, 071 222 2855
33 Bedford Street, WC2, 071 497 0310

North West

CAMDEN COFFEE SHOP

11 Delancey Street, NW1
071 387 4080

Station Camden Town underground

Bus 24, 29, 134, 168, 253

Open Mon–Wed, Fri–Sat 0930–1800
Thur 0930–1300

George, the Greek-Cypriot owner, learnt his craft of coffee roasting from his grandfather back in Cyprus and bought this little shop from a fellow Cypriot from the same village twelve or so years ago. There are no fancy jars — just bags and bags of raw beans. He does all the roasting himself in antique apparatus, which is small enough to mean that everything is freshly roasted. He doesn't have a huge number of different coffees, but he roasts each variety several ways — light, medium and very strong and is happy to roast to your own specification if you buy over 5lb. He is quite poetic about the simple coffee bean and obviously has a devoted following of long-standing customers, many of whom come from far away.

IMPORTERS LIMITED

3 The Green, W5
081 567 2981

Station Ealing Broadway
underground and BR

Bus 65

Open Mon–Sat 0830–1730

They roast the coffee on the premises and have a special Turkish mix. The Ealing Yugoslav and Polish communities also have their own favourites. There's a full range of coffees, exotic fruit teas, decaffeinated tea and coffee. A small selection of fine chocolates and biscuits. Some coffee-making equipment. The café offers tea, coffee and light snacks.

Also at 76 Golders Green Road, NW11, 081 455 8186 (open Mon–Sat 0900–1800, Sun 1000–1700), where a newly decorated café replaces the somewhat frayed but much loved predecessor – now selling Louis's pâtisserie to enjoy with the excellent coffee.

W. MARTYN

135 Muswell Hill Broadway, N10
081 883 5642

Bus 43, 107, 234

Open Mon–Wed, Fri 0930–1730
Thur 0930–1300
Sat 0900–1730

If you would like your children or grandchildren to see what a grocery shop looked like 'in the olden days', go no further than Muswell Hill. Mr Martyn likes nothing better than to be told his shop is old fashioned: 'And with counter service', he will tell you proudly. He's the fourth generation since the shop started in 1897 and the original interior is still there. They still weigh and pack dry goods, such as the large selection of dried fruits. Shelves and counters are crowded with tins and jars of the best-quality fruits – exotic, tropical in rum or liqueur and preserves and pickles, honeys and hazelnut butter. The shop is best known for its freshly roasted coffee, the smell of which lures you in. There are fourteen different coffees and Mr Martyn advises his customers to buy small amounts often. There is loose tea as well as bags, and fruit and herbal too.

South West

FORGET ME NOT TEAS

45 High Street,
Wimbledon, SW19
081 947 3634

Station Wimbledon
underground and BR

Bus 93

Open Tues–Sat 0930–1730
Sun 0930–1745

A real gem of a place, this quintessentially English tearoom sits on the edge of the Common. You feel you are entering a private parlour, each table being laid with a crisp fine cloth and a different set of beautiful old china – part of a collection belonging to the proprietress. Victorian bric-à-brac decorates the two small rooms. The fare matches the old-fashioned feeling perfectly. 'All food is cooked to order. We do not have a microwave,' says a prominent notice. Everything, needless to say, is made on the premises. A light menu is served throughout the day and there's a selection of set teas such as the Gentleman's Club tea, with Scotch woodcock, devilled ham on toast and other suitable re-freshments. Cakes are luscious. Weekends are exceed-ingly popular and queues are lengthy. Go during the week if you can, but don't miss this real treat.

TEA TIME

21 The Pavement, Clapham
Common, SW4
071 622 4944

Station Clapham Common
underground

Bus 45a, 88, 137, 137a

Open Tues–Fri 1100–1730
Sat–Sun 1000–1800

This café is known far beyond the area and attracts a young crowd who enjoy the comfort food (steak and kidney pie, spaghetti bolognese, homemade soup and baked potatoes) as well as the cakes and ice creams. Novelty cakes are made to order. There are pretty, old-fashioned tins for sale (filled with teas or coffees) and Charbonnel et Walker (see pages 123–4) chocolates.

South East

COFFEE SHAK

39 Lee High Road, SE13
081 852 1084

Station Lewisham BR + bus

Bus 21, 122, 178, 261

Open Mon–Sat 0900–2300
Sun 1000–2000

An inexpensive vegan and vegetarian coffee bar and restaurant (bring your own wine). Dreamy mango lassi, cappuccino, herbal teas with vegan cakes, or a gooey banana cake are fine for morning coffee. Lots of spicy dishes and salads are served all day.

PETER DE WIT

21 Greenwich Church
Street, SE10
081 305 0048

Station Greenwich BR

Bus 188, 286

Open Mon–Fri 1100–1830
Sat–Sun 1030–1900

In the midst of fairly nasty caffs and greasy-spoon restaurants, which is mostly what this centre of so much history and beauty can offer, this higgledy-piggledy shop, owned by decorative artists, is a cosy place for a cup of tea. In the best traditions of English eccentricity you are surrounded by hand-painted puppets, wooden soldiers, prints of old Greenwich and the odd packing case. The homemade cakes, scones with clotted cream and fruit pies help to revive the flagging tourist and there are light meals and savouries for hungrier customers. Sit in the courtyard on a sunny day.

Greengrocers

There are plenty of greengrocers in London, but the really top-class ones are few and far between. It could well be that the leading supermarkets have taken a lot of business away from smaller greengrocers, who are not able to offer quality and price because the spoilage in fruit and vegetables is inevitably so high. The shops we have selected are hand picked and we hope there's not a rotten apple in the barrel.

The following entries from other sections may also be of interest for their particularly good fruit and vegetables: Adamou; Baily Lamartine; Bumblebee Natural Food Store; Bushwacker Wholefoods; Camlik; Gideon's; A. A. King; Paul's; Viniron.

Central

W. BAXTER & SONS LIMITED

31a Leadenhall Market, EC3
071 626 8081/2960

Station Aldgate underground
Fenchurch Street BR

Bus 5, 15, 25, 40, 42, 67, 78, 100, 253, X15

Open Mon–Thur 0700–1630
Fri 0700–1730

This greengrocery shop has been in the same family for well over a hundred years and you get old-fashioned service suited to its location in this lovely Victorian market. The fruit and vegetables are well displayed and there's a good choice of both home-grown and exotic produce and of groceries as well. They deliver to the City and West End.

FRY'S OF CHELSEA

14 Cale Street, SW3
071 589 0342

Station South Kensington
underground

Paul Fry has to be everyone's idea of the perfect greengrocer – not only does he have impeccable produce in his shop, but he seems to be one of the family to many of his customers. They leave their car keys with him in case the clampers come around; he sends them baskets of fruit when they have babies. His

Bus 14, 45a, 49, 219

Open Mon–Fri 0500–1700
Sat 0500–1300

award for London's best greengrocer is obviously deserved when you see the strikingly good quality of everything – the rare mushrooms, seakale, red chicory, sugar-snap peas as well as the everyday stuff. He has milk, eggs, fresh bread every day and delivers locally.

North West

THE APPLE MAN

114 Goldhawk Road, W12
081 749 9986

Station Goldhawk Road
underground

Bus 94, 237

Open Mon–Sat 0930–2000

The Apple Man is Jonathan Pollitzer, and the produce on sale comes from his Apple Pie Farm in Kent. He sells up to twelve varieties of English apples – crispins, russets, spartans, Coxes, bramley, goldens, Laxton's superb, discovery, James Grieve, scarlet pimpernels and outside the shop there are boxes of small apples at bargain prices (like 10p a pound) simply because the greengrocers he supplies don't want small fruit. You can buy apple and other trees and shrubs, grape vines and plants to order. Also from the farm are some organic fruit and vegetables, apple juice and purées and, in the season, cobnuts. Duskin's juices in delicious apple varieties are available as well as Merrydown vintage cider and juice. A happy, friendly place, they have an all-year-round supply of apples.

BLYTH

24 Temple Fortune Parade,
NW11
081 455 2383

Station Golders Green
underground

Bus 13, 26, 260

Open Mon–Fri 0830–1700
Sat 0830–1300

Highly recommended by many very satisfied customers (one praised the staff, saying they are happy to oblige even if you don't buy very much), this shop is known for its consistently fine quality fruit and vegetables. There may not be the widest choice – but that in itself can be a good sign in a greengrocery where standards are so critical, bearing in mind the high wastage factor in these commodities. The fact that they only have 'simply the best of everything' as we were told, means they must have a rapid turnover and are prepared to discard any tired produce.

CRESCENT FRUITERERS

62 Belsize Lane, NW3
071 435 9444

Station Belsize Park
underground

Bus 268

Open Mon–Sat 0700–1900
Sun 0700–1300

Well-laid-out shop, friendly service with a particularly good range of basics and exotics at reasonable prices for Hampstead. Quality is always good. They'll do special orders from the market if asked in advance. There's usually a bargain table of produce that won't last another day.

T. J. ELLINGHAM

179 Ballards Lane, N3
ex-directory

Station Finchley Central
underground

Bus 13, 26, 260

Open Mon–Sat 0730–1700

DAVID KING

513 Finchley Road, NW3
071 794 2834

Station Finchley Road
underground + bus
Finchley Road and Frognal BR

Bus 13, 82, 113

Open Mon–Fri 0730–2000
Sat 0900–1800
Sun 1000–1400

BRIAN LAY-JONES

36 Heath Street, NW3
071 435 5084

Station Hampstead
underground

Bus 46, 268

Open Mon–Sat 0730–1800

PLUMB & APPLEBEE

104 High Road, N2
081 444 7796

Station East Finchley
underground

Bus 17, 102, 143, 236

Open Mon–Sat 0830–1830

A leading wholesaler in fruit and veg told us that there were a handful of greengrocers in London of real note – Johnny Ellingham is one (the others are Blyth, NW11 [page 89, Dave King in NW3 [below], Fry's in SW3 [pages 88–9], and outside Panzer in NW8 [page 64]. In all you will find produce of top quality, well presented in an immaculate shop. One customer sends his Rolls-Royce all the way from the West End to pick up his order at Ellingham's and others come from far and near. Pricing is important, as is personal service in this family-run business – everyone seems to be related – sons and brothers in law, uncles and dads. Everything is fresh daily and, curiously, they do a good trade in fresh farm eggs.

Y ou don't see a lot of pieds de mouton around, but this first-class greengrocer is likely to have these wild mushrooms along with other interesting items. Mâche and rocket, fresh herbs, mini vegetables and pattipan squash are just a few of the vegetables. Quinces, which must rank as exotic even though we grow them in Britain (but rarely see them in the shops), physalis and out-of-season soft fruit were all to be seen on a cold winter's day. The proprietor does the buying himself and has an eye for good quality and unusual produce. He delivers locally and goes out to Stanmore once a week.

E verything always looks wonderfully fresh and inviting at this greengrocery. They carry an extensive range of salads, plenty of out-of-season fruits and they make up fruit baskets for gifts. Free delivery in the area up to Golders Green.

D on't be put off by the slightly dotty name – this shop is a good source of exotic produce throughout the year. There's always something unusual here which you may not have found anywhere else – like the Afro-Caribbean hot little yellow and red peppers or Medjool dates from California. Prices are fairly reasonable, especially good for odd things like pawpaws, which sell well. There are all the everyday necessities as well as the rare and beautiful. They supply caterers and restaurants and deliver locally.

ROYS GREENGROCERS

5 Formosa Street, W9
071 286 2408

Station Warwick Avenue underground

Bus 6, 8, 16, 46

Open Mon–Sat 0830–1800
Sun 0930–1300

Customers of Roy's sing his praises and he is happy to join in – telling you he just gets everything that's good. It all looks excellent, especially his wide selection of salads, which he keeps chilled. He has rocket all the year round and all the other interesting leaves. Picturesque cauliflowers, exotic fruits and bizarrely spelled labels. In spite of the fascia saying 'groceries' the only non-greengrocery sold here is eggs.

SUPERFRESH LIMITED

133–5 Ealing Road,
Wembley
081 900 2607
fax 081 900 1669

Station Alperton underground

Bus 79, 83, 297

Open Sun–Sat 24 hours

There are a number of greengrocers along this stretch of road and good Indian shoppers are likely to go to each one, feeling the ripeness of the mangoes, smelling the freshness of the coriander, sizing up the aubergines, etc. If you only have time for one, this shop has a very good range of exotic fruit and vegetables, much of it imported by the owners from Kenya, Cyprus, India, Bangladesh and Egypt. Prices are keen, choice is tremendous and they never close.

Also at 113–15 Upper Tooting Road, SW17, 081 767 8214, Sun–Sat 0800–2000

Superfresh Limited

North East

GIBBER OF LONDON

116 Seven Sisters Road, N7
071 609 0113

Station Finsbury Park underground

Bus 14a, 253

Open Mon–Sat 0800–1600

T hough this is a shop, it's more like buying off a barrow – maybe it's just the chirpiness of the chaps. Gibber has been around for a quarter of a century as wholesaler and retailer – whatever quantity you want to buy 'from a pallet to a piece' there's a great choice and good quality. Prices are keen, especially if you need a whole box of anything. As well as a complete range of fruit and vegetables, they have a small selection of delicatessen, specialising in Mediterranean cuisine (hummus and taramasalata).

ANDREAS MICHLI & SON

405 St Ann's Road, N15
081 802 0188

Station Manor House/ Turnpike Lane underground + bus

Bus 29, 121, 171

Open Mon–Sat 0930–1930
Sun 1100–1530

A jolly shop with an international array of fruit and vegetables – especially Cypriot. Lots of wonderful olives and cooking pots which they import from Cyprus.

Peter Childs

South West

PETER CHILDS

8 Lichfield Terrace,
Richmond
081 940 2034

Station Richmond
underground and BR

Bus 27, R69

Open Mon–Tues, Thur–Sat
0830–1730
Wed 0830–1300

A highly regarded greengrocer with good-quality produce, a wide selection of the best of whatever is in season, fresh herbs and salads and you'll find some unusual items, like the spring shallots which resemble purple spring onions and the yellow courgettes.

EVERFRESH LIMITED

204–8 Upper Tooting Road,
SW17
081 672 7396

Station Tooting Bec/
Broadway underground

Bus 77, 155, 219, 355

Open Sun–Sat 0800–1900

We counted seven different types of aubergine in this large, mainly greengrocery, shop. Many different kinds of chilli, karelia, plantain, tindoori, white onion, tiandola, ponnangani, vallarai – and if you don't know what to do with all these unusual vegetables, the pater familias is strolling round the shop and bound to give you good advice. Mangoes of various types, bananas and other exotic fruit and jars of pickles and preserves. Opposite is the House of Fresh Fruit (at 197) and various market stalls along the road – all with excellent prices. Well worth shopping around.

Also at 119–21 Ealing Road, Wembley, 081 903 1058

South East

BARTLEYS FRUITERERS

29 Dulwich Village, SE21
081 693 2206

Station North Dulwich BR

Bus 37, P4

Open Mon–Sat 0830–1730

Old-fashioned quality greengrocers with an excellent selection of exotics and mundane – loquats, star fruit, lychees, English basil plants, pumpkins. They are always first in the area with English sprue and salsify. Plus a good choice of salads and of different cultivated mushrooms. Some organic vegetables and dried fruit sold loose. Parking outside.

⋟ *Green London* ⋞

Organic food has caught the imagination of the nation and is certainly here to stay, as proved by the move away from niche marketing to major supermarket chains. All the health-food shops we have listed are, we feel, particularly good examples of the genre.

The following entries from other sections may also be of interest for their organic produce: The Beer & Home Brew Shop; Gideon's; Natural Foods Limited; Neal's Yard Bakery; Nuthouse; G. C. Sparkes.

Central

CLEARSPRING

196 Old Street, EC1
071 250 1708

Station Old Street underground

Bus 5, 43, 55, 76, 141, 214, 243, 263a, 271

Open Mon–Fri 0830–1900
Sat 0930–1730

A macrobiotic mecca, stocking organic foods and products with no sucrose (good for diabetics). Everything is rigorously checked for additives. Fruit and vegetables are delivered fresh every day. Albi, a potato-like vegetable used for healing and recommended by the Kushi Institute next door, is always in stock. Many items from Japan, a good selection of cheeses, and plenty from the take-away counter for the many office workers in the vicinity, including good breads. Downstairs the light and welcoming basement has pretty giftware such as wooden bowls and an Indian tiffin box. Organic wines, lager and natural beers brewed without sugar. Best of all, for anyone unsure of what macrobiotic food and diet are all about, all the staff at Clearspring are encouraged to take courses at the Institute, where they hold seminars, offer diet counselling and run excellent cookery courses for those who need macrobiotic food advice. Mail order service.

EAST WEST RESTAURANT

188 Old Street, EC1
071 608 0300

Station Old Street
underground

Bus 5, 43, 55, 76, 141, 214,
243, 263a, 271

Open Mon–Fri 1100–2130
(last orders 2100)
Sat 1100–1500

If you want to sample macrobiotic food this would be a good place to visit, though you may not feel it is the greatest gastronomic experience. The food is hearty and portions are generous. Homemade soup (leek, potato and pea was good), a choice of salads with hummus, a daily hot dish with plenty of vegetables, pulses, tofu and rice – you'll not go hungry. Lots of desserts, all made without sugar or dairy produce (cashew nuts replace cream very successfully). Fruit juices, Bamchu tea and organic wines are available. Many dishes are made to recipes supplied by Clearspring/East West Centre for their courses and cookery lessons. Popular with city types (as well as the thonged sandal brigade).

NEAL'S YARD WHOLEFOOD WAREHOUSE

21–3 Shorts Gardens, WC2
071 836 5151

Station Covent Garden
underground

Bus 1, 4, 6, 9, 11, 13, 15, 77,
168, 171, 176

Open Mon–Wed 0930–1900
Thur–Fri 0930–1930
Sat 0930–1730
Sun 1030–1330

The grandaddy of all health-food shops has had a fresh lease of life with its new owners, who have refurbished it, but basically it is the same as before, only more so. All the familiar packs and sacks for bulk buying (in all senses) of seeds, nuts, dried fruits, etc, and a counter of cheeses from the near-by Neal's Yard Dairy (see page 38). They continue to make their own peanut butter, there's a good selection of unusual breads and everything always looks very appetising and, of course, healthy.

Also at Neal's Yard at the Garden Centre, Alexandra Palace, N22, 081 444 4533

WHOLEFOOD

4 Paddington Street, W1
071 935 3924

Station Baker Street
underground

Bus 2a, 2b, 13, 18, 27, 30,
74, 113, 159

Open Mon 0845–1800
Tues–Fri 0845–1845
Sat 0845–1300

This wholefood suppliers-cum-grocer's-cum-green-grocer's offers advice on organic food, healing and health. The chiller is filled with yoghurts made from the milk of organic cows, sheep and goats, salad stuffs, fresh yeast and a number of organic cheeses – parmesan, Montgomery's Cheddar; Charente butter from France; whey cream butter from Shrewsbury, Berrydales' frozen tofu ices, chemical free organic baby foods. Bach remedies and health supplements as well as beauty products are available. There's a huge area for books, with information on the Soil Association, Green guides, organic pest control and rare and out-of-print books. For home bakers there are gluten-free flours and Justin de Blank organic flour or take-away Cranks' breads.

North West

BUMBLEBEE NATURAL FOOD STORE

30, 32 & 33 Brecknock Road, N7
071 607 1936 (nut shop)
071 609 9446 (bakery)
071 284 1314 (veg)

Station Camden Town underground and BR

Bus 10, C12

Open Mon–Sat 0900–1800

There are three Bumblebee shops along this road. A wonderful smell assails the nostrils at 30, where they keep the nuts (great selection and good prices), dried fruit, pulses and general wholefood groceries. At 32 is the bakery with shelves of grains, cereals, different rices, couscous, organic wines and fruit juices. They make gluten-, yeast- and wheat-free sourdough bread and have a selection of hot and cold foods ready prepared to take out, including vegetarian haggis. At 33 they sell some of the best organic vegetables in town – large, succulent Jerusalem artichokes, firm celeriac, kale, pink fir-apple potatoes. At the back is a good selection of top-quality British and Irish cheeses. With plenty of helpful staff around, this collection of shops has to be without doubt one of the very best sources for organic food in London.

Also at 10 Caledonian Road, N1

BUSHWACKER WHOLEFOODS

59 Goldhawk Road, W12
081 743 2359

Station Goldhawk Road underground

Bus 94, 237

Open Mon–Tues, 0930–1830
Wed, Fri, Sat 0930–1800
Thur 0930–1430

A spotlessly clean and well-run wholefood delicatessen, it has its own packed and well-priced staples. Recommended for the choice of Clearspring products. There's a good range of rice, wholewheat pasta, and other dried goods. The frozen section includes Indian vegetarian products, the Tivall range, tofu ices and frozen Loseley shortcrust pastry. Unpasteurised cheese – Devon Garland, Exmoor – and fresh yeast and tofu products are in the chilled counter. Among the organic vegetables rarely seen Swiss chard and ungassed bananas were sighted. Some interesting bottles include gooseberry champagne, naturally fermented ciders, elderflower and organic wines. Produce is restocked on Tuesday and Friday.

CORNUCOPIA HEALTH FOOD

64 St Mary's Road, W5
081 579 9431

Station South Ealing underground

Bus 65

Open Mon–Sat 0900–1730

An exceptionally good health-food shop, well laid out and offering a great choice in all the lines you would expect to find. Plenty of ready-to-eat food – nutty flans, cheese and spinach 'larties' (whatever they may be!). You can buy water from their aquathin purifier – bring your own container if you like – guaranteed pure and fresh. A splendid cheese counter with over sixty cheeses including Montgomery's Cheddar, Lanark blue, Duddeswell organic. Weigh your own lentils, pulses, rice, beans, etc. Gluten-free products, flours, polenta, buckwheat flour, pasta. Organic and country wines, olive oil, lots of Japanese food and a big selection of cookery books. They have concentrated fruit juice by the litre. Very friendly and helpful staff.

EARTHWORKS

132 King Street, W6
081 846 9357

Station Hammersmith underground

Bus 27, 267

Open Mon and Sat 0930–1800
Tues–Fri 0930–2030

A first-class cheese counter with British and foreign representatives, lots of macrobiotic items, plenty of unusual as well as staple products. Grains, nuts, etc, are available loose; pastas both exotic and gluten free and at the back there's a section of lotions, potions, herbs and spices.

Also at 1 Devonshire Road, W4, 081 995 0588

SESAME HEALTH FOODS

128 Regent's Park Road, NW1
071 586 3779

Station Chalk Farm underground
Primrose Hill BR

Bus 31, 68

Open Mon–Fri 1000–1830
Sat 1000–1800
Sun 1100–1730

A well-stocked, clean and well-run shop with products from Clearspring, Dove's Farm, Whole Earth, Jordan's. Chunky wholesome loaves from a south London bakery (a cheese and herb loaf went down well). Hot food (all made downstairs) can be taken out or eaten in – in the summer tables outside are popular to watch the comings and goings along this colourful street. Soup, quiche, pizza, a rice dish and something vegan all look really appetising. Locals say the staff are great – they provide coffee and tea, with sympathy at no extra charge.

WILD OATS

210 Westbourne Grove, W11
071 229 1063
fax 071 221 1995

Station Notting Hill Gate/Ladbroke Grove underground

Bus 15, 28, 31

Open Mon–Fri 0900–1900
Sat 0900–1800
Sun 1000–1600 (but check first)

In a particularly pretty parade of shops, this spacious shop has exceptionally fresh and attractive-looking fruit and vegetables (some kept under refrigeration). Just about everything organic is available – oils, beers, wines, champagne, and a good selection of books. Over twenty different types of bread are sold and nuts, cereals, pulses and yoghurts are, naturally, available. A novel service is provided by an in-house adviser on a macrobiotic diet and the Clearspring macrobiotic range is well represented. The shop has recently expanded and will have the space to offer an even wider range of high-quality health foods.

North East

FRIENDS FOODS

1 Roman Road, E2
081 980 1843

Station Bethnal Green
underground

Bus 106, D6

Open Mon–Thur, Sat 0900–
1800
Fri 0900–1900

A good basic health store. Everything in packets. Organics, macrobiotic, breads and cosmetics – at reasonable prices.

Also at 113 Notting Hill Gate, 071 727 9382

South East

VEGANOMICS WHOLEFOODS

312–14 Lewisham Road,
SE13
081 852 7978

Station Lewisham BR

Bus 1, 180

Open Mon–Sat 1000–1800

A vegan enclave with a restaurant and wholefood shop, with original mahogany shop fittings to lend nineteenth-century atmosphere to this twentieth-century organic paradise.

☙ *Liquid London* ❧

London continues to be the wine capital of the world. We have the monopoly of the top wine writers, finest auction houses and many internationally respected shippers and merchants. Most wine-growing countries suffer from a chauvinism that prevents them from promoting any wine but their own. Not so the British, who now buy the best from the world's vineyards.

Ale and beer have enjoyed an extraordinary renaissance in recent years and there are specialist shops and pubs catering to a burgeoning band of enthusiasts. Spirit drinkers too are becoming more discriminating and seeking the more esoteric single malts, the more unusual eaux de vie and recherché examples of the distiller's art.

We have limited our choice to the smaller, private merchants, but recognise that leading supermarkets have done much to popularise wine drinking and take the mystique out of buying by helping to educate and bringing down the cost.

We raise a glass to London's wine and spirits shops.

Central

THE BEER & HOME BREW SHOP

8 Pitfield Street, N1
071 739 3701

Station Old Street underground

Bus 5, 43, 55, 76, 141, 214, 243, 263a, 271

Open Mon–Fri 1100–1900
Sat 1000–1600

This unprepossessing-looking shop hides a multitude of fascinating stories, if not sins. The original Victorian shopfront, inlaid with brass, is still there, making this a listed building. It was a gambling den in Victorian times and earlier still a plague pit. Today it is a repository for all things beery – including 500 different beers (out of 30,000 made around the world). You can find all the leading and many weird and wonderful varieties, such as Chimay from Belgium, which is considered to be the burgundy of the beer world. There are fruit beers (raspberry and cherry) with amazing aroma; the fruit is replaced at secondary fermentation, producing very complex flavours. And there are sloe wine, damson wine, mead, scrumpy cider, everything you need for home brewing. Organic wine from Italy. Glasses in many shapes and sizes.

BERRY BROS & RUDD

3 St James's Street, SW1
071 839 9033

Station Green Park underground

Bus 9, 14, 19, 22, 38

Open Mon–Fri 0930–1700

No other family has been selling wine from one building for so long – 300 years – and the shop has changed little in the past 200 years. Wood-lined walls, old chairs, wooden floor (all rather Dickens Sunday TV serial) enhance the old-fashioned feel of the place and the old-fashioned personal service. They offer a better range than supermarkets, you can buy half a bottle here and get all the advice you need, which is sound and readily proffered, and they give discounts on all orders of two dozen bottles upwards. The clients have been noteworthy – let us pause to drop some names: Byron and Beau Brummell, Pitt and Peel, Napoleon III, A. J. Balfour, Gertrude Lawrence, Rosa Lewis, Anthony Eden, Laurence Olivier, the French Rothschilds, André Simon, Duff Cooper. Old invoices and lists line the walls. Originally coffee, tea, spices

Berry Bros & Rudd

and snuff were also sold there. They will select and store wine for you, deliver free anywhere in the UK for one case and more (which can be a mixed case). For parties they'll supply wine and spirits on sale or return and they have glasses for hire.

THE HUGH JOHNSON COLLECTION

68 St James's Street, SW1
071 491 4912

Station Green Park underground

Bus 9, 14, 19, 22, 38

Open Mon–Fri 1930–1730

A collection of modern and antique wine bits and pieces chosen by Hugh Johnson could be the answer to that question – what to give the wine lover who has everything. Here you'll find 'everything for the modern connoisseur using traditional designs or modern reproductions of the perfect design, aesthetically and functionally perfect'. Among the vast array there are racks, cradles, corkscrews, salvers, glasses, carafes, decanters, punch bowls – all in swish, satin-lined green boxes with gilt clasps. Some exquisite prints and, needless to say, all Hugh Johnson's many best-selling wine books and videos. There are amazingly beautiful redesigned wine coolers – tall elegant and silver plated. All very, very grand.

JUSTERINI & BROOKS

61 St James's Street, SW1
071 493 8721

Station Green Park underground

Bus 9, 14, 19, 22, 25, 38

Open Mon–Fri 0900–1730

You can buy one bottle or a whole cellar here – the advice will be the same. These wine suppliers to the Queen have a big cellar in east London which services their small shop. They specialise in cellar plans and have a special projects manager to help organise your own 'selected cellar plan' to your price range. They will cellar wines for you too and lay down port and claret. Their wide range is appreciated by writers and companies for wine tastings. They have plenty of offers and bin ends and wines are priced from as little as £3 up (a long way up). Deliveries are free in London for over two cases and mainland UK for over five cases.

LEA & SANDEMAN

301 Fulham Road, SW10
071 376 4767

Station South Kensington underground + bus

Bus 14

Open Mon–Sat 0930–2030

This independent wine merchant specialises in French wines, with an emphasis on wines from domaines and growers. Starting at around £3 the wines go up to £200 a bottle with the widest choice from £4 to £15 a bottle. The staff, most of whom have gained their Wine & Spirit Education Trust diplomas, are well versed in wine lore and able to give sound advice. There are wine-related prints for sale. Free local delivery and if you buy over £100 worth of wine they'll deliver anywhere in London.

MILROY'S SOHO WINE MARKET

3 Greek Street, W1
071 437 9311

Station Tottenham Court Road underground

Bus 7, 8, 10, 14, 19, 22b, 55, 73, 134, 176

Open Mon–Fri 0900–1900
Sat 1000–1800

Whisky galore at this famous Soho shop where every whisky available is to be found. They stock a huge range of malts, not too much blended and some high-strength whiskies. This is the place to come if you are looking for old rare whisky like a White & Mackay's thirty-year-old or a Ballantyne's ten-year-old. And for that very special present, how about a little something from their splendid range of single malts, like a fifty-year-old Dalmore at £2,750 or a 1938 Macallan or a Balvenie. A fine collection of Bell's decanters. Apart from the hard stuff, they do a goodly selection of wines – the mainstays being Bordeaux and Burgundy.

LA RESERVE

56 Walton Street, SW3
071 589 2020

Station South Kensington/ Knightsbridge underground

Bus 14, 30, 74, C1

Open Mon–Fri 1000–2000
Sat 1000–1800

There are five shops in a group of independent wine merchants with La Reserve, each with its own distinct character and stocking different wines. They all have certain standard wines, but it is up to the individual manager to choose special wines for his own shop. La Reserve has old wines, often bought from private sources of top quality. The major part of the wine is French at this shop, though they have a good showing of Californian and Australian and an eclectic range of Italian. They run a series of wine tastings in spring and autumn with classes on 'How to Taste', 'Ageing' (the wine not the consumer), and experts on particular regions. One of the services Mark Reynier offers his customers is to decant wines for them.

Also: Le Sac à Vin, 203 Munster Road, SW6, 071 381 6930
Le Picoleur, 47 Kendal Street, W2, 071 402 6920
The Heath Street Wine Company, 29 Heath Street, NW3 071 435 6845
Clapham Cellars, 13 Grant Road, SW11, 071 978 5601

REYNIER'S WINE LIBRARY

16 Upper Tachbrook Street, SW1
071 834 2917

Station Pimlico/Victoria underground and BR

Bus 2, 11, 16, 24, 25, 29, 76, 82, 135, 239

Open Mon–Thur 1100–1830
Fri 1100–1900

A novel idea, and very appealing to serious wine drinkers, you buy your wine from the wide range of vintages and varieties (something for everyone), and if you choose you can drink it, accompanied by a simple buffet of English and continental cheeses and pâtés, at the adjoining wine bar. You pay a corkage of £1 for the privilege, but it gives you the chance to drink wines at shop prices with your lunch. Good advice is to go for the more expensive wine for best value (i.e. you'd pay a lot more in a wine bar).

LA VIGNERONNE

105 Old Brompton Road,
SW7
071 589 6113

Station South Kensington
underground

Bus 30, 74

Open Mon–Fri 1000–2100
Sat 1000–2000

A particularly good shop, say people in the trade. Liz Berry is La Vigneronne, and she has the largest selection of Alsace wines in the country as well as old vintage clarets and Madeiras, French country wines, vins doux naturels, eaux de vie, vintage cognacs and much more. There are books and wine accessories. Especially recommended are the tastings, held once or twice a week throughout the year at Imperial College. They cover the full gamut of wines from 1961 clarets to more modest recent vintages.

North West

AMAZING GRAPES

94 Brent Street, NW4
081 202 2631

Station Hendon Central
underground

Bus 83, 183, 240

Open Mon–Wed 0930–1800
Thur 0930–1900
Fri 0930–1500
Sun 1000–1400

This shop has the largest selection of kosher wines in Europe – quite a claim and you might be surprised to find such classy numbers as Baron Edmond de Rothschild, Gevrey Chambertin, Piper Heidsieck and not a few other wines which you might not have imagined were kosher. In fact most wine-producing countries make some kosher wines and Israel now has some world-class wines from the Golan, produced under the watchful eye of a Californian winemaker in the most modern winery. There's also a big range of grape juices and brandies (not the well-known French makes as they aren't kosher), whiskies (which, being made of grain are kosher anyway). You can also hire chairs, tables and glasses and buy paper tableware.

BIBENDUM WINE LIMITED

113 Regent's Park Road,
NW1
071 722 5577
fax 071 722 7354

Station Chalk Farm
underground
Primrose Hill BR

Bus 31, 168

Open Mon–Sat 1000–2000
Sun 1100–1800

If a warehouse can be said to be inviting, then this manages to be so. This firm offers immediate free delivery within London postal districts with a minimum order of one mixed case. They have a comprehensive range – basically anything, including a good range of half bottles and magnums. Bin-end sales in January. In addition to the free tastings in the store, they hold one main big tasting each year – usually at the Inn on the Park – to which anyone is welcome to come (those on the mailing list are invited automatically). They also hold four or five tastings a year throughout the capital. There's a section of accessories, glasses, corkscrews, etc, and books and oils. Easy parking in the forecourt is a bonus in this area, where a car can be a nuisance.

GROGBLOSSOM

253 West End Lane, NW6
071 794 7808

Station West Hampstead
underground and BR

Bus 28, 159

Open Mon–Thur 1100–2200
Fri–Sat 1000–2200
Sun 1200–1500, 1900–2200

A beer lover's dream . . . 250 different beers, including an aphrodisiac with ginseng and herbs, the world's strongest beer from Switzerland, loads of Belgian, Polish and more being added all the time. The staff are jolly (no wonder since they have to taste all this new stock) and happy to proffer advice. Bin-end bargains in wine are a regular feature, with very good prices. They carry over fifty champagnes, thirty malt whiskies, Irish whiskies, Bourbons, French ciders and try to specialise in unusual lines. There's a collection of posh olive oils and mustards. Free glass loan and local deliveries, sale or return and tastings every weekend.

Also at 66 Notting Hill Gate, W11, 071 792 3834
160 High Road, East Finchley, N2, 081 883 3588

THE HERMITAGE

124 Fortis Green Road, N10
081 365 2122

Bus 43, 107, 234

Open Mon–Sat 1030–2000
Sun 1200–1430

Very desirable collectables and accessories, decanters, glasses, posters, cute handmade baskets, books – all packed into a Tardis-like shop. Good and affordable wines from Alsace and bin-end sales (25 per cent off) represent really good value. There's an interesting range of half bottles and champagnes to suit all palates and pockets. At Christmas presentation boxes are made up – with champagne and chocolates, port and Stilton. Other tasty items – mustards, oils, olive pastes, etc, and wine-related greetings cards – all go to make this a pleasant and useful local wine shop.

RICHARD KIHL

164 Regent's Park Road, NW1
071 586 3838

Station Chalk Farm
underground
Primrose Hill BR

Bus 31, 168

Open Mon–Fri 0930–1700
Sat 1100–1700

Looking for a present for a wine enthusiast? There are cheap and cheerful ideas here – from bottle tags or wine thermometers for a few pounds up to silver and crystal decanters at £4,000. In between there's a shop full of charming wine-related antiques, pictures, port tongs, barley-sugar-like glass candlesticks, etched glass sets of most covetable port glasses, spittoons and Heath Robinson wine cradles worked by crank (popular in the United States and Japan), and every kind of corkscrew. Richard Kihl is also a wine shipper and broker.

CHRIS MILIA

11–13 Pratt Street, NW1
071 485 5032
fax 071 482 4557

Station Camden Town/
Mornington Crescent
underground

Chris Milia claims to have over 1,000 wines in his wine warehouse, which is actually an area at the back of his grocery shop. They come from everywhere and he specialises in unusual wines. He won't offer you just one ouzo – you can choose from six or seven. Similarly with retsinas, and he has thirty different champagnes, a wide range of liqueurs and ports from £6 to

Bus 24, 29, 134, 168, 253

Open Mon–Thur 1000–2000
Fri 1000–2100
Sat 1000–1900
Sun 1200–1400

£100. There are also plenty of beers from all over the world. You can buy by the case. For foodies the front of the shop may be the more interesting area – especially if you are looking for a good selection of Greek food. In the chiller you'll find jars of tarama paste to make your own taramasalata, packs of sausages, smoked pork loin and other meats suitable for a barbecue – he will even sell you the barbecue equipment. Large packs of pulses, pourgouri (bulghur), drums of oil, kebab skewers, wonderful olives – all things Cypriot. The fruit and vegetables are not particulary interesting, though you may be able to find unusual things – but Inverness Street market (see page 181) near by is probably better.

The Barnes Wine Shop

South West

THE BARNES WINE SHOP

51 High Street, Barnes,
SW13
081 878 8643
fax 071 221 1995

Station Barnes Bridge BR

Bus 9

Open Mon–Sat 0930–2030
Sun 1200–1400

Lovely wooden racks and showcases of decanters and glasses make this an unusually good-looking wine shop. Tastings are held every Saturday and they have regular tutored events with a Master of Wine. Free glasses supplied for parties, free local delivery and other vinous related goods are there – books, gadgetry, table mats. They carry a fair selection of everything, but are particularly good on pudding wines. They go for new cult wines – Shaw & Smith sauvignon blanc from Australia, a few English wines, and Chilean and Italian reds. James Rodgers is wine buyer and the staff are keen to help.

CAVES DE LA MADELEINE

82 Wandsworth Bridge Road, SW6
071 736 6145

Station Fulham Broadway underground + bus

Bus 28, 295

Open Mon–Sat 0930–2030

U nder new management since being bought from Layton's, the name's the same in this lovely old tiled shop. They have wines 'straight from the vineyard' – lots of white Burgundy and plenty of New World wines. They specialise in malt whiskies – the lesser known and difficult to find brands. Saturday morning tastings and a party service, free delivery in central London, and advice on setting up your cellar.

THE FULHAM ROAD WINE CENTRE

899 Fulham Road, SW6
071 736 7009

Station Parsons Green/Putney Bridge underground

Bus 14

Open Mon– Sat 1000–2100

A n exciting place for wine enthusiasts, this spacious shop (second cousin to the Barnes Wine Shop, see page 105) offers marvellous service and advice – all the assistants have obtained diplomas. Wines are arranged by grape variety rather than country, so people who like a certain style can try others in that range. And what a huge and adventurous range of wines they have, available by bottle or case. They also sell modern and antique wine glasses, prints and books. They once sold a strip of land in a vineyard and will advise on starting a cellar (particularly if you have a few thousand pounds to invest). Local deliveries. During the week there's always a bottle or two open and they have regular tastings every Saturday when 12–14 wines will be opened. Each week a different country is featured. In addition to these shop tastings they run courses throughout the year. (See also under Food and Wine Schools, page 191).

WHITE HART LIQUOR STORES

115 White Hart Lane, Barnes, SW13
081 878 7881

Station Barnes Bridge BR

Bus 9

Open Mon–Sat 1000–2200
Sun 1000–1400, 1900–2200

T his firm specialises in champagne and has over fifty in stock, as well as other sparkling wines. Prices are good. They have more than fifty beers, 400 different wines, seventy-five spirits and liqueurs.

Also at 567 King's Road, SW6, 071 731 0773

South East

THE BITTER EXPERIENCE

129 Lee Road, SE3
081 852 8819

Station Blackheath BR + bus

Bus 21, 75, 122, 261

Open Mon–Fri 1100–2130
Sat 1000–1400, 1500–2130
Sun and Bank Holidays 1200–
1400, 1900–2100

Not just any old beer shop – this is for the cognoscenti, with a huge range of Belgian beers (over thirty) and others from all around the globe. Interesting and unusual are the draught beers from Adnam's – choose from mini pins (18 pints), poly pins (36 pints), firkins (72 pints). There's a fair range of wines at a spread of prices.

☙ *Pots and Pans* ❧

Our *batterie de cuisine* shops range from where to buy good basic kitchen-ware to the ultra design conscious David Mellor. In between we visited the best of the hotel and restaurant suppliers and those specialists who can provide the paraphernalia for the ambitious amateur cook.

The following entries from other sections may also be of interest for the food- and drink-related items they sell: Bibendum; General Trading Company Café; the Hugh Johnson Collection; Richard Kihl; Liberty Coffee Shop; the Tea House.

Central

BODUM SHOP

24 Neal Street, WC2
071 240 9176
fax 071 497 8064

Station Covent Garden underground

Bus 1, 4, 6, 9, 11, 13, 15, 77, 168, 171, 176

Open Mon–Sat 1000–1800

'Kitchen design for everyday chefs' is how this Danish firm describes its wares. Each Bodum shop (Paris, New York, Milan, etc) has a small coffee bar so their coffee-makers can be seen in action. There's a great deal of difference in taste among the various methods of brewing the same blend of coffee. Here you can buy Coffee Bay, Café d'Or and Taylor's coffee beans or ground – nineteen varieties in all, along with every shape, colour and size of cafetière you could wish for. They make excellent presents, as do their kettles, tea-pots, jugs and salad bowls. They offer a useful spare-parts service.

Also at Whiteleys, Queensway, W2, 071 792 1213 (where they sell tea too)

DIVERTIMENTI

45–7 Wigmore Street, W1
071 935 0689

A spacious place to browse and to enjoy looking at and buying cooking utensils and tableware both for professionals and home cooks. Everything of high quality, mostly imported from France. You'll find good equipment such as Cuisinox pans. The large,

Station Bond Street/Oxford Circus underground

Bus 6, 7, 8, 10, 12, 13, 15, 16a, 25, 73, 88, 94

Open Mon–Fri 0930–1800 Sat 1000–1700

solid chopping boards should last a lifetime. A few of the assistants are knowledgeable but others should stick to polishing the copper (as proved by a farcical situation with a highly trained French chef – incognito – who asked for help in choosing a set of knives and was proffered somewhat fanciful information). A lovely range of French earthenware baking and serving dishes and pretty china, plus the famous painted mugs. They also do wedding lists.

Also at 139–41 Fulham Road, SW3, 071 581 8065 (open as here, but until 1800 on Saturdays)

LEON JAEGGI & SONS LIMITED

124 Shaftesbury Avenue, W1
071 434 4545

Station Leicester Square/ Piccadilly Circus underground

Bus 3, 6, 9, 13, 15, 19, 22, 38, 53, 88, 94

Open Mon–Sat 0900–1730

This is a family-run business supplying the catering trade (and HM the Queen) with pots, pans and pan scrubbers, but delighted to serve non-professional cooks. Service is important and the staff are certainly most helpful, pointing out (repeatedly) that ALL prices are exclusive of VAT. No wonder they seem good value. Not as extensive, maybe, as Pages (see page 110), but friendlier atmosphere and loyal customers. An excellent choice of knives. Larger items delivered.

Also at 231 Tottenham Court Road, W1, 071 631 1080

DAVID MELLOR

Butler's Wharf, 24 Shad Thames, SE1
071 407 7593

Station Tower Hill/London Bridge underground

Bus 47, 188, P11

Open Tues–Sat 1030–1800 Sun 1130–1730

You might easily think you have wandered into an extension of the near-by Design Museum in this latest addition to David Mellor's empire. It is huge, airy, stylish, the ultimate cook's paradise. Prices are fearsome, but you can consider it a cultural outing and just gaze and admire. Apart from the equipment – a comprehensive selection and all well made – there are design-conscious china, glass, tableware, books, baskets, wooden bowls, boards, tables. Great place for gift inspiration . . . they hold wedding lists.

Also at 4 Sloane Square, SW1, 071 730 4259

NEAL STREET EAST

5–7 Neal Street, WC1
071 240 0135
fax 071 836 8395

Station Covent Garden underground

This is a fascinating shop selling anything and everything to do with the Orient – thus a very good source of books on all eastern cuisines and a few not so far east (Africa?). These are all down in the basement alongside a useful collection of Chinese and Japanese cookery gear – a Mongolian brass steamboat for your hotpot, bamboo steamers, African peanut spoons, chopsticks galore with pretty rests. The Japanese lacquerware is very attractive and other items

Bus 14, 19, 22b, 24, 29, 38, 176

Open Mon–Sat 1000–1900

from that country include table mats and cast-iron cook and serve pots. There are masses of Chinese plates, bowls, spoons, etc. A section devoted to tea includes pretty pots, cups and other related things.

David Mellor (see page 109)

PAGES

121 Shaftesbury Avenue, W1
071 379 6334

Station Leicester Square/
Piccadilly Circus underground

Bus 3, 6, 9, 13, 15, 19, 22, 38, 53, 88, 94

Open Mon–Fri 0900–1800
Sat 0900–1700

'Cutlery sold by the dozen' and 'All prices exclusive of VAT'. The signs are bold and business is brisk. If you're stocking a guest house, factory canteen, holiday camp, restaurant, or your own domestic kitchen you can get everything under this one roof from heavy-duty ovens to potato peelers. Along with all manner of strictly useful professional equipment there are good and pretty china and glassware. You can buy an espresso machine for your own cappuccinos or a Royal Stafford eight-cup cafetière with bone-china insert if you want a change from the glass variety. Quick service. Plenty for home cooks – tools of the trade, Le Creuset, baking dishes, saucepans, etc.

North West

BUYERS & SELLERS

120 Ladbroke Grove, W10
071 229 1947

Station Ladbroke Grove underground

Bus 15, 52, 52a

Open Mon–Wed, Fri–Sat 0900–1700
Thur 0915 1430

This is the place to find really great bargains in major kitchen equipment – cookers, extractor fans, dishwashers, both built in and free standing. They deal in 'frustrated exports' and are able to pass on the benefits to their customers. There's more than a little old-fashioned courtesy and consideration from the ever-helpful Cynthia Coyne, who runs an advice line and offers armchair shopping with delivery all over the country.

RICHARD DARE

93 Regent's Park Road, NW1
071 722 9428

Station Chalk Farm underground
Primrose Hill BR

Bus 31, 168

Open Mon–Fri 0930–1800
Sat 1000–1600

Lovely to look at are the handmade baskets, pottery urns and crocks for bread, the copper moulds and solid, well made, practical cookware in this shop – all to be used as well as to decorate a kitchen (not just the twee ornamental stuff). It is sensible gear for proper cooks. The basement is crammed full of French china, which is Richard Dare's speciality. The Véritable Faience de Quimper range of painted, specially glazed French earthenware is not cheap, but very beautiful. Unusual is the Provençal fabric, probably intended for cloths, but almost certainly made up into skirts by the trendy Hampstead customers.

FAIRFAX KITCHEN SHOP

1 Regency Parade, NW3
071 722 7648

Station Swiss Cottage underground

Bus 13, 31, 82, 113

Open Mon–Sat 0930–1730

Semi-professional is how one could describe the equipment sold in this useful shop. There are large sizes of platters, pans and utensils which serious home cooks might appreciate. A better than average range of pasta- and coffee-making equipment (they import from Italy). Everything is good quality – practical rather than designer cookware. Sound advice given, particularly on technical questions about equipment and sizes. Good sale-time bargains.

POPAT STORE

138 Ealing Road, Wembley
081 902 4182

Station Alperton underground

Bus 79, 83, 297

Open Mon–Sat 1000–1830
Sun 1100–1730

A marvellous hotchpotch of all manner of Indian goods, but for us the interesting side of the shop is where the cooking utensils are ranged. Moulds to make kulfi, tawas for making doosa, steamers, pressure cookers, rolling pins to roll out chapattis and enormous pestles and mortars for grinding spices or making pastes.

JOHN RUSSELL KITCHENWARE SHOP

128 Chiswick High Road, W4
081 994 5790

Station Turnham Green underground

Bus 27, 237, 267

Open Mon–Sat 1000–1800

A handy shop both for serious cooks and browsers, there is a little bit of everything. The stock is well chosen – obviously by someone who cooks. There are Danish stainless-steel pans and other professional cookware, including Cuisinox and Le Creuset. Stylish tableware from France, a small range of books, table linen, coffee makers. Have your knives sharpened free.

South West

LA CUISINIERE

299 New King's Road, SW6
071 736 3696

Station Parsons Green underground

Bus 14, 22

Open Mon–Sat 0930–1800

A well-stocked shop with a big range of stainless-steel saucepans from France, Portugal and Italy. They will hire out special cake tins and can supply most domestic equipment. There's a lovely table full of little gadgets – irresistible if you are so minded or need an inexpensive present. They have Emma Bridgewater pottery and lots of blue and white plates and bowls. Pretty baskets. A small selection of cookbooks. They also do wedding lists.

Also at 81–3 Northcote Road, SW11, 071 223 4487

DENTON'S CATERING EQUIPMENT LIMITED

2–4 Clapham High Street, SW4
071 622 7157
fax 071 622 5546

Station Clapham North underground
Clapham High Street BR

Bus 45a, 88, 155, 355

Open Mon–Fri 0830–1730
Sat 0830–1300

It may lack the sophistication of West End kitchenware shops, but you'll probably find most things at this well-stocked suppliers. There is a wide range of good professional icing equipment with bags, nozzles, tubes and decorations for every conceivable occasion. They also stock cake boards and boxes. Professional quality chefs' knives include Gustav Emil and Sabatier. Dishes are mainly for restaurants but there are several makes familiar to home cooks. Domestic-sized cafetières and professional cookware, baking dishes, tins of all shapes and sizes are available. Upstairs is for serious, commercial caterers. The staff are friendly and happy to order virtually anything you want in the way of catering equipment. Delivery is free in the London area.

THE DINING ROOM SHOP

62–4 White Hart Lane, Barnes, SW13

A truly original idea this – a whole shop devoted to everything you could conceivably associate with dining rooms. Go there for instant heirlooms such as the handsome decanters or old china. There are antique tables and chairs, or modern reproductions can be made

The Dining Room Shop

081 878 1020

Bus 9

Open Mon–Fri 1000–1730
Sat 1015–1730

THE
KITCHENWARE
COMPANY

36 Hill Street, Richmond,
Surrey
081 948 7785

Station Richmond
underground and BR

Bus 27, R69

Open Mon–Sat 0930–1730

to your or their designs. They do wedding lists and will find any item you need. Delightful pictures (of diners, buffets, etc) and a host of accessories make this a charming place to browse and a useful source of presents.

A comprehensive selection of very classy yet practical cook and bakeware. From pricey David Mellor and Wilkins cutlery to lots of inexpensive gadgets. Knives by Sabatier and Henckles. Famous names from Cuisinox to Le Creuset and unusual items like proper paella pans, couscous pots, fish smokers, etc. Copper pans for the seriously rich. Chopping blocks/butcher block tables. A super selection of modern pottery and pretty Mexican recycled glass, Thomas glass and china. Watch out for their incredible sales, January and July.

LINE OF SCANDINAVIA

44 Lower Richmond Road,
SW15
081 788 3256

Station Putney Bridge
underground + bus

Bus 265

Open Mon–Fri 1000–1800
(closed 1330–1430)
Sat 1000–1700

The best and most elegant table and glassware, kitchen utensils, fabric, candles and candleholders are to be found here, along with bowls and vases (lots of Orrefors). Everything is Scandinavian, which says it all. A lovely shop for browsing, treating yourself or buying gifts.

VERRALL'S LIMITED

89 The Broadway, SW19
081 543 1010

Station Wimbledon
underground and BR

Bus 57, 93, 155, 352

Open Mon–Sat 0930–1800

A family-run business, this is a general cookware shop with good quality products. They have a pretty range of Italian hand-painted bowls and some unusual cookware. Spaghetti steamers, Le Creuset, Sabatier, lots of pretty oriental tableware, a good selection of coffee machines, including Gaggia and Bodum, bakeware and copper moulds. They hire out speciality cake tins in every conceivable shape and size. Frequent special offers make this a useful stopping-off point when shopping in Wimbledon.

❧ *Specialists and Traiteurs* ❧

These specialist food shops offer you the equivalent of having a chef in your own kitchen, unlike the supermarkets with their industrially prepared dishes. Most also offer upmarket delicatessen and almost by definition most of them will do outside catering. Some of our traiteurs have a small area where you can sit and sample their wares.

The following entries from other sections may also be of interest as traiteurs: Cannelle; Rosslyn Hill Delicatessen; La Salumeria; La Sienne.

Central

JUSTIN DE BLANK PROVISIONS LIMITED

42 Elizabeth Street, SW1
071 730 0605

Station Victoria underground and BR

Bus 11, 239, C1

Open Mon–Fri 0900–1900
Sat 0900–1500

This company has been providing ready-made dinner-party food to many a smart hostess around town for years. It is all cooked on the premises and the large repertoire can be put into attractive dishes for minimal hassle. This shop is more of a deli than the others (see below) and tries to cover a bit of everything.

46 Walton Street, SW3, 071 589 4734, Mon–Fri 0730–1800, Sat 0800–1300. Basically take-out food – hot and cold. They are cheaper than the other shops ('inter-branch competition', we were told).
60 New King's Road, SW6, 071 736 4323, Mon–Fri 0830–1800, Sat 0830–1700. A smaller version of Elizabeth Street. ('We have smoked salmon, but not caviar.')

BOUCHERIE LAMARTINE

229 Ebury Street, SW1
071 730 3037

Station Victoria underground and BR

The nearest London gets to Paris's Fauchon – exquisite French food and produce (at exquisite prices). There's a butchery counter where your meat will be beautifully cut and tied to order, a charcutier and traiteur, with pâtés, readymade dishes (à la Roux brothers), breads, including a selection of Poilâne and brioches, croissants and pâtisseries from the Roux

Bus 11, 239, C1

Open Mon–Fri 0800–1900
Sat 0800–1600

CARLUCCIO'S

28a Neal Street, WC2
071 240 1487

Station Covent Garden
underground

Bus 1, 4, 6, 9, 11, 13, 15, 77,
168, 171, 176

Open Mon 1200–1900
Tues–Sat 1000–1900

FINNS

4 Elystan Street, SW3
071 225 0733

Station South Kensington
underground

Bus 14, 45a, 49, 219

Open Mon–Fri 0800–1800
Sat 0800–1400

HOBBS OF MAYFAIR

29 South Audley Street, W1
071 409 1058
fax 071 491 2374

Station Bond Street
underground

Bus 6, 7, 8, 10, 12, 13, 15,
16, 25, 73, 88, 94

Pâtisserie. There are salads, fresh fruit and the prettiest baby vegetables, wild mushrooms and seasonal treats all outside the shop to tempt you to venture in. Their own stocks, truffles and many more delights.

For Antonio Carluccio – mushroom king, TV chef, chef/patron next door at the Neal Street Restaurant – this glorious shop is the realisation of a dream. 'I want to sell the real taste of Italy in London,' he told us. This encompasses fresh produce with lots of 'wild things' such as wild rocket, garlic and hops, plus, obviously, every possible variety of wild mushroom – fresh, dried, prepared – and truffles in season. There's a selection of imports from Italy, all exclusive, hams, handmade amaretti, their own-label goods, including bottled grilled aubergines and dried pasta. And to round off the menu there are about thirty fresh dishes each day, prepared in the restaurant kitchens to take home.

Lazy residents are well catered for around Chelsea Green with The Pieman (see page 117) on one side and Finns on t'other. There's a weekly menu and the prepared dishes are on view or can be ordered from the list, which gives you plenty of suggestions, but they can do anything with two days' notice (and in your own dishes so it looks like YOUR homemade, not THEIRS). They have ham on the bone, imported and unusual English cheeses, their own homemade lemon and lime cordials. They use top-quality ingredients – for which the clientele is happy to pay. Soups include Thai hot and sour chicken and bortsch, there are roulades and terrines, vegetarian dishes and all manner of meat, chicken and fish from which to choose. Their cold dishes find their way into many a smart picnic hamper.

This exceedingly pretty shop sells food which you might think is merely for decorating your pantry or dining room. The shelves are lined with elegant jars in the company's stylish livery and the contents, created especially for Hobbs, are appetising – lots of interesting combinations of pickles, preserves and sweetmeats that you are unlikely to see elsewhere. Flavoured oils and vinegars and overflowing wicker baskets make it a great place for all-year-round gifts if price is no problem, with particularly gorgeous Christmas ideas. For everyday groceries there's a small selection of Neal's

Open Mon–Fri 0900–1900
Sat 0900–1700

IVANO

38 Tachbrook Street, SW1
071 630 6977

Station Pimlico/Victoria
underground and BR

Bus2, 11, 16, 24, 25, 29, 76,
82, 135, 239

Open Mon–Sat 0800–1800

KASPIA

18–18a Bruton Place, W1
071 493 2612

Station Bond Street
underground

Bus 6, 7, 8, 10, 12, 13, 25,
73, 88, 135, 159

Open Shop Mon–Sat 1000–
2300
Restaurant Mon–Sat 1200–
1500 and 1900–2330

THE PIEMAN FOOD COMPANY LIMITED

16 Cale Street, SW3
071 225 0587

Station South Kensington
underground

Bus 14, 45a, 49, 219

Open Mon–Fri 0900–1830
Sat 0900–1300

Yard cheeses and other staples. Free delivery in May-fair; credit card telephone orders on 071 638 1230 or fax 071 638 1231.

This is a very jolly sort of place, obviously much appreciated by hungry local workers and residents who can choose a substantial meal from the many dishes on offer. It can be zapped in the microwave, whisked back to the office and enjoyed at your desk. It's all real comfort food, mainly Italian, with a large selection including vegetarian lasagne, liver Veneziana, seafood curry, Spanish omelette and a dish of the day. Large spinach and ricotta pastries, trifle and other sweets are all made in the kitchen downstairs and served with a smile. They also do outside catering.

A little corner of Paris, this London branch of the caviar specialists oozes chic and luxury. What else when you can buy Beluga, Oscietra, Sevruga and pressed caviar from Russia and Iran, Polish and Russian vodka, the best Scottish smoked salmon, which is expertly cut fresh daily, French foie gras, canned Russian crab (as good as fresh it is said). Russian food – blini, piroshki and bortsch – ready to go, from their adjoining restaurant, which offers set menus of varying prices, depending on the caviar input. For a very special treat, it's a pretty place to eat – open after the theatre too.

Simple Simon would be delighted to meet this pie-man in Chelsea. The food is all prepared in their own kitchens and there is a daily menu which is especially popular at lunchtime. There's always a vegetarian choice among the two or three dishes and hot potatoes, salads, generously filled sandwiches and baguettes, most of which are sold by 1400 (expect to queue between 1200 and 1400). As you'd guess, pies are their speciality and they encourage customers to bring in their own dishes to be filled. Cakes and pre-cut cheeses, breads and fruit juices as well as homemade jams, oils, vinegars, condiments, dried herbs. The larger and even better-stocked shop in Kensington carries cold meats and sausages, pastas and more of everything. Phone 071 627 5232 for their catering arm.

Also at 20 Stratford Road, W8, 071 937 3385

LES SPECIALITES ST QUENTIN

256 Brompton Road, SW3
071 225 1664

Station South Kensington
underground

Bus 14, 30, 74, C1

Open Mon–Sat 0900–2000
Sun 0900–1600

Part of a group which includes several near-by restaurants, this shop has a small but mouth-watering selection of pâtisseries, sweet and savoury, breads and some terrines. While there's not an enormous choice of food, what they have is first class.

LE TRAITEUR FRANÇAIS

142 Notting Hill Gate, W11
071 229 7185

Station Notting Hill Gate
underground

Bus 12, 27, 28, 31, 52

Open Mon–Sat 0900–1900
(but check for variations)

From humble beginnings in a tiny space at Whiteleys this first-class company moved to a spacious shop in Notting Hill. There they are able to display the fine pâtés, terrines, ballotine of salmon, rillettes de porc and all the other mainstays of a good French traiteur. There is a monthly menu of dishes which are always available (order one day in advance) as well as daily specials. These might include flan de St Jacques with sauce Noilly, fricassée de volaille sauce diable or six escargots de Bourgogne. Everything is made upstairs including the superb pâtisserie. If you want really fresh pasta, they will make it when you telephone to be picked up within an hour. As well as the

Le Traiteur Français

Villandry

ready-prepared food, there's a good selection of charcuterie such as jambon de Cobourg, cheese (French of course) and épicerie fine. House wines start at under £4 and there are ciders from Brittany and Normandy.

VILLANDRY

89 Marylebone High Street, W1
071 487 3816

Station Baker Street underground

Bus 2a, 2b, 13, 18, 27, 30, 74, 113, 159

Open Mon–Sat 0930–1900

French traiteur/greengrocer/charcutier/fromager – par excellence. Not cheap, but according to many people of taste one of the best in town. Direct from Rungis comes the pick of France – vegetables, fruit, mushrooms, herbs all arranged in *paniers*. Oils, mustards, French honeys, calissons d'Aix and other French biscuits. This shop is the only one in the UK buying Pain Poilâne from Max Poilâne's bakery – it is not factory made, so this is the real stuff. There's a small range of pâtisserie from Blanc Pâtisserie in Oxford and daily deliveries of Sally Clarke's bread. The French cheeses, in excellent condition, are from Philippe Olivier, and there's an unusual selection, mainly from small specialist producers, of British and Irish cheeses (no chauvinism here – just the best of everything). And the Gorgonzola is a must. A superior selection of wines. Coffee shop open till 1730 for tea, coffee, filled baguettes, soup, charcuterie and cheese, light lunches and for dinner the third Thursday in every month – must book. Also by special arrangement.

North West

GIACOBAZZI

150 Fleet Road, NW3
071 267 7222

Station Belsize Park
underground
Hampstead Heath BR

Bus 24, 168

Open Mon–Sat 0900–1900
Sun 1000–1400

Definitely a rosticceria with some deli items rather than the other way round, this welcoming shop, with its Italian-trained chef, is run by three young Londoners with firm roots in Italy. There's a wide selection of ready-prepared dishes, with more up their sleeves to suit all occasions. They can produce a three-course meal (from £10 a head) – just take it home and relax. Also staples such as loose rice and dried goods.

TOM'S

226 Westbourne Grove,
W11
071 221 8818
fax 071 221 7717

Station Notting Hill Gate/
Ladbroke Grove underground

Bus 15, 28, 31

Open Mon–Sat 0800–2000
Sun 0930–1500

Tom's a Conran so it goes without saying that this is a very attractive place to shop. The friendly team try to create personal contact and if you want something special they do their best to get it for you. From Kendal mint cake to fresh foie gras there's something for everyone – though at quite a price. Large counter of prepared dishes, charcuterie and sausages all look tempting. The pâtisserie, from Philippe Dadé, is first class and there's a speciality cake maker on tap. At the back the small greengrocery section receives twice-weekly deliveries direct from France. Downstairs the grocery section has all the fine food packs you'd expect to find, from France, Italy and a good selection of US favourites.

WESTSIDE CATERERS

92 Pitshanger Lane, W5
081 991 5576

Bus E7

Open Mon–Sat 0730–1830

The friendly Iranian proprietors of this shop are only too delighted to explain some of the more unusual items they sell – like kashk, which is a yoghurty dressing to put on meat and vegetables. Their cooked food is international with Indian, Mexican and Californian as well as Iranian dishes – mostly cooked on the premises and deliciously fresh. They do a lot of vegetarian dishes like cutlets with coriander and parsley, and, as you might expect, food is delicately spiced. The menu changes every day and there are always new things arriving from the kitchen to whet your appetite. Homemade cakes, Iranian biscuits and sweetmeats sit side by side with English buns and iced Danish pastries. They cater for parties small and large.

South West

CAREYS

20 Barnes High Street,
SW13
081 878 8594

Station Barnes Bridge BR

Bus 9

Open Mon–Fri 0800–1830
Sat 0800–1800

Gourmet sandwiches and hot homemade soup are some part of the many take-away possibilities from this high-quality delicatessen and outside catering company. They will make dishes to order, novelty wedding cakes, barbecues, buffets and children's teas. Salads look fresh and wholesome, nut and vegetable pâtés are appetising as are the cold raised meat pies. The menu changes weekly. The raspberry meringue roulade and carrot cake both drew sighs. As well as the ready-cooked foods there are deli items, sun-dried tomatoes, loose wild rice and some gift ideas.

SONNY'S FOOD SHOP

92 Church Road, Barnes,
SW13
081 878 1898/741 8451

Bus 9

Open Mon–Fri 0900–1800
Sat 0900–1700
Sun 0900–1400

A designer deli, with metal display shelves stacked with own-label jars of olives, homemade rouille, cornichons and mustards, beans, oils, honeys. Baskets of metre-long pasta flavoured with sage, or chilli and garlic, porcini, beetroot, nettle, made by Conforti – the packages are beautiful! A small but select cheese counter with perfect Brie and Neal's Yard cheeses (Montgomery's Cheddar and Duckett's Caerphilly among them) and super bread – nine types including bacon and onion, raisin and hazelnut. Everything on the deli counter is homemade. Toulouse sausages and portions of osso bucco, duck-liver parfait and other dishes are readily called up from their adjoining restaurant.

LA TOURAINE

48 White Hart Lane,
Barnes, SW13
081 878 6861

Bus 9

Open Tues–Fri 0915–1800
Sat 0900–1700
Sun 1000–1400

Gene Tunney, co-owner of this delicatessen, also a pâtisserie and wine shop, is an English master chocolatier/pâtissier and makes everything on the premises. The superb collection of pâtisserie has pride of place, but there is a small deli counter with foie gras, jambon persillé and other delicacies, including gourmet gifts. There are baps, baguettes and sandwiches to take out and they cater for local office parties. The mainly French wines come, not surprisingly, from the Loire.

South East

FOOD PARCELS

20 Royal Hill, Greenwich, SE10
081 858 2268

Station Greenwich BR

Bus 18, 286

Open Mon–Thur 0900–1700
Fri 0900–1730
Sat 0900–1600

There's plenty of action here with local business folk coming in for take-out lunches and hosts arriving to pick up the first courses for their elegant dinner parties. Almost everything is made on the premises and though there are plenty of interesting vegetarian dishes, the juiciest piece of red beef confirms that they cater for all tastes. Indeed this is a catering business as much as a deli, though the shelves display useful jars and packs to augment home cooks' food. They will deliver locally such original dishes as salmon and sweet-cure bacon with rosemary or homity pie, the soupe du jour or whatever is on the daily changing menu.

Sweet Treats

How gracious it must have been to take a cup of chocolate in Nash's Regency London. Since the marketing men are now selling 'luxury' chocolate in all its forms and ice cream as 'better than sex' (their words, not ours), perhaps the time is ripe for us to rediscover chocolate houses.

The British have the possibly unenviable reputation for being the biggest consumers of sweets in the world, so it is good to see that increasingly we are able to buy quality confectionery, as witnessed by the high-street chain of Thornton's (whose motto could be 'Eat a toffee, make a dentist happy').

As well as the shops listed, don't forget that department stores all have chocolate counters and some have ice-cream bars as well.

The following entries from other sections may also be of interest for their specially good ice cream and/or chocolates: Annabel; Art de Thé Tearooms; J. F. Ayre; Cannelle; Le Connaisseur; Golders Hill Park Cafeteria; Harrods (American Ice Cream Bar and various chocolate counters); Sara Jayne; Maison Sagne; Mimma; Newens – the Original Maids of Honour Tearoom; Pechon; Tea Time; La Touraine; Victoria Bakery.

Central

CHARBONNEL ET WALKER

One The Royal Arcade, 28 Old Bond Street, W1
071 491 0939
fax 071 495 6279

Station Green Park/Bond Street underground

Bus 9, 14, 22, 25, 38

Mme Charbonnel worked for one of Paris's best chocolate shops and was persuaded by the future Edward VII to come and make chocolates in London. In 1875 she met up with Mrs Walker, hence the curious name of this firm. Everything that is wonderful and best in the British chocolate world is sold from a chocolate-box shop in this stunning, bright orange painted arcade. Not just pretty packaging, they use at least 70 per cent cocoa solids in the chocolate products (made in Tunbridge Wells, with Belgian couverture made to their own specification). The drinking chocolate is the

Charbonnel et Walker

Open Mon–Wed, Fri 0930–1730
Thur 0930–1800
Sat 1000–1600
(longer opening hours at holidays)

highest cocoa-fat content available (51 per cent) – hugely popular ('It's walking off the shelves'), fudge sauces, cooking chocolate (70 per cent cocoa fat), marvellous biscuits. Chocolates are English style, bitter sweet, nearer French than Belgian and almost all handmade, as are the truffles. You can have your personal selection and they keep a record of it. Sold through Selfridges, Partridges and elsewhere, but always under their own name. Courier service if you can't wait to taste these chocolates, and mail order.

LES CHOCOLATS D'ALICE

43 Pimlico Road, SW1
071 259 9424

Station Sloane Square underground

Bus 11, 137, 239

Open Mon–Sat 1000–1800

The young Belgian proprietress sells chocolates handmade by an artisan chocolatier from her home village. She has a large selection, as well as marzipan fruits, pâte de fruits, fruit liqueur chocolates, marrons glacés and at Christmas lots of chocolate figures wrapped in gold foil to hang on the tree. There are also papier mâché boxes, baskets or porcelain bowls into which you can put your choice of chocolates, which will be gift wrapped free.

ROCOCO

321 King's Road, SW3
071 352 5857

Station South Kensington/ Sloane Square underground

Bus 11, 19, 22, 45a, 49, 219

Open Mon–Sat 1000–1830

Chantal Coady dreamed of owning a chocolate shop while she was studying at art school. Being a determined young lady, she made her dream come true and Rococo is the charming result. There's simply the best of everything in chocolates there, from the sublime to the ridiculous. Valrhona truffles and Easter eggs at one end of the scale down to quail's eggs for 30p. It's heaven, both for the serious chocolate lover and for people who have a sense of humour.

North West

ACKERMAN CHOCOLATES LIMITED

9 Goldhurst Terrace, NW6
071 624 2742

Station Finchley Road
underground
Finchley Road and Frognal BR

Bus 13, 82, 113, C11, C12

Open Mon–Fri 0930–1800
Sat 0930–1700

Established in the 1940s, this Swiss-owned choco-latier is considered by many to be the finest in town. It supplies members of the royal family. The chocolates are made by hand in Camden Town – tiny, exquisite, almost black chocolates filled with violet cream (favourite of elderly ladies), coffee or mint cream. Truffles 'to die for' and sophisticated continental type like Mozart kugel, marzipan truffles, nut discs, mint wafers, chocolate animals, Christmas figures and chocolate coffee beans. They also have serious chocolate bars made by Feodora and their own Callebaud cooking chocolate which gives good results (available in large blocks to order).

ANONA

13 Highgate High Street, N6
081 348 5213

Station Highgate
underground

Bus 210, 271

Open Tues–Sat 1000–1800
Sun 1100–1400

This chocolate specialist shop has the very best chocolate – Neuhaus and Godiva from Belgium and Ackerman (see above) from London. There's a wide range of novelty chocolates and the finest quality bars of Valrhona cooking chocolate – with 61 per cent cocoa solids (normal English choc bars contain around 40 per cent). They also have a good selection of diabetic chocolate. The shop is air-conditioned to keep everything in tip-top condition.

THE EXCLUSIVE CHOCOLATE SHOP

797 High Road, North
Finchley, N12
081 446 2560

Bus 125, 263

Open Mon–Sat 0930–1800

Continental chocolates from Mondose and Daska-lides and Italian ice cream from Inghilterra. They'll fill boxes and baskets and vases for gifts.

HÄAGEN-DAZS

75 Hampstead High Street,
NW3
071 794 0646

Station Hampstead
underground

Bus 46, 268

Open Mon–Thur 1000–2300
Fri–Sun 1000–2330

Every child's dream – an ice-cream parlour serving sixteen different ice creams made from natural ingredients, pure cream, no stabilisers and Belgian chocolate. You can have a cone or a cup or a sundae with a choice of toppings, to eat in or take out, plus hot and cold drinks (hot chocolate comes from Charbonnel et Walker (see pages 123–4) and in addition you can buy the ice cream in tubs to take home. Cookies and cream, we were told, is the most popular combination. The chocoholic sundae is Belgian chocolate ice cream with-chocolate chocolate-chip ice cream, chocolate vermicelli, hot chocolate fudge sauce and whipped cream. Fresh cream ice-cream cakes to order for those 'push the boat out occasions' (quite pricey but sophisticated).

Also at 14 Leicester Square, WC2, 071 287 9577

LESSITERS

167a Finchley Road, NW3
071 624 5925

Station Finchley Road/Swiss Cottage underground

Bus 13, 82, 113, C11, C12

Open Mon–Sat 0900–1800

Passions run high where chocoholics gather – which is the best of all – Belgian, Swiss or French chocolate? Each has its supporters and if you are in the Swiss camp, Lessiters is the shop for you. They have been here (appropriately at Swiss Cottage) since 1911 and the chocolates are all made in their own factory, as is the ice cream. There are masses of gift items, and the fresh cream truffles (all made with Lindt couverture) are extremely popular.

Also at 16 Poultry, EC2, 071 248 7664
75 Davies Street, W1, 071 499 3691

MARINE ICES LIMITED

8 Haverstock Hill, NW3
071 485 3132

Station Chalk Farm underground
Primrose Hill BR

Bus 31, 168

Open Mon–Sat 1030–2245
Sun 1130–2000

There can't be a family in north-west London that does not have childhood memories of this ice-cream parlour – which includes a restaurant serving light meals. The ice cream is made in the Italian style on the premises and the long queues outside on a hot summer's day testify to its enduring popularity. Inside you can indulge in various bombes, all named after the place in Italy from where the family Manzi hailed – Ravello.

North East

AMBALA

55 Brick Lane, E1
071 247 8569

Station Aldgate East underground
Shoreditch BR

Bus 8, 15, 25, 40, 67, 253

Open Sun–Sat 1000–2000

Part of a successful chain, with outlets all over London and throughout Britain selling very high quality, not too sweet, Pakistani sweets (though most people would call them Indian) based on ancient recipes handed down in one family for generations. The shops sell only what is made in their own factory in Hackney. Try the divine burfi or the excellent rasmalai or any of a dozen or more sweetmeats and a few savoury items such as pakoras and samosas. Daily deliveries ensure freshness and they will post goods abroad for you.

Also at 284 Green Street, E7, 081 472 6004
680 High Road, Leyton, E10, 081 558 0385

48 Upper Tooting Road, SW17, 081 767 1747
330 Ballards Lane, N12, 081 446 4432
6 Glenmore Parade, Ealing Road, Wembley,
   081 903 9740
112 Drummond Street, NW1, 071 387 3521
89 The Broadway, Southall, 081 843 9049

South West

SANDRINE

233 Upper Richmond Road
West, SW14
081 878 8168

Station Putney BR

Bus 37

Open Mon–Sat 1000–1730

A useful local place to buy handmade (mostly Belgian) chocolates made from natural ingredients. The pretty packaging can be made up to your own requirements.

South East

CRITERION ICES

118 Sydenham Road, SE26
081 778 7945

Station Sydenham BR

Bus 75, 108b, 194, 194a

Open Sun–Thur 1030–1730
Fri 1030–1830
Sat 1030–1900

For more than half a century the Valenti family have been making fine dairy ice cream in Sydenham and they never stand still – new flavours are constantly being introduced to the already long list of favourites. Recent additions include deep cherry crisp, deep chocolate truffle and strawberry yoghurt. Ginger lovers will adore the stem ginger and vanilla, with huge chunks of ginger. Peanut-butter fudge is an extraordinary translation into ice, with lumps of chocolate. The mango sorbet is the best we've tasted. Light snacks and homemade cakes and coffee are served in the café.

RUDI'S

23 Greenwich Church
Street, SE10
081 858 5441

Station Greenwich BR

Bus 188, 286

Open Sun–Thur 1030–1830
Fri–Sat 1030–2230

German Mövenpick ices in sugar cones are pretty classy in this part of Greenwich. Delicious dairy ice cream and very fruity sorbets (the lemon is recommended for long hangovers – it's very powerful). There's also some of the finest chocolate – Neuhaus, Valrhona and Mondose.

⮽ *Bar None* ⮽

Perhaps it is no accident that there are no English equivalents for *simpatico, sympathique, sympatisch*; it may also be the reason why, by and large, cafés in London have a long way to go before they acquire that very special charm of their continental cousins.

Our seemingly strange bedfellows here – wine bars, pubs, sandwich bars, juice bars, tapas bars and cafés – do have something in common, all being places where you will find a light snack and/or something particularly good to drink.

A welcome addition to the London scene is the fairly recent appearance of the superior sandwich bar, for which praise should go to Marks & Spencer for showing us that sandwiches can be interesting, substantial and tasty. On the other hand opprobrium can still be heaped upon British Rail for its pitiful cafés and sandwiches.

London should be famous for its pubs, but sadly any pub in possession of a microwave and a chip frier feels entitled to claim that it serves 'traditional home cooking'. While wine bars have come of age, tapas bars, still in their infancy, need to prove themselves. The good ones are all too rare.

That said, during the course of our researches we have been able to enjoy many a happy hour in some delightful and often serendipitous places.

The following entries from other sections may also be of interest for light meals as well as good tea, coffee and cakes: Annabel; Aroma; Aziz Baba Deli Pastahanesi; Bibendum; Books for Cooks; Celebration Cakes by Suzelle; the Coffee Gallery; the Cooler; Criterion Ices; Dominique's; East West Restaurant; Florians; Importers Limited; Lisboa Pâtisserie; Louis Pâtisserie Hampstead; Luigi's Euroteca Centre; Maison Bertaux; Maison Bouquillon; Maison Sagne; Marine Ices Limited; Neal's Yard Bakery; Pâtisserie Bliss; Pâtisserie Valerie; Pechon; Pizzeria Castello; Primrose Pâtisserie; Reynier's Wine Library; Rippon Cheese Stores; Sesame Health Foods; Waitrose.

Central

BETJEMAN'S WINE BAR

44 Cloth Fair, EC1
071 796 4981

Station Farringdon
underground and BR

Bus 55, 63, 221, 259

Open Mon–Fri 0730–2300

Tucked away behind the venerable St Bartholomew's church, a mere meat hook away from Smithfield market, this one-time residence of the late poet laureate is now a wine bar. Open for breakfast and bar food (until 2130), the wine is rather more interesting than the food. The multi-national list is extensive with choice numbers. Eaux de vie by the glass, exceptional choice of port both by the glass and bottle and sherry.

BIRLEY'S SANDWICH BAR

12–13 Royal Exchange, EC3
071 626 5134
071 929 0822 for delivery
fax 071 623 2210

Station Bank underground

Bus 6, 8, 9, 11, 15b, 21, 76,
133, 149

Open Mon–Fri 0700–1500

A most attractive chain of sandwich bars in the City providing sandwiches and salads. Early birds can have breakfast – sausage in Italian bread or egg and bacon muffin. A fortnightly changing menu of special salads such as fillet steak cooked medium rare with Cheddar cheese and assorted peppers, or roast leg of lamb with peppers, potato and mangetouts can be delivered to your office along with your choice of sandwiches, or platter boxes presented on a silver tray. Delivery (within EC1–EC4) guaranteed within fifty minutes – if ten minutes' late it's free. They have an evening service delivery until 2100.

Also at 17 Cullum Street, EC3, 071 621 0763
5 Bow Lane, EC4, 071 248 0358
Unit 2, Cannon Street Station, EC4, 071 626 8594
14 Moorfields, EC2, 071 628 9701

BONNE BOUCHE CATERING

40 Tachbrook Street, SW1
071 630 1626

Station Victoria underground
and BR

Bus 2, 11, 16, 24, 25, 29,
76, 82, 135, 239

Open Mon–Sat 0800–1800

This shop, part of a chain of Bonne Bouche, is blessed with a manageress who doesn't believe in standing still. Mina, from Laos, has her cousin cook special spicy-style chicken to go with pickled vegetables into the well-stuffed Vietnamese sandwiches which bring in the local office workers at lunchtime. When one variety palls she goes to work inventing another set of fillings. Best-seller is tuna which, like all the sandwiches made on the premises, can be in any bread you choose. Individual pieces of nougat sticks, walnut and honey or almond slices are popular carry-out cakes for lunches, and there are gâteaux (also sold by the slice), carrot cakes and many others. The sunflower bread loaves are popular and on Saturday they have a number of special breads – herb, onion, pepper and sesame.

Other shops (not necessarily so inventive in their

sandwiches) are at 22 Bute Street, SW7, 071 584 9839
129 Praed Street, W2, 071 724 5784
2 Thayer Street, W1, 071 486 9584
70 Cannon Street, EC4, 071 236 3353

M. J. BRADLEYS

43 Bedford Street, WC2
071 836 2830

Station Charing Cross/Covent
Garden/Embankment
underground

Bus 6, 9, 15a, 15b, 30, 77,
77a, 176

Open Mon–Fri 0730–1600
Sat 0930–1600

A sandwich bar and tiny (four tables) café, which serves breakfast of muesli with fruit and yoghurt or croissants, then goes on to sandwiches, baps and salads. Good and interesting choice. Homemade soup of the day (like pea and mint), some cakes, pastries, tea and coffee. 'The creative eater can design his own sandwiches' sounds a bit pretentious, but around Covent Garden anything goes. They will deliver for orders over £12 if you telephone before 1130.

BRUNEL

134 Great Portland Street,
W1
071 636 0674

Station Oxford Circus
underground

Bus 7, 8, 10, 13, 15, 25, 73,
135, 159

Open Mon–Fri 0730–1600

Cheerful and very rapid service is what you need in a sandwich shop, and this one certainly provides that. Daily specials might include hot ciabatta filled with mozzarella, tomato and olives or seafood salad. All sandwiches are made to order. There's a soup of the day, espresso, desserts. Local delivery.

Also at 9 Aldwych WC2, 071 240 2601
211 Strand, WC2, 071 353 1972

CHIMES

26 Churton Street, SW1
071 821 7456

Station Victoria underground
and BR

Bus 2, 11, 16, 24, 25, 36,
38, 52, 73, 76, 135

Open Sun–Sat 1200–1430 and
1800–2215

A delightful find to take foreign friends to for English food. Traditional recipes like Shropshire fidget pie or Gloucestershire lamb pie with rosemary and apples provide a nostalgic touch. The puddings are a must – bread and butter, orange treacle tart or crumble, all with hot custard – guaranteed to restore faith in our native cuisine. Liquid accompaniments include a fine selection of draught cider (pulled by hand pump), vintage cider, English perry (made from pears), fruit wines like elderflower, gooseberry, damson or apple and various soft drinks, with traditional lemonade. There are also ports, sherries and mead and a list of grape wines. On Sundays they have a roast lunch. Posters and prints relating to cider and wine making, and a lively atmosphere with robust classical music.

Also 91 High Street, Wimbledon, SW19, 081 946 2471

THE CHURCHILL ARMS

119 Kensington Church Street, W8
071 727 4242

Station Notting Hill Gate underground

Bus 27, 28, 31, 52

Open Mon–Sat 1200–1430 and 1800–2130
Sun 1200–1430

Popping down to the local takes on a whole different meaning here, where Thai food makes an interesting alternative to the usual pub fare. This one gives you a choice of the standard English favourites – steak and kidney, liver and bacon and moussaka (English?), but go for the Thai dishes of pork, beef, chicken, duck and prawns with stir-fried vegetables, noodles or rice. You can choose from very mild to spicy to very hot (and they mean hot in Thailand/Notting Hill). The pleasant conservatory is a lepidopterist's delight. Food is really tasty and very reasonable.

CORK & BOTTLE

44–6 Cranbourn Street, WC2
071 734 6592

Station Leicester Square underground

Bus 14, 19, 22b, 24, 29, 38, 176

Open Mon–Sat 1100–2300 (food served 1230–2245)
Sun 1700–2230 (food and wine bar)

A first-class example of the genre: good food served in generous portions, and an excellent wine list with plenty of Australian wines from owner Don Hewitson's territory. This is a good spot to know because the dross in short-order food round and about Leicester Square is pretty dismal. Handy for theatre-goers.

THE EAGLE

159 Farringdon Road, EC1
071 837 1353

Station Farringdon underground and BR

Bus 55, 63, 221, 259

Open Mon–Fri 1200–2300

Usually when a brewery decides to gentrify one of its pubs it pulls in a designer and lets rip with the chi-chi. The tenants of this old pub have left the décor intact and encourage punters to come in for a pint if that's what they want. If you are looking for some up-to-the-minute Italian/Californian-style food at very good prices and you don't mind the rather loud music, this is a great place to be. The field mushroom soup was positively bursting with mushrooms and the vegetarian dishes we tried were oozing with good flavours – grilled vegetables with pesto and sun-dried tomato paste served with focaccia and a tian of Mediterranean vegetables. A short but not expensive wine list is chalked up on the board with the rest of the menu. If you go late (perhaps after the Barbican or South Bank), the food may have run out but they do try to find something.

GENERAL TRADING COMPANY CAFE

144 Sloane Street, SW1
071 730 0411
071 730 6400 for evening
reservations

Station Sloane Square
underground

Bus 11, 19, 22, 137, C1

Open Mon–Fri 0900–1715
Sat 0900–1345
and 1800–2215 for suppers

The café, run by Justin de Blank (see page 115) in this very English, very nice store, is full of young duchesses and elderly countesses, so the table talk is likely to be amusing. Breakfast, hot or cold, until 1100 then till 1200 there are cakes and pastries, all made on the premises and pretty yummy. Lunch is served between 1200 and 1500 – hot casseroles, puddings, with a good wine list and well priced, as is the set cream tea. In the evenings there are candlelit suppers and a quite different atmosphere. There are two set menus (two or three courses) as well as light 'theatre' suppers. In summer eat in the garden and conservatory.

The kitchen shop in the store is much loved by Sloane Rangers. A good hunting ground for gifts for classy cooks. The buyer travels to India, Italy and France seeking out unusual items. They do wedding lists.

HAMINE

84 Brewer Street, W1
071 439 0785

Station Piccadilly Circus
underground

Bus 3, 6, 9, 13, 14, 15, 19, 22, 38, 53, 88, 94

Open Mon–Sat 1200–2400

Save yourself the price of a fare to Tokyo – this must be a clone of many noodle bars in Japan. It attracts a predominantly Japanese clientele, whose heads are bowed over the huge bowls filled with noodles in soya sauce (shoyu larmen) or noodles in soya bean soup (miso larmen) or noodles and mixed vegetables in salt soup (tang men). The menu is short with only a few other possibilities such as grilled dumpling in spicy hot sauce or a curry with rice. Décor is clean cut, black and white with no frills. You order at the till as you go in and then wait (rather long at the height of the lunchtime rush). The steaming food is obviously freshly cooked to order, plentiful and very tasty. Suntory beers and soft drinks add further liquid refreshment. Upstairs is a Karaoke bar.

KATIE'S OF MAYFAIR

15a Pall Mall, SW1
071 976 1630
fax 071 839 8521

Station Green Park/Piccadilly Circus underground

Bus 3, 6, 9, 13, 14, 15, 19, 22, 38, 53, 88, 94

Open Mon–Fri 0600–1700

A clean, modern and bright sandwich bar with reasonable prices for the location, where you can eat in or take out. Hot dishes include soup of the day, dish of the day and a selection of pastas. You can order by phone or fax and they deliver (free for orders over £15). Fast service, fresh food and cappuccino. Open for breakfast.

THE LUTINE BELL

35–6 Leadenhall Market, EC3
071 283 3827

Station Aldgate underground
Fenchurch Street BR

Bus 5, 15, 25, 40, 42, 67, 78, 100, 253, X15

Open Mon–Fri 1030–1430

A take-away and snack bar, with an Italian restaurant upstairs, which offers inexpensive food. Soup, macaroni cheese, quiche, chilli, liver and bacon on rice, pastas, Spanish omelette and the like.

MARKS & SPENCER SANDWICH BAR

Moorgate, EC2
071 387 5232
fax 071 628 8688

Station Moorgate underground

Bus 9, 11, 21, 43, 76, 141, 214

Open Mon–Fri 0730–1800

As Britain's largest sandwich supplier, M&S have opened their first take-away sandwich bar in London's square mile (with a 'conventional' food hall next door). 'Everything is geared up to the customer/ office worker who wants a quick lunch.' There's a super range of 100 interesting, well-constructed sandwiches plus thirty different rolls. The senior selector of sandwiches spent three months in America researching new lines. And for early risers there are microwaveable breakfast baps. They make up platters to order.

MESON DON FELIPE

53 The Cut, SE18
071 928 3237

Station Waterloo underground and BR

Bus 1, 68, 76, 168, 171, 176, 188

Open Mon–Fri 1200–1500 and 1700–2400
Sat 1830–2400

The décor is not overwhelmingly Spanish but the food leaves no doubt. The tapas menu is not huge, but all the expected dishes are there plus a few more. Chorizo, riñones al Jerez, gambas gabardinas, fresh sardines, etc, and of course the inevitable flan for dessert. Service is efficient by the all-Spanish staff. There are seven sherries including half bottles of fino, and most of the important regions of Spain are represented. Port is the only non-Spanish wine. If you want to eat before a show at the near-by Old or Young Vic go promptly when it opens at 1830 – by 1845 it is really swinging on a Saturday night and you might not make it to the theatre.

THE NARROW GAUGE (SHOP)

18–20 Creechurch Lane, EC3
071 283 2337

Station Bank/Aldgate underground
Fenchurch Street BR

The arrival of The Narrow Gauge in the City has given desk-bound gourmets an opportunity to sample the delights of Kate Catleugh's successful concept in healthy, low-calorie food. Her original approach to 'diet food' makes a pleasing alternative to the many sandwich bars in the area or to the heavy business lunch, but you don't have to be watching your weight to enjoy the 'Broad Gauge' dishes which are also

Bus 5, 15, 25, 40, 42, 67, 78, 100, 253, X15

Open Mon–Fri 0800–1900

available in this pretty shop. All the prepared food is packaged with cooking advice and the Narrow Gauge dishes carry calorie counts which are surprisingly low given the exotic contents. You can eat there, your meal zapped in the microwave. Only the best of everything is on sale – teas, coffees and chocolates and an attractive collection of tea and coffee pots and paraphernalia. Early opening for breakfast and late closing (by City standards) means bankers and stockbrokers can eat well at odd hours. Deliveries within the City.

See also The Narrow Gauge (pages 197–8) for home-delivered diet plan.

NATURE'S DELIGHT

96 Drummond Street, NW1
071 387 6405

Station Euston underground and BR
Euston square underground

Bus 10, 14, 18, 24, 27, 29, 30, 73, 134, 135

Open Tues–Wed, Sat–Sun 1100–2100
Thur–Fri 1100–2130

Here's your chance to try paan – that extraordinary Indian digestive which cleanses the palate, sweetens the breath and is very much an acquired taste. It is made to order for you from ingredients in lovely brass containers – red honey, coriander, cardamom, other spices and a perfumed concoction, all rolled together in a leaf. Before, or perhaps after, try one of the freshly prepared fruit juices – sugar cane, coconut, ortanique are just a few. Falooda is an experience not to be missed, as are the dry-fruit milk shakes.

NUTHOUSE

26 Kingly Street, W1
071 437 9471

Station Oxford Circus underground

Bus 7, 8, 10, 13, 15, 25, 73, 135, 159

Open Mon–Fri 1030–1900
Sat and Bank Holidays 1100–1800
Closed Christmas Day

The food in this vegetarian health-food restaurant is very good, extremely sustaining, though the dreary décor might not inspire you. Everything is freshly made and there's a choice of up to ten hot dishes, with daily specials which might be fried vegetables in wine sauce or a mixed bean casserole. Plenty of original salads and homemade soup. Tempting desserts include a great hot fruit crumble. Prices are reasonable with no minimum charge. This small place gets very busy at lunchtime so advice (unlikely as it may seem) is to reserve a table. There's also a small area selling health food.

THE PIE & ALE SHOP

37–9 Pimlico Road, SW1
071 730 5984

This is actually a restaurant beside a pub/brewery rather than a shop. There's always a choice of pies, usually steak and kidney and chicken and mushroom, as well as a hot vegetarian dish, and on Sunday there's a roast joint of meat. Most food is under a fiver. The shop

Station Sloane Square
underground

Bus 11, 137, 239

Open Mon–Sat 1100–2300
Sun 1200–1500 and 1900–
2230

is part of the Orange Brewery Pub, on the corner of Pimlico Road and St Barnaby's Street, and it boasts an in-house brewer and brewery in its own cellar. They are very proud of their range of bitters – choose from Pimlico porter – dark and with hidden strength; Pimlico light – a better choice for lunchtime; SW1, said to be the locals' favourite; the original Orange Brewery beer and SW2 for the connoisseur – dark and powerful. Private parties of up to thirty are catered for.

RANOUSH

43 Edgware Road, W2
071 723 5929

Station Marble Arch
underground

Bus 6, 7, 8, 10, 12, 15, 16,
30, 36, 135, 137

Open Sun–Sat 1100–0100
(summer until 0200)

Part of a small empire of Lebanese restaurants, this place is a real delight if you like Middle Eastern food but don't want to get involved in a serious eat-in. Clean and fresh, with marble floors, on one side of the narrow shop are the savoury foods. There are baba ganoush, hummus, stuffed vine leaves, labneh (drained yoghurt thick enough to cut with a knife), and meat dishes like sweetbreads, brain, lamb's testicles – all Lebanese favourites which can be warmed up and eaten in or taken away, wrapped in pitta with salad and gherkins. On the other side are pastries – all nuts and honey in beautiful shapes. To wash these delicacies down there are freshly pressed juices – mango, tamarind, pineapple, carrot and other less exotic fruits. Jalab is a mixture of dates, raisins and incense (not 'incest' as we were told) – very sweet but at the same time refreshing. At the back of the shop you can while the time away with men sitting over their hubble-bubbles.

LOS REMOS

38a Southwick Street, W2
071 723 5056

Station Paddington
underground and BR

Bus 7, 15, 27, 36

Open Mon–Sat 1200–2400

The Galician proprietor of this establishment (upstairs a restaurant and downstairs a tapas bar) is passionate about authenticity and sad that London has so very few genuine tapas bars. His is certainly a model with more than fifty dishes including all the classic tapas favourites. On show at the counter are albondigas, tortilla with onion, courgettes with tomatoes, gambas al ajillo (with a wonderful lemony garlic sauce), pulpo alla gallega and daily specials marked on the board. The all-Spanish wine list, plus some unusual spirits and liqueurs and the fabulous turron (soft and hard), membrilla (quince paste) and other Spanish sweetmeats, all go to make this a delightful stop in an otherwise fairly gloomy area. Although open all day, note that the menu is limited between 1530 and 1800 – though a phone call to Roberto Lopez will ensure he will be there to rustle up one of his specialities.

TARTE JULIE

5 Vigo Street, W1
071 734 8353

Station Piccadilly Circus
underground

Bus 3, 6, 9, 13, 14, 15, 19,
22, 38, 53, 88, 94

Open Mon–Sat 0900–1830

Part of a French franchise, Tarte Julie is a welcome addition to the area where a fair amount of tat is more usual than a good tarte. The window display will set your mouth watering with its 'tartes salées', ranging from a classic quiche lorraine to périgourdine au confit d'oie, from provençale to fruits de mer. The sucrées embrace a variety of apple tarts through to rhubarb with cassis, fromage blanc aux pruneaux, and a whole gamut of chocolate confections. All these can be taken out (slice by slice) together with salads, or if you prefer, settle down to enjoy yourself with a glass of wine or a herbal tea, espresso or chantilly chocolate. Guaranteed to take the pain out of shopping in Regent Street. Service can be erratic.

THE VAULTS

Chiswell Street, EC1
071 588 2551

Station Barbican underground

Bus 4, 279a

Open Mon–Fri 1100–2100

Not a bowl of taramasalata in sight, this wine bar has a most imaginative choice of salads. Curried lamb, smoked chicken, kofta with raita and rice, the house special of mixed cold meats, all served in generous portions. There's a daily hot dish (lunchtime only) such as chicken chasseur. Desserts are in the order of chocolate fudge cake, profiteroles, crème brûlée and a fresh fruit salad. Drinks a'plenty from the bar. A really pleasant atmosphere in these picturesque cellars opposite and underneath Whitbread's brewery. The adjoining restaurant serves lunch only.

The Vaults

THE WREN CAFÉ

33 Jermyn Street, SW1
071 437 9419

Station Piccadilly Circus
underground

Bus 3, 6, 9, 13, 15, 19, 22,
38, 53, 88, 94

Open Mon–Fri 0800–1900
Sat 0900–1900
Sun 1000–1700

Next to the exquisite Wren church of St James in Piccadilly is this wholefood, vegetarian restaurant (except for the turkey and ham pie!). Everything is cooked on the premises, with a daily menu of specials. The chilli-bean casserole is a winner – as are the prices of main courses, which are well under £5. Also salads, pastries and substantial homemade cakes which are really delicious. In summer you can sit in the courtyard of the church to eat. They deliver to local offices free of charge on a pre-order arrangement.

North West

ART DE THE TEAROOMS

236 High Street, Hadley
Wood, Barnet
081 441 7929

Station High Barnet
underground + bus

Bus 34, 84, 234, 263

Open Mon–Fri 0900–1700
Sat 0900–1800

Downstairs Sarah sells Belgian chocolates, Crabtree & Evelyn preserves and exclusive gifts of unusual ceramics (teapots, mugs, cake tins, etc). Upstairs Jane makes gooey cakes and mainly vegetarian food. Hot dishes at lunch, special dishes of the day, sandwiches and full tearoom menu (not very expensive). Homey and jolly atmosphere.

THE CLIFTON

97 Clifton Hill, NW8
071 624 5233

Station Maida Vale/St John's
Wood underground

Bus 8, 16, 46

Open Mon–Fri 1100–1500
and 1700–2300
Sat 1100–2300
Sun 1200–1500 and 1900–
2230

A most elegant pub – Grade II listed in fact – part of a hotel and restaurant, situated in a classy residential area. Inside is pretty with Persian rugs, pine panelling, leather seats. Outside seating is also good. The bar menu is well above average – good-sized portions, good quality, huge baps filled with cream cheese and smoked salmon, prawns and mayonnaise, or steak. There's a dish of the day and traditional Sunday lunch.

LE COCHONNET

1 Lauderdale Parade, Maida
Vale, W9
071 289 0393

Station Maida Vale
underground

In a pretty part of Maida Vale, this is a pleasant place to sit and watch the world go by – the conservatory on the pavement looks quite continental and provides a bright and airy feel to the wine bar. The food is fairly standard but it's worth a journey for the wine, which is well priced and interesting. There's a good choice of wine by the glass, lots of New World wines, a big list

Bus 6, 28, 31, 36

Open Drinks Mon–Sat 1200–2300
Sun 1200–2230
Food Sun–Sat 1230–1500 and
1830–2300 (Sun 2230)

of clarets. Zero marks for bringing an open bottle of wine to the table. Sunday brunch and various social activities makes this popular with the locals.

MAGNUM'S

4 Fleet Road, NW3
071 485 3615

Station Belsize Park
underground
Hampstead Heath BR

Bus 24, 168, C11, C12

Open Sun–Sat 1100–2300

This is a useful local hostelry offering better than normal wine-bar food. Starters might include vegetable croquette with tomato coulis or goat's cheese and spinach filo parcels; main dishes range from duck and orange salad or sautéed chicken livers to sirloin steak. Good desserts. There's a very reasonable lunch menu offering a choice of starter and main course, and drinks and snacks are served all day. Afternoon coffee and Sunday brunch are featured. A comprehensive wine list.

The Clifton (see page 137)

MAJJO'S FOOD

1 Fortis Green Road, N2
081 883 4357

Station East Finchley underground

Bus 17, 102, 143, 236

Open Mon–Sat 1130–2200

Majjo relates that lamb passanda was one of the dishes her grandparents would take on long train journeys because the meat was preserved in the yoghurt sauce and spices and so lasted long enough to be enjoyed until they reached their destination (they didn't like to buy food from the hawkers on the stations along the way). Her lamb passanda might not have to last quite so long if you take it home from East Finchley together with some of the other delicious dishes, which are on the daily changing menu. You can see the spotlessly clean kitchens behind where everything is cooked from four every morning. They grind all the spices – just as an Indian housewife would do. Friday is baked fish day, Saturday chicken tikka. Warm parathas, chapattis, samosas and three different rice dishes – all basmati, needless to say. And there's kulfi to round off your meal. Generous portions and reasonable prices make this an excellent alternative to your local tandoori restaurant, particularly if you like to see what you are buying.

North East

WILLOUGHBY'S CAFE-BAR

26 Penton Street, N1
071 833 1380

Station Angel underground

Bus 153

Open Mon 1200–1500
Tues–Sat 1200–2300

Although for north Londoners it could be en route for the Barbican or Sadler's Wells, Penton Street might not be the hub of the universe – unless you are a cab driver visiting the taxi-training school. But what was once what the French call a 'rendezvous pour chauffeurs', or in plain English a driver's caff, has been transformed into a simple café-bar, open to all comers from breakfast on. Coffee is good and the all-day menu featuring wine-bar staples is supplemented by daily specials. Homemade soup, fish and a vegetarian dish are the theme on which variations are played. The wine list is well balanced and the house wines (served in ¼l glasses) are excellent. Interesting sandwiches to take out.

WISTERIA TEA ROOMS

14 Middle Lane, N8
081 348 2669

Station Finsbury Park underground and BR + bus

Down among the Lloyd loom chairs and flying ducks on the walls this oddball café serves excellent home-cooked dishes to a surprisingly young clientele, who obviously appreciate the Art Deco bric-à-brac that is an integral part of the establishment. Tea arrives in an old china teapot and the daily specials, like aubergine with cheese or tuna aïoli, are served on pretty

Bus 14a, 41, W2, W7

Open Tues–Fri 1130–1800
Sat–Sun 1000–1800

plates (nothing matches). Healthy portions, always with accompanying fresh salad and granary toast, compensate for somewhat erratic service. A cafetière of your chosen coffee can be enjoyed with first-class puds or cakes. Cheap and very cheerful, but it gets very busy so claim your table early for lunch. Garden at the back.

South West

BRIXTONIAN

11 Dorrell Place, SW9
071 978 8870
fax 071 737 5521

Station Brixton underground
and BR

Bus 2, 3a, 12, 45, 109, 133, 159, 250

Open Sun 1730–2300
Mon–Tues 1730–2400
Wed–Sat 1100–2400

The best-selling cocktail in this 'Rhum-Shop-Café-Restaurant-Bar' is called Brixton Riot, and like all their drinks, it's rum based, using one of the more than 180 rums they stock. Service is friendly, coffee and divine ginger and honey cake is an option if you can't face rum at 11 a.m. Lunch is served between 1200 and 1400 – creole chicken and rice, pasta, salads and the like. Upstairs is a restaurant serving mainly French West Indian food – they have a different 'island-hopping' menu each month. We haven't tried it, but it sounds good. Booking advisable.

REBATOS

169 South Lambeth Road, SW8
071 735 6388

Station Stockwell
underground

Bus 2b, 88

Open Mon–Fri 1200–1430
and 1900–2315
Sat 1900–2315

The tapas at this Spanish-looking bar may be more Balham than Barcelona, but taste good (the fresh anchovies in vinegar are particularly fine). Behind the tapas bar is a dining room for which you have to book weeks ahead, and indeed on a wintry Monday with snow, recession et al in London it seemed very full where everywhere else was empty. A really good-value set menu at lunch and dinner consists of three courses, with a choice of starters (seafood salad, crab au gratin, grilled sardines, soft roes on toast, gazpacho, fish soup Cantabrica). Main dishes are fish oriented.

THE TEA GALLERY

103 Lavender Hill, SW11
071 350 2564

Station Clapham Junction
BR + bus

Bus 45a, 77, 77a, 156

Open Sun–Sat 1100–2300

'Tea and kitsch' could perhaps best describe the studied quirkiness of this café. There are faded velvet chairs, old curtains on the tables and odd, but pretty, china, including novelty teapots. 'Imperial' toasties are their speciality; the freshly made egg mayonnaise sandwich (served hot) is recommended. Unusual teas, cheerful service and light snacks throughout the day. In the evening it transforms into a restaurant spreading into the next room, with a bright blue shrine-like bar and a sofa with well-loved teddies. A French chef produces country food (untried by us).

South East

THE CROWN & GREYHOUND

73 Dulwich Village, SE21
081 693 2466

Station North Dulwich BR

Bus 37, P4

Open Mon–Thur 1100–1500
and 1730–2300
Fri–Sat 1100–2300
Sun 1200–1500 and 1900–
2230

Agreat pub – very large and grand with a lovely smell of spices. There's a family room with fire, wood benches and a pretty garden with tables. Choose either pub snacks or the restaurant with salad bar. The menu includes casseroles, curries, vegetarian choice, wonderful door-step sandwiches, fresh vegetables and huge portions all the way. Food is available every day from 1200 to 1430 and Tues–Sat for à la carte menu from 1700 to 2230. There are also bar snacks Mon–Sat from 1730 to 2100.

PHOENIX & FIRKIN

5 Windsor Walk, Denmark
Hill (on station), SE5
081 701 8282

Station Denmark Hill BR

Bus 40, 68

Open Mon–Sat 1100–2300
Sun 1200–1500 and 1900–
2230

Denmark Hill station was destroyed by fire in 1980, but has now been restored to full Victorian station glory as a pub, complete with wonderful station clock, open fire, wood floor and old railway posters. They specialise in real ales such as Old Peculiar, Stonehend, Dog-Bolter, Phoenix, Adnams Bitter and Cameroon, as well as the excellent Old Rosie scrumpy from York-shire. The food bar serves filled baps, salads, pies, quiches and a hot dish on weekdays. Food bar closes at 1400.

SEYMOUR BROTHERS

2 Grove Lane, SE5
071 701 4944

Station Denmark Hill BR

Bus 176, 184, 185

Open Mon–Thur 0900–2000
Fri 0900–1900 Sat 0900–1800
Sun 1000–1400

The two eponymous brothers run this tea-shop cum deli. Food to eat in or take away. Italian olive oil breads with ritzy fillings, homemade soup of the day, fudgy cakes and a great fresh-fruit cheesecake. There's a good selection of salamis, cheeses, coffees and a few smart deli provisions. Eat in the garden in good weather. What makes this special is the exhibition of (good) art – all to buy. Next door is an amazing craft shop which is well worth a look.

≱ *Fish and Chips* ≱

Though this art form is very much a north of England speciality, there have been fish and chip shops (fondly known as 'chippies') in London since the mid-nineteenth century. They are all take-aways, and some additionally have seating inside. Whether these are called 'restaurant' or 'shop' defines their class. Apparently the best way to tell a really good fish and chip shop is to look for the cab drivers parked outside, as at the Fryers Delight. Toffs in Muswell Hill is most decidedly a restaurant, with the north London equivalent carriage being the chauffeur-driven Rolls.

Central

THE FRYERS DELIGHT

19 Theobald's Road, WC1
071 405 4114

Station Holborn underground

Bus 8, 22b, 25, 38, 45, 46, 55, 68, 168, 171

Open Mon–Sat 1200–2200 (take-away till 2300)

Here you'll find the best-value fish and chips in London in the opinion of many of those who profess expertise in this field. There are certainly no frills and no cheques in this chippy run by an Italian family in the best British tradition – complete with an excellent cup of tea and jaw-cracking bread and butter 'doorsteps'. The portions of fish are more than adequate though not enormous. The batter is crisp, chips are homemade and good. The fastest service in town – your order is sitting in front of you almost before you've given it.

GEALE'S FISH RESTAURANT

2 Farmer Street, W8
071 727 7969

Station Notting Hill Gate underground

One of the area's most popular fish and chip shops, as confirmed by the long queues, the simple décor means you can concentrate on enjoying the fish and chips. In fine weather you may be lucky enough to get a table outside. Bypass the soups and get stuck into what they do best – haddock, plaice, Dover or lemon sole, skate, rock salmon or a daily special. Everything comes

Bus 12, 27, 28, 31, 52

Open Tues–Sat 1200–1500
and 1800–2300

THE GOLDEN HIND

73 Marylebone Lane, W1
071 935 4905

Station Bond Street
underground

Bus 2a, 2b, 13, 18, 27, 38,
74, 113, 159

Open Mon–Fri 1130–1430
and 1700–2030

ROCK & SOLE PLAICE

47 Endell Street, Covent
Garden, WC2
071 836 3785

Station Covent Garden
underground

Bus 1, 4, 6, 9, 11, 13, 15,
168, 171, 176, 188

Open Mon–Sat 1130–2300

THE SEA SHELL

45–51 Lisson Grove, NW1
071 723 8703

Station Baker Street
underground
Marylebone BR

Bus 2a, 13, 18, 27, 30, 74,
82, 113, 159

Open Mon–Fri 1200–1400
and 1715–2230

in fresh daily, so if they are sold out don't be disappointed. Prices are reasonable but, unlike some chippies, do not include the chips or the tartare sauce. Licensed.

Nostalgia reigns supreme here with a 1940s interior complete with Bakelite fittings and a real old northern frier with lids. Run by a charming family of Italian ladies from Parma, there are lots of nice little touches such as fresh flowers, a choice of sauces and condiments and embroidered mats. Take away or eat in (there's another room downstairs) and choose small, medium or large portions of fish, sausages, fishcakes or cod's roe served with chips or salad.

Cramped, chaotic and busy, this is a sit-down or take-out fish bar. You are likely to share a table with some colourful characters. Not a large range of fish – cod, rock, haddock, plaice, skate, but all fresh and quickly cooked to order. Espresso coffee. A reasonably priced and filling meal for such an expensive area.

Lisson Grove may be known as the home of Eliza Doolittle, but its other claim to fame must surely be the Sea Shell, where you can almost always find a long queue waiting patiently to buy what might be among the capital's best fish and chips. There is a restaurant beside the take-away and if you arrive early enough you should get a table, but be prepared to wait – it's well worth it. The fish, fresh daily, is fried in good ground-nut oil and if you like it served cold, ask for it prepared with matzo meal. The choice is from top-priced halibut down to cod's roe and the portions are more than fair. The fish is crisp, the chips – real, old-fashioned – are great. And there's a good strong cup of tea to wash it all down – or wine if you prefer. The set lunch is reasonably priced.

North West

NAUTILUS

29 Fortune Green Road,
NW6
071 435 2532

Station West Hampstead
underground

Bus 28, 159, C11

Open Mon–Sat 1130–1430
and 1700–2300

The limited menu is all you need when the quality is as good as this. All fish is fried coated in matzo meal, which gives a crunchy finish. From cod to Dover sole, all served with excellent chips. Licensed.

TOFFS

38 The Broadway, Muswell
Hill, N10
081 883 8656

Station Highgate
underground

Bus 43, 107, 234

Open Tues–Sat 1130–2200
Sun 1230–2100, closed Mon,
3 weeks August, Christmas,
Easter and Bank Holidays

Many devotees of fish and chips agree that Toffs is tops. The Ttofalli family (second-generation Greek Cypriots) has won a number of prestigious awards – including the Seafish Authority's best for Great Britain in 1988 and 1990. This involves food technicians and hygienists inspecting the premises to test both food and cooking. They only buy grade one fish – never frozen, with fresh supplies bought for the next day at midnight. Have your fish fried, grilled or poached, and choose from an impressive array – John Dory (which might be marinated in olive oil, Greek parsley and garlic), halibut, skate, red snapper,

Mrs Ttofalli with her daughter

salmon, sea bass, kalamari as well as all the old British favourites. Mrs Ttofalli makes the most sensational taramasalata you will ever taste. Huge portions are likely to make you simply look at the sweet trolley, but the homemade fresh fruit tarts, steamed puds and roulades might tempt you. There's a small wine list and beers and a reasonably priced set menu is served between 1200 and 1700.

TWO BROTHERS FISH RESTAURANT

297 Regents Park Road, N3
081 346 0469

Station Finchley Central underground

Bus 13, 26, 260

Open Tues–Sat 1200–1430 and 1730–2215 (2130 for take-away)

'Not yer avridge chippy' is how this busy fish restaurant is billed. It's licensed and air-conditioned for a start. Plaice, cod, skate, haddock, halibut, trout or salmon can be steamed or grilled, but most punters go for fried. The chips are extra-ordinarily well cooked in ground-nut oil. At lunchtime there's a choice of standard or large portions. Interesting fishy starters (smokies in a creamy sauce, marinated herrings) plus dish of the day and traditional puds (though we couldn't see anyone who could manage one). Be prepared to queue, or you can phone for take-away orders.

North East

FAULKNER'S

424–6 Kingsland Road, E8
081 254 6152

Station Dalston Kingsland BR + bus

Bus 22a, 22b, 67, 149, 243

Open Mon–Fri 1200–1400 and 1700–2200 (Fri 1615–2200)
Sat 1130–2200

This company originally owned the Sea Shell (see page 145) and established a fine name for the best in fish and chips. Fish is the freshest (they have a wet-fish shop a few doors away at 394). Take-away prices are very reasonable. Restaurant is licensed, but you can bring your own (and, quirkily, they only charge corkage on red wine).

UPPER STREET FISH SHOP

324 Upper Street, N1
081 359 1401

Station Highbury and Islington underground and BR

Bus 4, 19, 43, 263a, 279

Checked tablecloths and hanging plants signify a rather superior fish and chip shop and several items from the menu confirm that impression. Halibut poached or fried in egg with herb sauce, or a daily special from the board of mussels fried in batter and served on a skewer are among the sophisticated items you can order here. They sometimes have exotic Seychelles fish as well as the usual varieties of fried fish. Starters include homemade fish soup, served hot and herby, smoked salmon pâté and fresh rock oysters. Delicious nursery puds such as jam roly-poly, served with custard or cream. No licence but no corkage if you bring your own wine.

Open Mon 1730–2200
Tues–Fri 1130–1400 and
1730–2200
Sat 1130–1500 and 1730–
2200

South West

FULHAM'S PIE AND MASH

140 Wandsworth Bridge
Road, SW6
071 731 1232

Station Fulham Broadway
underground + bus

Bus 28, 295

Open Mon–Wed 1145–1800
Thur–Fri 1145–2000
Sat 1145–1700

A real London treat is stewed eels, but if you haven't the stomach for that have a beef pie (well filled with good mince) with mashed potatoes and the traditional 'liquor' – parsley sauce. 'Add a touch of salt and vinegar' was the advice given to liven up the sauce, and it works wonders. Old blue and white tiles on the walls, wooden benches and a menu offering jellied eels, sausages, onions as well as the aforementioned eels, pie and mash, make this a typical (but perhaps higher quality) eel and pie shop. They can cater for your Cockney party, sell live eels and supply uncooked fresh or frozen pies for the freezer.

⇒ *Out and About* ⇐

L ondon is so well endowed with fine museums, galleries and beautiful parks, but however much you may enjoy visiting places of interest the time comes when a cup of tea or a light meal is welcome. Many museums and galleries have woken up to this fact and are now offering good food to fuel you for further forays into the cultural or scientific world.

Cafés in London's parks have in the past been more miss than hit, but we have been able to find a few good watering holes among the greenery. We have also included in this section ideas for where to eat in places of entertainment and, so that you don't have to shop till you drop, restaurants and cafés in stores.

Because so many of our national monuments seem to take pleasure in ripping off tourists, it was good to discover some purveyors of good food at reasonable prices that can grace rather than disgrace the milieu in which they are placed.

When it comes to street food, unfortunately we feel a government health warning might be appropriate to the vast majority of food you are likely to see being sold from foodcarts around town. And *caveat emptor* should be the words inscribed on everyone's heart when in search of sustenance on the streets of London.

The following entries from other sections may also be of interest for light meals as well as good tea, coffee and cakes: Peter de Wit; Forget Me Not Teas; Fortnum & Mason.

Central

ARTS THEATRE CAFE

6 Great Newport Street, WC2

D on't mind the slightly drab look of this little café in the basement of the Arts theatre. The food is delicious, service pleasant and it is well placed for pre-theatre or post-shopping. The daily changing menu has dishes which you would be likely to find at an

071 497 8014

Station Leicester Square
underground

Bus 14, 19, 22b, 24, 29, 38,
176

Open Mon–Fri 1200–2100

CHELSEA PHYSIC GARDEN

66 Royal Hospital Road,
SW3
071 352 5646

Station Sloane Square
underground

Bus 11, 137, 239

Open Wed & Sun 1400–1700
from mid-March to mid-
October and 1200–1700
during Chelsea Flower Show
week

THE COFFEE GALLERY

23 Museum Street, WC1
071 436 0455

Station Holborn underground

Bus 7, 8, 14, 19, 22b, 24,
29, 38, 73, 134, 176

Open Mon–Fri 0830–1730
Sat 1000–1730
Sun 1230–1830

HARRODS RESTAURANTS

Knightsbridge, SW1
071 730 1234

Italian village restaurant – rather a sophisticated village at that. The house wine is reasonable and available by the glass. There's always an exhibition of photography to please the eye.

You can enjoy a good cup of tea in the blissful surroundings of this 'secret' garden, founded in 1673 by the Society of Apothecaries, thus making it Europe's oldest botanic garden. Amongst the 3½ acres between the river and Swann Walk is the oldest rock garden in Europe, which dates from 1772. There are more herbs than you could ever have imagined existed for culinary and medicinal use. See the largest olive tree outdoors in Britain. Teas (and lunches in Chelsea Flower Show week) and plants for sale. Entrance via Swann Walk. No dogs. There's also a reference library with some books on food. Contact the curator.

But a step away from the British Museum, this is a relaxed and pleasant place to stop for breakfast, lunch or afternoon tea amidst a changing exhibition of paintings or photography and ceramics from Amalfi, home town of Piero Amodio. As well as having an eye for attractive art, Signor Amodio and his wife know how to make a mean bollito misto – one of the soups you are likely to find on the lunchtime menu. There are usually three sandwiches and three salads (but go early to be sure of a choice). We tried the smoked salmon and scrambled egg and a salad of rocket, spinach, mozzarella and sun-dried tomatoes. Together with a soup and a very good tart (sometimes they are homemade and some are from Pâtisserie Valérie) you can create a substantial meal – or, if you aren't so greedy, a splendid snack.

There are eleven restaurants and bars in Harrods so you don't need to go hungry while being relieved of your money. The fourth-floor Georgian restaurant serves traditional British food. There is a set two- or three-course lunch (you select from the *à la carte* menu).

Station Knightsbridge
underground

Bus 9, 14, 22, C1

Open Times vary according to
restaurant

This restaurant also serves afternoon tea (with pianist
tickling the ivories) with everything you could want
including unlimited pastries (so don't eat lunch).
On the ground floor the West Side Express (Hans
Road door) opens for breakfast at 0745 – US style
(though Americans might need to suspend belief just
a bit). There's also an ice-cream parlour, a cheese bar,
espresso bar, health-juice bar, pasta bar and self-service
restaurants. The basement pub opens from 1100 for traditional pies, ploughman's lunches and (for husbands
weary of accompanying their wives) a quiet pint of
beer.

THE IMPERIAL
WAR MUSEUM

Lambeth Road, SE1
071 820 9817

Station Lambeth North
underground

Bus 3, 44, 109, 159

Open Sun–Sat 1000–1730

Run by de Blank Restaurants, this café offers good-
value light meals which are also to be found in a
number of other venues (see below). There are always
robust salads, several hot dishes and desserts (often
worthy, wholemeal confections). It makes museum
visiting even more interesting if you can rest your feet
and tempt your tastebuds.

Also at The Barbican Centre, Silk Street, EC2, 071 588
8391
British Museum, Great Russell Street, WC1, 071 323
8256
Museum of Mankind Café de Colombia, 6 Burlington
Gardens, W1, 071 287 8148
Natural History Museum, Cromwell Road, SW7, 071
938 9185
Science Museum, Exhibition Road, SW7, 071 938
8149
Habitat, 206 King's Road, SW3, 071 351 1211
Mansard Café, the Heal's Building, 196 Tottenham
Court Road, W1, 071 580 2522

Opening hours vary from place to place. Check if it is
critical.

INSTITUTE OF
CONTEMPORARY
ARTS

Nash House, The Mall, SW1
071 930 0493
fax 071 873 0051

Station Charing Cross/
Piccadilly Circus underground

Easily the best of any gallery/museum café in the
capital, the food is classy, authentic Italian, such as
you might eat at Riva, the River Café, Santini's, but at
a fraction of the cost. There's always something interesting and new on the limited menu, which changes
daily. Soup, starter, good salads, three main dishes,
imaginative vegetarian choices, pasta with pumpkin or
octopus or porcini, puds (homemade tiramisu). Chocolate truffle cake and pâtisserie from Nadell's (see page

Bus 1, 3, 6, 9, 11, 12, 13, 15, 24, 29, 53, 77

Open Café Mon–Sat 1200–2200
Sun 1200–2100
Bar Mon–Sat 1200–1430 and 1730–2300
Sun 1200–1400 and 1730–2230

JAPAN CENTRE

66–8 Brewer Street, W1
071 439 8035
fax 071 437 0878

Station Piccadilly Circus underground

Bus 3, 6, 9, 13, 14, 15, 19, 22, 38, 53, 88, 94

Open Shop Mon–Fri 1000–1930
Sat and Sun 1000–1800
Restaurant Mon–Fri 1100–1900
Sat 1100–1800

LIBERTY COFFEE SHOP

Regent Street, W1
071 734 1234

Station Oxford Circus underground

Bus 7, 8, 10, 13, 15, 25, 73, 135

Open Mon–Sat 0930–1730

NATIONAL GALLERY

Trafalgar Square, WC2
071 839 3321

Station Charing Cross underground

Bus 3, 6, 9, 13, 15, 53, 88, 94, 159, 170, 176

19). There's no minimum charge – have a baguette, cappuccino, soup or a three-course feast. Non-members pay £1.50 for daily membership, but the food's so good it's worth the £20 annual membership of the ICA, which gives entrance to the refurbished galleries, café and bar as well as exhibitions and films. A private (Nash) room is available for parties.

In a small strip of London which has become a mecca for Japanese restaurants, cafés and shops, the Centre has all of these. Upstairs the bookshop has a good corner for oriental cookbooks and guides to Japan (food and travel). Downstairs amongst the videos there's a small selection of foods in the 'minimarket'. (A larger food shop in the same group is at Yoshino, see pages 66–7.) Most interesting though is the sushi bar with very reasonable prices and portions to suit all appetites (medium, large and extra large), all served with tea. The chef in pale blue tunic looks like a brain surgeon, the sushi, tonkatsu and other dishes look great. Be prepared to wait – there's always a huge queue.

Liberty is a store on many tourists' lists, and rightly so for its handsome building and covetable goods. When the shopping palls, the basement café, where even the tables not surprisingly are covered in Liberty fabric, is a pleasant oasis. Light bites, delightful desserts, perfect pastries (menuspeak) are all fresh and appetising. Individual cafetières and wine.

After feasting on the sight of the most wonderful paintings, the light and airy restaurant in the basement of the National Gallery is an agreeable place for a light meal or just a drink (though coffee might be disappointing). A lunchtime hot buffet with three choices or several substantial salads which are all tasty and freshly prepared. Sandwiches and snacks are available throughout the day. For a more sophisticated ambience go to the brasserie restaurant in the stunning

Open Mon–Sat 1000–1700
Sun 1400–1700

new Sainsbury Wing. The décor is pleasing, the view exciting and the food (and coffee) can be delicious. Snacks at the bar or *à la carte* or set menu until 1½ hours before the gallery closes.

THE NEW SERPENTINE RESTAURANT

Hyde Park, W2 (Exhibition Road side)
071 402 1142

Station Knightsbridge underground

Bus 9, 10, 52, 52a

Open From mid-March–end September
Mon–Sat 1030–2230
Sun 1030–1730
October–end Dec 1030–1630
Jan–mid-March closed

Part of Prue Leith's empire, this has to be without doubt the restaurant with the best view in London, right on the water's edge, surrounded by beautiful old trees and wildlife (both animal and human). In the summer you are a mere splash away from the Lido's diving boards. Eat inside or out – inside it's light, spacious and with lots of weeping fig trees. An all-day menu until 1730 offers light dishes and salads. A £4.50 minimum charge at lunchtime, with grills, hot dishes ranging from bangers and mash to spinach and pine-nut-stuffed artichoke with wild rice and mushroom sauce, and puddings and cheeses. Available for private parties. A short distance away in the park (near the Hyde Park Hotel) is The Dell (telephone 071 723 0681), which is a self-service café with excellent coffee and cakes, a hot dish of the day and good soup. You can eat outside by the water on a sunny day. Open in the summer daily 0900–2000, with a Pimms Bar in good weather. Oct–mid-March 1000–1700.

Somewhat further away at Hampton Court Palace, Leith's have the Tiltyard restaurant and Garden Café. See also The Orangery, Kensington Gardens, below.

THE ORANGERY

Kensington Palace, Kensington Gardens, W8
071 376 0239

Station Kensington High Street underground

Bus 9, 10, 33, 49, 52, C1

Open Summer season only
Sun–Sat 0930–1730

Designed by Hawksmoor and Vanbrugh and built in 1704, this was originally a 'stately greenhouse' and used by Queen Anne for summer picnic suppers. So if you want to say you lunched at Kensington Palace you can eat here – set lunch (two or three courses) or choose from the menu. Lots of light dishes and an enchanting ambience. Lovely for cream teas. Available for private parties through Leith's Good Food, 86 Bondway, SW8, 071 735 6303, fax 071 735 1170.

ROYAL ACADEMY OF ARTS RESTAURANT

Burlington House, Piccadilly, W1

The recently refurbished restaurant downstairs at Burlington House lacks the jolliness of the former room, with rather a mish-mash of styles, but there's certainly more space and more seats than before. At lunchtime there's a cold or hot buffet, filled baps, open sandwiches and plenty of vegetarian dishes. Later on

071 439 7438 (recorded information 071 439 4996/7)

Station Green Park/Piccadilly Circus underground

Bus 9, 14, 19, 22, 25, 38

Open Sun–Sat 1000–1730 (closed Good Friday and Christmas)

you can indulge in a cream tea or a huge wedge of chocolate fudge cake. Prices are reasonable and the food looks very wholesome. There are papers to read too.

SIMPSON (PICCADILLY) LTD

203 Piccadilly, W1
071 734 2002

Station Piccadilly Circus underground

Bus 3, 6, 9, 13, 15, 19, 22, 38, 53, 88, 94

Open Mon–Wed, Fri–Sat 0915–1715
Thur 0915–1800

This lower-ground-floor restaurant is in one of the few stores in London to have the distinction of being a listed building. They serve a traditional British breakfast until 1130, which includes kippers and omelettes as well as continental pastries. From 1200 until 1430 their lunch menu consists of more British food – potted shrimps, brown Windsor soup, shepherd's pie or roast from the trolley, Welsh rarebit. Teatime, from 1530 to 1715, brings savouries and light tea specials (omelettes, cakes and pastries). At one side of the restaurant is a sushi bar, open just at lunchtime. There's a good range of raw and marinated fish dishes – ika (cuttlefish), tako (octopus), toro (tuna), uni (sea urchin) and awabi (abalone). You might find it easier to try one of the two set lunches, the less expensive includes hot miso soup and tea, the other adds sashimi to the other items. There is also an *à la carte* menu available. On the ground floor the Gallery Coffee Shop serves tea, coffee and light snacks and is open from 1900 to 1715 (1830 on Thursday).

TATE GALLERY RESTAURANT AND COFFEE SHOP

Millbank, SW1
071 834 6754 (for **restaurant** reservations)

Station Pimlico underground

Bus 2, 36, 77a, 88, 185

Open Mon–Sat 1200–1500 (restaurant)
Mon–Sat 1030–1730 and Sun 1400–1715 (coffee shop)

Restaurant: for years this has been praised for its wine list – interesting and very reasonably priced. The food is noteworthy with an *à la carte* menu offering good roast beef with trimmings and steak pie. Some well-cooked, fine tasting, modern dishes deliver all that the menu description promises. Not cheap – there is a minimum charge, but the surroundings are elegant for a basement. Coffee shop: a self-service modern café with its wooden space-ship design (a futuristic Ark, perhaps). Great attention to cleanliness – pity the coffee tastes a bit stale. The cold buffet has some good-looking dishes like vegetable terrine en croûte, set among the gala pies, and some excellent ethnic vegetarian dishes. Also a good range of sticky cakes and pastries. Reasonable prices.

The Orangery (see page 151)

TERRACE CAFE AT THE NATIONAL THEATRE

South Bank, SE1
071 401 8361

Station Waterloo
underground + BR

Bus 1, 68, 76, 171, 176, 188, P11

Open Mon–Sat 1200–2000

This relatively new café at the National Theatre fulfils many needs. It provides tasty food in small portions, so you can build up a meal to suit your appetite and pocket as well as any time constraints you may have pre- or post-theatre. And there's a wonderful river view which is missing from the more formal Ovations Restaurant in another part of the complex. The daily soup has proved excellent on several occasions, salad of baby spinach leaves with bacon and hazelnuts in profusion is first class. Timbale of fish or smoked chicken salad have both been much enjoyed. Desserts are tempting, coffee is served with chocolates and if you have the time and inclination there are wines and beers too. This is a delightful and long-overdue watering hole on the South Bank – Festival Hall please take note.

WHITECHAPEL ART GALLERY

80 Whitechapel High Street, E1
071 377 6182

Station Aldgate East underground

Bus 8, 15, 25, 40, 67, 253

Open Sun–Tues, Thur–Sat 1100–1630
Mon 1100–1530
Wed 1100–1830

A really good self-service café for soup, pasta, salads – plenty of vegetarian and fish dishes. Portions are generous, prices are reasonable. And the apricot and apple crumble is out of this world. Licensed.

The art gallery is open Tues–Sun 1100–1700 (Wed till 2000).

North West

COLLEGE FARM

45 Fitzalan Road, N3
081 349 0690

Station Finchley Central/ Golders Green underground+bus

Bus 13, 26, 260

Open Sat–Sun 1400–1600

A greeting from a tailcoated young man might seem a little extravagant for a humble farm teahouse, but this is a slightly oddball place, so no matter. The farm has unusual breeds of cattle, sheep, pigs, and some way-out looking chickens with punk hair-dos. Round off your visit with a cream tea – lashings of Devonshire cream, good scones and an excellent pot of tea. Served on pretty blue and white crockery in the slightly crumbling café, this is all good fun for a weekend outing in suburban Finchley.

CREPES

beside the King William IV, Hampstead High Street, NW3

Station Hampstead underground

Bus 46, 268

Open Sun–Sat 1200–2300

The word ephemeral could have been invented for Hampstead, where shops, cafés and restaurants come and go with monotonous regularity. This box on wheels (though they don't turn round) has been a fixture on the High Street for quite a few years, and visitors and locals alike queue to buy the delicious crêpes, which come sweet or savoury. They are all made fresh to order – bulging with good things like spinach, garlic, cream and cheese, asperges au poivre, or ratatouille, ham and cheese. The sweet ones come with banana and butterscotch, almond maple cream – or plain old Suzette, an enduring favourite.

GOLDERS HILL PARK CAFETERIA

Golders Hill Park, NW11

Station Golders Green underground

An Italian family run the self-service cafeteria in one of north-west London's prettiest parks (which includes a mini-zoo much loved by local children). On a warm summer's day sit on the terrace, hung with flowering baskets and overlooking the park (though there is plenty of seating indoors for chilly weather).

Bus 13, 28, 82, 83, 102, 210, 226, 240

Open Daily from beginning of March to end October 1030–1800

Some claim the espresso to be the best in the area; a choice of teas or herbal tea and light hot and cold snacks are always available. The pâtisserie is good, catering as they do for a cosmopolitan clientele. The ice-cream specialities are based on their own homemade ice cream.

Golders Hill Park Cafeteria

THE GROVE GALLERY

69 The Grove, W5
081 567 0604

Station Ealing Broadway underground and BR

Bus 65

Open Mon–Sat 1100–2300 Sun 1100–2230

This is an oasis of calm and charm just near the bustling Broadway. Upstairs the gallery shows a wide variety of covetable arts and crafts – paintings, jewellery, glassware, ceramics. Downstairs, and something of a surprise, is a chic little wine bar restaurant which serves wonderful, mainly Polish, food. Hot bortsch, just like your babushka made, served with uska (rather like agnolotti); a plate of piroshki (or pierogi depending where you come from) filled with beef, cabbage, spinach; real buckwheat blinis – all the favourite Polish and Russian specialities. Stunning cakes – apple, cheesecake, poppy seed. Excellent coffee. And all served on elegant black and white china. The wine list includes glühwein and of course a choice of vodka – cherry, honey, etc.

South West

NEWENS – THE ORIGINAL MAIDS OF HONOUR TEAROOM

288 Kew Road, Kew Gardens
081 940 2752

Station Kew Gardens underground and BR

Bus 27, 65

Open Mon 0930–1300
Tues–Fri 1000–1730
Sat 0900–1730

This quaint little bakery cum tearoom just opposite Kew Gardens boasts an impressive lineage back to the days when Henry VIII munched the delicate pastries (light and fluffy with a curd filling) known as Maids of Honour. They are a must if you have tea – whether with the full set blow-out or just a pot. Light lunches (a set menu if you like) with homemade pies using Real Meat Company meat. Everything looks so good, including the crocheted table mats and fresh roses on the tables. The shop sells bread, old-fashioned cakes, and the well-stuffed meat pies.

South East

BLUEPRINT CAFE

Butler's Wharf, 28 Shad Thames, SE1
071 378 7031

Station Tower Hill/London Bridge underground

Bus 47, 188, P11

Open Mon–Sat 1200–1500
and 1900–2230
Sun 1200–1530

Elegant and unfussy as befits a restaurant at the Design Museum, with stunning views (both of the river and Terence Conran, who is regularly seen lunching). It's like being on an inland ocean liner. Modern Italian/Californian food with a daily changing menu. Prices are moderate and there are good wines. Service can be slow.

CROWDERS, GREENWICH THEATRE

13 Nevada Street, SE10
081 858 1318

Station Greenwich BR

Bus 177, 180, 286

Open Mon–Sat 1000–1500
and 1800–2300

If you are planning a bite before the theatre, give yourself plenty of time as it gets very crowded before curtain up and you have to queue for the food and then struggle to find a table. But the food is good, with ample portions of tasty salads, quiches, pies and the usual wine-bar menu. Sam Smith's real ale at pub prices.

THE DESIGN MUSEUM

Butler's Wharf, 28 Shad
Thames, SE1
071 403 6933

Station Tower Hill/London
Bridge underground

Bus 47, 188, P11

Open Tues–Sun 1130–1830
(incl Bank Holidays)

Strikingly situated by the river, this mecca of fine design has several food-related exhibits such as equipment, books and wedding cakes. The self-service café has tea and coffee (including espresso) and baguettes, cakes, croissants and is licensed. There's a superb river view, which you can enjoy both outside and in. It's worth the walk from the Tower of London to sit and have a snack here.

See also Blueprint Café (page 156).

Restaurants

Our idiosyncratic collection of restaurants represents our personal favourites from a year's eating out, during which we encompassed a wide range of styles, prices and neighbourhoods. The great and famous are here (though by no means all of them), but principally our aim has been to seek out some good-value meals not only in posh and expensive places, but also in humbler establishments.

Since there are plenty of excellent restaurant guides to London, we have not tried to compete with them, especially given the scope of our book. Indeed many of our favourites might not even feature in the mainstream guides.

In our experience set-price lunches always prove to be remarkably good value, whether in a simple Indian vegetarian restaurant like Chutneys, where we ate a three-course lunch for under £5, or the justifiably exalted La Tante Claire, where the set lunch will cost only a small fraction of what you would pay in the evening.

We felt there was little point in giving specific prices as they invariably increase, therefore we have put our choices into three rough categories. Low £ = under £15. Medium ££ = £15–25. High £££ = over £25, all per person. The cost of wine is not included.

Bear in mind that it is worth booking at even quite small restaurants to avoid disappointment.

The following entries from other sections may also be of interest as they have restaurants in addition to their main business: Brixtonian; Kaspia; Rebatos; Villandry.

Central

ANDREA'S

22 Charlotte Street, W1
071 580 8971

Elegant – in a Greek way – with chandeliers and pillars, lace cloths, candles and a mini-Acropolis, to which is added for extra atmosphere relentless Greek music – sub Nana Moussaka. The service is very good,

Station Goodge Street
underground

Bus 24, 29, 134

Open Sun–Fri including Bank
Holidays 1200–1500 and
1730–0100
Sat 1730–0100

Credit Cards All

Price Range £–££

Type Greek

BIBENDUM

Michelin House, 81 Fulham
Road, SW3
071 581 5817

Station South Kensington
underground

Bus 14, 30, 45a, 74, C1

Open Mon–Fri 1230–1430
and 1900–2330
Sat 1230–1500 and 1900–
2330
Sun 1230–1500 and 1900–
2230

Credit Cards All

Price Range £££

Type French and English

CAPITAL HOTEL

Basil Street, SW1
071 589 5171

Station Knightsbridge
underground

Bus 9, 10, 14, 19, 22, 30,
52, 74, 137, C1

Open Mon–Sat 1230–1430
and 1830–2230
Sun 1230–1430 and 1830–
2200
and after-theatre dinners (last
orders 2300) on request Mon–
Sat

Credit Cards Access, Diners,
Visa

both friendly and helpful, and the restaurant is very clean. All the staple Greek restaurant fare is here with excellent hummus and taramasalata, good moussaka with rice, stifado (a house speciality) and a well-cooked spicy beef casserole with large pieces of tender, juicy meat. Vegetarians are catered for with dolmades, felafel and a special vegetarian moussaka. The sweets, which are bought in, are not brilliant, but who can eat anything after the huge portions? There's a selection of Greek and other European wines.

Stylish, light, spacious restaurant, just as you would expect from Terence Conran. It's a delight on a bright sunny day. Simon Hopkinson's cooking owes much to Elizabeth David – good, honest, unpretentious bourgeois food, with exceptional vegetable dishes, and pudding is not to be missed. Set lunch is good value but wines are pricey. Downstairs there's a small oyster bar, and the Conran shop is always worth a look for cooks.

A tiny doll's house of a hotel just behind Harrods. The restaurant is small, pink and a bit frou-frou. But service is old-fashioned and charming. The two set menus at lunch are incredible value for money, each including three courses (with a choice of three dishes in each course) plus nibbles before, coffee and petits fours after and mineral water during the meal, as well as VAT and service. The food is beautifully cooked. Chef Philip Britten has earned his Michelin star. If the lobster bolognese is on, it's a delight. The wine list is French and expensive – even the house wine is pricey, so be warned.

Afternoon tea is wonderful if you need a break from shopping, your feet ache and you can't face Harrods' queues. In the evening there are also two set menus costing rather more than at lunchtime but offering

Price Range ££–£££

Type French inspired

great gastronomic treats (one fish based, one meat based) for a minimum of five courses. Also *à la carte* menus at lunch and dinner.

For first-rate British dishes we recommend The Greenhouse Restaurant, 27 Hay's Mews, W1, 071 499 3331, under the same ownership. The chef is Gary Rhodes.

DAQUISE

20 Thurloe Street, SW7
071 589 6117

Station South Kensington underground

Bus 14, 30, 45a, 49, 74, 219, C1

Open Restaurant and café daily 1000–2330
Lower restaurant Mon–Fri 1200–1500 and 1730–2330
Sat and Sun 1200–2330

Credit Cards None

Price Range £–££

Type Polish

Not much has changed here since this restaurant opened just after the Second World War. It's still a haunt for visiting or emigré Poles and hungry students. Go early if you want to try their Polish poppy-seed cake with coffee. The main dishes on the restaurant menu are hearty and filling, but very tasty and well cooked – beef goulash with Hungarian potato pancake and stuffed cabbage rolls with kasha are favourites with regulars. Small wine list. Staff, all Polish, are charming and helpfully explain the menu.

ANDREW EDMUNDS

46 Lexington Street, W1
071 437 5708

Station Piccadilly Circus/ Leicester Square underground

Bus 3, 6, 9, 13, 14, 15, 19, 22, 38, 53, 88, 94

Open Sun–Sat 1230–2300

Credit Cards Access, Visa

Price Range £–££

Type Modern

Not a slick city operation, this friendly unfussy restaurant with paper cloths offers a short menu which changes daily. There's always a soup and a decent selection of non-meat dishes – the Piedmontese peppers with feta and rocket is one of the most expensive first courses but large and splendid. There are usually four or five main dishes. Beef stew is cooked with sun-dried tomatoes and chilli, salmis of partridge comes with spinach and courgettes. Good, wholesome, interesting and not insubstantial food. Very good value, especially if you go easy on the wine. Owned and run by Andrew Edmunds, who has the super old print shop next door – you can whet your appetite on the John Bull and Rowlandson gastronomic prints (though you'll need a deep pocket for these).

THE FOUR SEASONS, INN ON THE PARK

Hamilton Place, Park Lane, W1

Chef Bruno Loubet came from Raymond Blanc's Petit Blanc in Oxford to inspire the kitchens of this hotel. It's not the most *intime* venue, but the lunchtime *menu du jour* is one of London's best buys and the staff make up for the surroundings by being very

071 499 0888

Station Hyde Park Corner
underground

Bus 9, 14, 19, 22, 25, 52, 74, 82, 135, 137

Open Sun–Sat 1200–1500
and 1900–2300

Credit Cards All

Price Range ££–£££

Type French

down to earth and smoothly efficient. Food is undeniably French, with some unusual combinations (which don't always work, but top marks for trying). Pâtisserie is out of this world – we had a white chocolate confection with praline cream set on a prune and armagnac sauce. The cheese board is worthy of attention – all in perfect condition. Wines are expensive. The adjacent Lanes restaurant has one of the best lunchtime buffets in town – great value; the three different menus all include wine. There's a well-priced evening buffet which includes a glass of champagne, served between 1800 and 2000. In the lobby breakfast is served until midday and light meals until two in the morning or just have a dessert. Choose afternoon tea from the embroidered menu – to the tune of the resident harpist.

LE GAVROCHE

43 Upper Brook Street, W1
071 408 0881

Station Bond Street
underground

Bus 2a, 2b, 6, 7, 8, 10, 12, 88, 94, 113, 135

Open Mon–Fri 1200–1400
and 1900–2300

Credit Cards All

Price Range £££

Type French

Among London's most notable restaurants (of which we have much to be proud), Le Gavroche is the capital's only three-star Michelin restaurant. French chef/patron Albert Roux and son Michel don't rest on their laurels, the huge menu is constantly evolving, the food superlative, the service faultless. This is eating in truly grand style. One can't but be impressed by the sheer attention to detail, except for the gloomy décor (dark green). Prices are second mortgage stuff, so take advantage of the set lunch to try London's most exquisite *haute cuisine*.

GOLDEN CHOPSTICKS

1 Harrington Road, SW7
071 584 0855

Station South Kensington
underground

Bus 14, 49

Open Sun–Sat 1200–2330

Credit Cards All

Price Range ££

Type Chinese

We were directed here by Yan Kit So, who recommends the special seabass dishes (order twenty-four hours ahead). A bright, smart restaurant with friendly and helpful service, the food is delicately cooked (not swamped in soy, salt, sugar, MSG or sticky with cornflour). The menu is comprehensive, but they can cook you any dish you fancy with spicing to suit. They're very obliging and adapted several dishes to suit children. There's a minimum charge of £10 per person.

L'Hippocampe

L'HIPPOCAMPE

63 Frith Street, W1
071 734 4545

Station Tottenham Court
Road underground

Bus 14, 24, 29, 176

Open Mon–Fri 1200–1500
Mon–Sat 1800–2400

Credit Cards Access, Amex,
Visa

Price Range ££–£££

Type French fish

Here's a real delight – a French fish restaurant serving absolutely beautiful food, with a very reasonable set-price menu at lunch and dinner. And for oyster eaters, owner Pierre Condou has Cancale oysters sent over from Brittany by his stepbrother, thereby missing out the middle man. They make the best seafood sausage/boudin in town. The *menu du jour* has a choice of two starters and two main courses, so go with someone you want to share with and swop plates half way! Our red-pepper mousse with salad and morilles and the nage of seafood were perfect, as were the salmon with asparagus and oyster mushrooms and filo parcels of cod and crab with a hint of fennel. Accompanying vegetables were just right. Dessert on the menu is pâtisserie (the lemon tartelet came with a tangy sorbet) or a plate of French cheeses. Good coffee and delicious petits fours (extra to the menu) and wine is New World and French. Well placed for pre- or post-theatre dinner.

IKKYU

67 Tottenham Court Road,
W1
071 636 9280

Station Goodge Street
underground

Bus 7, 8, 10, 14, 19, 22b,
24, 25, 134, 176

Open Mon–Fri 1230–1430
and 1800–2230
Sun 1800–2230

Credit Cards All

Price Range £–££

Type Japanese

If you have always thought Japanese food was beyond your pocket, this is the place to go – especially at lunchtime when the list of set meals is extensive and exceedingly reasonable. They come as a package deal, which helps the uninitiated. The 'grilled salmon set' is two pieces of salmon (perfectly cooked and well seasoned) on a wooden board, with shredded cabbage and tomatoes, a generous bowl of rice, slices of pickled vegetable and a bowl of miso soup (which arrives with most of the set meals). The vegetarian lunch produced a jewel-like tray of bright little parcels of rice with carrots, pickled vegetables and cucumber encompassed in a black band of seaweed – exquisite to behold and clean and fresh tasting. There's a daily dish chalked on the board above the bar and a set menu in the evening as well as lunch. Service is somewhat erratic, though kindly. Tea is free – Japanese beer and saké are available.

THE INN OF HAPPINESS

St James's Court Hotel, 51
Buckingham Gate, SW1
071 834 6655

Station St James's Park
underground

Bus 11, 24, 29

Open Sun–Fri 1230–1430 and
1930–2315 Sat 1930–2315

Credit Cards All

Price Range ££–£££

Type Chinese

The St James's hotel is not only very glamorous but imaginatively offers a choice of good restaurants – the Auberge de Provence – an off-shoot of the three-star restaurant at Les Baux de Provence, France, as well as the Inn of Happiness for smart Chinese food. It backs on to a delightful courtyard and serves 'modern' Chinese food well cooked. *A la carte* is pricey but the set-lunch menu is good value.

JOY KING LAU

3 Leicester Street, WC2
071 437 1132

Station Leicester Square
underground

Bus 14, 19, 22b, 24, 29, 38,
176

Open Mon–Sat 1130–2330

Credit Cards All

Price Range £–££

Type Chinese

Dim sum (a large and not too expensive selection) both savoury and sweet are served up to 1730 as well as the main menu – which is extensive, to say the least. The set menus begin at under £10 a head for two or more people. If you want a really special meal (stir-fried strips of jelly fish, braised lobster, steamed scallops in the shell, crispy aniseed duck and rice cooked in lotus leaf) it's wise to book ahead and plan your own menu. Eat upstairs if possible – regulars always do. You could eat well for under £15 and feast for £20. Stick to tea or soup to drink.

ALASTAIR LITTLE

49 Frith Street, W1
071 734 5183

Station Tottenham Court
Road/Leicester Square/
Piccadilly Circus underground

Bus 7, 8, 10, 19, 24, 25, 29,
38, 73, 134, 176

Open Mon–Fri 1230–1430
and 1930–2315
Sat 1900–2315

Credit Cards Access, Visa

Price Range ££–£££

Type Eclectic

For many, Alastair Little is one of London's best chefs – and happily he has recently put a set menu into play which gives his many admirers a chance to enjoy his superb cooking more often than before. The two- or three-course menu offers a choice only in the first course. An asparagus risotto, wonderfully moist and oozing with asparagus, followed by corn-fed chicken with masses of ceps in a strongly flavoured sauce and served with spinach lightly tossed in olive oil made for a substantial lunch. Gourmands would find the dessert hard to pass up – a duo of tarts – pecan and cherry served with a perfect vanilla ice cream. This menu is served until early evening for pre-theatre diners. There's a bar downstairs for snacks such as cock-a-leekie soup made with truffles instead of prunes and the *à la carte* menu, which is full of memorable (if pricey) dishes.

MAGNO'S BRASSERIE

65a Long Acre, Covent
Garden, WC2
071 836 6077

Station Covent Garden
underground

Bus 168, 188, 196

Open Mon–Fri 1200–1430
and 1800–2230
Sat 1800–2230

Credit Cards All

Price Range £–££

Type French

This very French restaurant, within easy walking distance of the Opera House and many theatres, is ideal for an excellent value pre-theatre dinner menu. The two courses might include a seasonal soup or seafood quiche or salad, followed by gigot d'agneau (nicely rare), truite aux amandes or a chicken dish. Delicious warm bread and coffee are included, and there are tempting desserts if you have the time and inclination. Their regular menu is slightly more exciting, but the food is just as good pre- as post-theatre.

MUSEUM STREET CAFE

47 Museum Street, WC1
071 405 3211

Station Holborn underground

Bus 7, 8, 14, 19, 22b, 24,
29, 38, 73, 134, 176

Open Mon–Fri 1230–1430
and 1930–2300

Minimalist décor, maximum flavours. Menu displayed on blackboard at lunch is a small four or five choices for each course, but you can eat as much or as little as you like. Co-proprietor Gail Koerber is a wonderful pâtissière – producing marvellous bread and memorable desserts. Evening is a limited-choice set menu with lots of char-grilled fish and meat, and salads and roasted vegetables dressed with the best olive oil. Food is light although not insubstantial, of the Italo-Californian school. Always a good selection of Neal's Yard cheeses. Unlicensed (no corkage) so take your own

Credit Cards None

Price Range ££

Type Modern

NEW WORLD

Gerrard Place, W1
071 734 0677

Station Tottenham Court
Road/Piccadilly Circus/
Leicester Square underground

Bus 14, 24, 29, 176

Open Mon–Sat 1100–2345
Sun 1100–2300

Credit Cards All

Price Range £–££

Type Chinese

(wine shop next door). You must book since Gail and partner Mark Nathan have garnered many prizes and they have a loyal clientele.

This is the nearest to one of those giant Hong Kong restaurants that you are likely to find in London. Saturday lunch is the time when all the local Chinese come in *en famille* for dim sum, which is a great way to eat a light and very inexpensive meal. You can also choose from the extensive menu, which is available throughout the week. The parade of trolleys, pushed by not always very communicative girls (a good time to practise your Mandarin perhaps), offers a wonderful opportunity to try a selection of dishes which you might hesitate to order from the menu. Since the portions are small, you can be quite adventurous, for instance you could taste the chicken feet in a black bean and chilli sauce. Aubergines and peppers are fried fresh to order, dumplings arrive in little steamers, bowls of noodles with pork or duck are served from a great vat on a trolley. Tea comes automatically, but there is an extensive wine list. A number of reasonably priced set menus available at lunch and dinner.

New World

PIED A TERRE

34 Charlotte Street, W1
071 636 1178

Station Goodge Street
underground

Bus 24, 29, 134

Open Mon–Fri 1215–1430
and 1830–2200 (last orders)
Sat 1830–2200 (last orders)

Credit cards Access, Visa

Price range: ££–£££

Type Modern French

It's still early days, but this new restaurant looks like becoming a good bet. The cooking is first class (chef Richard Neat is ex-Harvey's) and portions are on the extravagant side of generous, making the cheaper set-lunch menu (under £20) very good value. We had a choice of two dishes for each of the three courses. VAT and service are inclusive, coffee and excellent petits fours are extra. The other menu is twice the price, but the choice is extensive and includes warm foie gras salad, oysters and a dish of braised pig's cheek. In the evening this is the only menu available. Wines are eclectic and pricey. We wish it well.

QUALITY CHOPHOUSE

94 Farringdon Road, EC1
071 837 5093

Station Farringdon
underground and BR

Bus 19, 38, 63, 171, 196, 259

Open Mon–Fri 0700–0930,
1200–1500 and 1830–2330
Sat 1830–2330

Credit Cards None

Price Range £–££

Type Brasserie

'Progressive working-class caterer' declares a slogan on the menu of this restaurant. Like the décor, the sentiment is left over from the days when this was genuinely a chop house serving the local community. Its new owners have left everything intact, except happily the cooking, which is very much *à la mode*, brasserie style. Their day starts with a hearty breakfast and then the daily changing menu takes over, with American classics like eggs Benedict, Caesar salad and French frisée aux lardons – all of which can be taken as first or main courses. Sausage and mash, calf's liver and bacon or corned beef hash seem suited to the surroundings, but are definitely NOT cooked in the manner of a working man's caff. There are some pricey wines, but stick to the more modest bottles and you can have a reasonable night out.

THE SAVOY

Strand, WC2
071 836 4343

Station Charing Cross/Covent
Garden underground

Bus 1, 6, 9, 11, 13, 15, 77,
170, 176, 196

The Savoy prides itself on many things, but it claims to have been the first hotel to use pink tablecloths. One guest entertained his guests to a gondolier party (it is the home of D'Oyly Carte, after all) in 1905, when Venice was recreated. The courtyard was flooded to a depth of four feet, painted scenery erected around the walls, gondolas built for costumed guests to dine in on the 'Grand Canal'. Caruso sang and 100 white doves were released. There were even a five-foot cake and a baby elephant (though heaven knows why). So from

Open Various times
depending on restaurants –
phone to check

Credit Cards All

Price Range Various

Type Various

Escoffier to Edelmann (the current chef), the hotel has always been known for the excellence of its cuisine – it's the home of pêches Melba and Melba toast (after Dame Nellie) and omelette Arnold Bennett. All that said, you can choose from the banqueting rooms (including kosher licence), the American Bar, the Thames Foyer for afternoon tea, breakfast in the River Restaurant (with sunrise over the Thames) or lunch or dinner without the sunrise, or pre- or après-theatre dinner in the Grill Room.

SIMPLY NICO

48a Rochester Row, SW1
071 630 8061

Station Victoria underground
and BR

Bus 2, 11, 16, 24, 25, 29,
36, 38, 52, 73, 76

Open Mon–Fri 1200–1415
Mon–Sat 1845–2300

Credit Cards Access/Visa

Price Range ££

Type Bistro

Bistro food at its very best. A set-price menu for lunch and dinner offers three courses to include vegetables with daily specials. It's a lovely menu with generous portions well presented on 'own-label' plates. You have an *embarras de choix* – smoked haddock with spinach and poached egg or perhaps warm potato salad with confit of duck with mustard dressing, or fresh pasta with wild mushroom sauce. The sizeable main dishes – beef with caramelised shallots, chicken with tomato sauce and couscous or confit with lentils – all come with delicious frîtes or creamed spuds. Puddings are light, old favourites – crème brûlée, chocolate mousse, caramel ice cream, rum baba. The elegant, thin dining room is charming with unfussy décor and beautiful Val Archer pictures. The only disappointment is the service – too familiar and too casual. That apart, this is real value.

If you want to taste the cooking of the master himself, book ahead at Chez Nico, 35 Great Portland Street, W1, 071 436 8846. It's pricey but you won't be disappointed.

SIMPSON'S-IN-THE-STRAND

100 Strand, WC2
071 836 9112

Station Charing Cross/Covent
Garden underground

Bus 1, 6, 9, 11, 13, 15, 77,
170, 176, 196

Open Mon–Sat 1200–1400
and 1800–2245

This famous restaurant has evolved from a 'home of chess' (1828) through Simpson's Divan and Tavern to 1848 when a caterer, John Simpson, joined owner Samuel Reis to provide large joints of meat, on silver dinner wagons, cooked by the great Chef Alexis Soyer (previously of the Reform Club), to today's London institution. Simpson's still serves classic British food – roast sirloin of beef (chef Adam Sherif says 'It's what Simpson's is all about') – average consumption twenty-five sirloins a day with all the trimmings; saddle of lamb – twenty-five saddles carved daily, roast

Credit Cards All

Price Range ££

Type British

Aylesbury duck and the like. A daily special (Monday – roast pork, Tuesday steak, kidney and mushroom pudding, etc). Puddings are traditional too – treacle roll, spotted dick. Everything is very British – there's a bill of fare rather than a menu (nasty foreign word) – and rather club-like, with heavy panelling and grand rooms. Set-price menu available 1800–1900 and Saturday lunch – three courses and coffee includes a choice of roasts.

AL SULTAN

51–2 Hertford Street, W1
071 408 1155
fax 071 287 1953

Station Hyde Park Corner underground

Bus 2a, 9, 10, 14, 16, 19, 22, 25, 30, 36, 38

Open Sun–Sat 1200–2400

Credit Cards All

Price Range ££–£££

Type Lebanese

The area around Shepherd's Market has several Lebanese restaurants – the menu varies little from one to another, but the quality at Al Sultan is of the highest. The décor is cool and elegant – the food is spicy and also elegant. If you don't know this most delicious of cuisines, ask the restaurant manager for advice on how to construct a meal; tell him what you want to spend and he'll deliver the goods. And what tasty and intriguing flavours will be brought to your table, dish after beautiful dish of hot and cold hors d'oeuvres, grilled meats and fish and, if you are still able, wonderful sweets from the trolley. You can have just a few small dishes if that's all you want – Lebanese food is very flexible.

LA TANTE CLAIRE

68 Royal Hospital Road, SW3
071 352 6045/351 0227

Station Sloane Square underground

Bus 11, 137, 239

Open Mon–Fri 1230–1400 and 1900–2300

Credit Cards All

Price Range £££

Type French

Without doubt one of the best-value and best-cooked set lunches in town; you can choose from two menus – one meat based and one fish, plus 'specials'. There's also the *à la carte* menu at lunchtime, but only *à la carte* at dinner. The lunch menu of three courses includes bottled water, unlimited coffee and petits fours, service and VAT. Chef Pierre Koffmann is acknowledged to be 'the chef's chef' and many leading chefs eat at La Tante Claire when they are 'off'. The food is in a class of its own, paying respect to Pierre's Gascon upbringing. It ranges from the simplest poached turbot to a richly satisfying braise of cheek of beef with an indecent amount of red wine. All breads are homemade and there is an excellent selection of cheeses. Service is friendly and first rate (Maitre d' Jean Pierre Durantet is one of London's best). Décor is simple but gracious.

The set lunch at La Tante Claire

TERRACE GARDEN, LE MERIDIEN, PICCADILLY HOTEL

21–2 Piccadilly, W1
071 734 8000

Station Piccadilly Circus underground

Bus 3, 6, 9, 13, 14, 15, 19, 22, 38, 53, 88, 94

Open Sun–Sat 0700–1100 and 1200–2330

Credit Cards All

Price Range ££

Type French

On a bright sunny day the conservatory of Le Meridien has to be one of London's prettiest and most stunning dining rooms with its plants hanging from the ceiling and its fabulous flowers. Service starts with breakfast and then goes on all day, with lunch, afternoon tea and dinner. There's a reasonable set-price lunch menu, or choose *à la carte* from the mainly French dishes – peasant-like boudin noir, or more *soigné* dishes such as a tranche de foie gras. Calorie-counted and vegetarian dishes are so marked. The pâtisserie is remarkable – a tarte paysanne and truffé de chocolat amer were particularly well received. Good coffee and efficient service.

North West

ADAM'S CAFE

77 Askew Road, W12
081 743 0572

Station Shepherd's Bush
underground and BR + bus

Bus 12, 207, 260, 266

Open Mon–Sat 1930–2230

Credit Cards None

Price Range £

Type Tunisian

A relatively new phenomenon in London is the transformation of a daytime greasy spoon caff into a candlelit dinner restaurant. This west London version has been pulling in the crowds – booking is essential – for the Tunisian specialities created by the proprietor, Abdel Boukaraa. From the daytime chips with everything it becomes harissa with everything – the fiery pepper sauce beloved of Tunisians, who even eat it on their breakfast bread. A plate of it arrives with the appetisers (meatballs and olives) and then on to the essential brik à l'oeuf, couscous, gargoulette and other spicy dishes. Take your own wine – no corkage – which makes this a really reasonable evening out.

BEDLINGTON CAFE

24 Fauconberg Road, W4
081 994 1965

Station Turnham Green
underground + bus

Bus E3, E4

Open Mon–Fri 0730–1600
and 1830–2200
Sat 0730–1400 and 1830–2200

Credit Cards None

Price Range £

Type Thai

Unprepossessing Thai café (painted bright red and yellow outside) with Formica tables crammed up together, lino floor and full of ever-so-trendy folk. The extensive menu includes a selection of Laotian dishes. They 'aim to serve authentic Thai prepared food, to order from fresh ingredients', now at lunch as well as in the evening. The Laotian som tarm (carrot and lime salad) was excellent. We can recommend the fresh spring roll and Thai beef salad. Everything was well cooked, but don't go if you can't bear chillies. Choose to eat outside on the pavement in hot weather as it can get steamy inside. The tea comes in large mugs. The food is so much better than many of the swish Thai restaurants in town – robust rather than elegant. Unlicensed. Small corkage charge. Must book.

BILLBOARD CAFE

222 Kilburn High Road, NW6
071 328 1374

Station Kilburn underground
and BR

Bus 16, 16a, 28, 31, 32

Open Mon–Sat 1830–0045
Sat and Sun 1200–1500

Credit Cards Access,
Mastercard, Visa

Price Range ££

Type Californian/Italian

An unpretentious café with a dedicated local following, it sits in the midst of the wasteland of Kilburn – not the most inviting of areas but worth a visit. The cheerful and chatty Greek owner has an adventurous spirit and though his food is 'labelled' north Italian/Californian, don't be surprised to see dishes from many other parts of the world. The pasta is homemade with some interesting sauces; the fish might include trout with a tamarind sauce, which tastes more of Thailand than Torino. A hearty pasta and fagioli soup or garlic toast with bell peppers, gamberetti with basil or bresaola are among the starters. Everything is cooked to order. All-Italian wine list with a Corvo as house wine. Live jazz Monday to Thursday.

THE CAFE DELANCEY

3 Delancey Street, NW1
071 387 1985

Station Mornington Crescent underground

Bus 24, 29, 134, 168, 253

Open Sun–Sat 0800–2400

Credit Cards Access, Visa

Price Range £–££

Type Brasserie

In a cheeky example of teaching your grandmother to suck eggs, the Café Delancey recently opened a branch in Paris. Their stated aim is to run their cafés (also in New York) along the lines of a continental café, where you can eat any dish at any hour. This original establishment in Camden Town has proved popular since it opened some years ago and has expanded considerably. Daily specials are chalked up on the board – char-grilled chicken or stir-fried rice perhaps – and the standard menu has the sort of food you would find in any similar French brasserie. Soup of the day is always vegetarian. There are plenty of lightweight dishes for late-night eating and breakfast can be anything from a croissant to a fry-up. Wine by the glass or half bottle for lone drinkers.

Also at 32 Proctor Street, WC1, 071 242 6691

CHUTNEYS

124 Drummond Street, NW1
071 388 0604

Station Euston underground and BR
Euston Square underground

Bus 10, 14, 18, 24, 27, 29, 30, 73, 135

Open Sun–Sat 1200–1445 and 1800–2230

Credit Cards Access, Visa

Price Range £

Type Indian vegetarian

In a street where Indian restaurants are cheek by jowl, Chutneys may well be the best-value restaurant food not only here but in all of London if you go for the weekend buffet lunch. For under £5 you can eat as much as you like, returning as often as you like. There are twelve different dishes, including nan bread, rice, salad and chutneys. The main courses are curries of potatoes, mixed vegetables, lentils, etc – all very tasty and sustaining. But go early if you like your food hot (in temperature). Three desserts – a wonderful kheer (rice pudding with cardamom), a good fresh fruit salad, and gulab jamun – are part of the buffet. A bonus, if you need one at that price, are freshly pressed fruit juices, including a wonderful apple juice prepared to order, and lassi. There is also a large and descriptive *à la carte* menu with thalis from Gujarat and the chef's selection of dishes from south India. It is possible to have a complete meal for around £6 from the menu.

KENNY'S

70 Heath Street, NW3
071 435 6972
fax 071 431 5694

Station Hampstead underground

Bus 46, 268

Noisy (good jazz/blues music), busy (best to book at weekends), all-American restaurant (the Scottish owner is an honorary citizen of New Orleans), serving well cooked nicely presented Cajun and Creole food. The service (American waitresses) is efficient and mercifully without the 'Have a nice day' refrain. The wine list is limited and expensive – best to stick to beer. Choose fish: the crab cakes with spicy hot sauce

Open Mon–Sat 1200–2345
Sun 1200–2230

Credit Cards Access, Amex,
Visa

Price Range ££

Type Cajun Creole

are good, and soft-shell crabs (Wednesday is crab-boil night) are a house speciality, or try the blackened fish. Daily specials are chalked up on a board which is carried from table to table. If the bluefish is on – eat it. Don't miss the puddings either – the best, deepest pecan tart and a surprisingly light Cajun bread pudding – made with bourbon, hazelnuts and chocolate. Portions are large.

QUINCY'S

675 Finchley Road, NW2
071 794 8499

Station Golders Green
underground

Bus 13, 28, 82

Open Tues–Sat 1900–2300

Credit Cards Access, Visa

Price Range ££

Type French/English Bistro

A friendly, intimate, little local restaurant serving Franglais food mainly to regulars. The set-price menu changes monthly. Seasonal produce is used to good effect. Fish is a speciality. There's always a choice of three or four dishes, plus imaginative vegetarian dishes and homely puds, such as rhubarb crumble and egg custard. Air-conditioning recently installed for balmy nights.

RANI

7 Long Lane, N3
081 349 4386

Station Finchley Central

Bus 13, 26, 82, 260

Open Sun–Sat 1800–2400
Wed–Fri and Sun 1230–1500

Credit Cards Access, Visa

Price Range £–££

Type Indian vegetarian

The head chefs at this family-owned Indian vegetarian restaurant are proudly listed as 'proprietor's mother' and 'proprietor's wife', which neatly sets the tone. It's a large, noisy place, but obviously there's a large family running it and all the staff are charming. Another nice touch is that there's no service charge – any change left behind is donated to charities. They display the list of the thousands of pounds sent to Save the Children, VSO and other worthy causes. Now to the food, which is excellent. A long menu can be circumvented by choosing from the various 'Options', which give a fair spread of dishes. Grander meals come under the Rani Super Table, which gives you a wider choice. The variety of flavours and textures is a revelation for anyone unversed in this cuisine. Portions are generous – be wary of over-ordering. Desserts are brilliant – saffron-laden gulab jambu, shrikhand plain and fruity. Licensed.

SIMON'S BISTRO

41 Church Road, NW4
081 203 7887

In an area mainly serviced by ethnic restaurants (including several kosher Chinese!) it's surprising to find Simon Rapkin in his bistro offering straightforward Anglo/French food. There may not be anything incredibly original here, but the cooking is sound,

Station Hendon Central
underground

Bus 143, 183

Open Tues–Fri 1200–1500
and 1800–2230
Sat 1800–2300
Sun 1800–2230

Credit cards Visa, Access

Price range £–££

Type Bistro

THAI GARDEN

109a Golders Green Road,
NW11
071 494 4373 (before 1800)
081 458 3221 (after 1800)

Station Golders Green
underground

Bus 18, 183

Open Sun–Sat 1800 until late
Sat and Sun 1200–1530

Credit Cards All

Price Range ££

Type Thai

UNCLE IAN'S

8, 9 & 10 Monkville Parade,
Finchley Road, NW11
081 458 3493

Station Golders Green/
Finchley Central underground

Bus 13, 26, 260

Open Sun–Thur, Sat 0900–
2400
Fri 0900–1600

Credit Cards Access, Visa

Price Range £–££

Type Jewish

portions are very generous and the welcome is warm. Tuscan fish soup, homemade pasta or goat's cheese and spinach parcels are among the starters, which are all priced the same. The main courses are at two price levels and include steamed salmon and sole wrapped in spinach with a saffron and fresh tomato sauce, swordfish or rack of lamb. Desserts are not for the waist watchers. The set lunch is excellent value – reason enough to go to Hendon.

A bewildering choice of dishes beckons in this charming restaurant, but the staff are so friendly you should have no difficulty finding your way through the maze of a menu. There are a number of set meals, which is always a good way to get your teeth into a new cuisine, and they offer excellent value. The steamboat soup is offered chilli hot or mild – unless you want the top of your head blown off, be warned – hot in Thai food means HOT. Take care not to over order as the food is quite substantial. Marvellous coconut ice cream and Thai rice pudding for dessert.

Good Jewish cooking is, for some inexplicable reason, not easily translatable from the domestic to the restaurant kitchen. Maybe it needs a Yiddisher momma to agonise over it all. That being so, Uncle Ian seems to have found the right formula and people flock from miles away to enjoy all the old favourites - matzo-ball soup, chopped liver, salt beef, latkes, lochshen pudding and all the other low-calorie delights that Jewish food is heir to. There are very reasonably priced lunch and supper set menus. Service is bright and breezy, décor serviceable (with wise-cracking notices about your spouse's affair – which they will cater!). Noise rather high, but the food is good. Not kosher. Enjoy!

VERSILIA RESTAURANT

250 Finchley Road, NW3
071 794 7640

Station Finchley Road
underground
Finchley Road and Frognal BR

Bus 13, 82, 113

Open Tues–Sun 1200–1400
and 1700–2300 (Closed Sat
lunch)

Credit Cards All

Price Range ££

Type Italian fish

A pretty restaurant with a warm Italian welcome, the mainly fish menu offers Tuscan specialities. As you sit down a dish of toast with anchovy spread and a crab mayonnaise is placed on the table while you mull over the menu. Then the amuse gueule of small fresh sardines in vinegar and oil arrives. A further taster might arrive if one of the party has declined a first course and is waiting for her companions to eat theirs. Cacciucco, a classic Tuscan fish soup, is a meal in itself; main courses include sole baked in foil, red mullet in a livornese sauce, sea bream with radicchio, and are reasonably priced considering the size of the portions. A choice of pasta with lobster or other seafood would make a less expensive meal. A varied wine list includes several inexpensive Italian house wines. The set lunch is great value.

VIJAY INDIAN RESTAURANT

49 Willesden Lane, NW6
071 328 1087

Station Kilburn underground
and BR

Bus 16, 16a, 32

Open Sun–Thur 1200–1445
and 1800–2245
Fri and Sat 1200–1445 and
1800–2345

Credit Cards All

Price Range £–££

Type Indian

South Indian cuisine usually means vegetarian but at Vijay's, recently awarded a Red M in the Michelin guide, you can eat all the dishes familiar from more general Indian restaurants. The house specialities are a must to start with though – dosas, adai and other light and crispy pancakes, all served with coconut chutney. They are huge and nearly a meal in themselves and, since the portions are generous, this is a place to go with a number of hearty appetites so you can order a good choice of main dishes. The salt lassi is pleasantly spicy, mango juice is refreshing. A full licence offers a good basic spread of wines (though badly described) and of course Kingfisher beer. You need to like ice cream if you want a dessert – there's not a great choice. Décor is simple – wicker-lined walls and rather gloomy lighting, and the tables are a bit small. But the service is excellent, efficient and friendly, and you will have a hard task to spend an enormous sum of money, especially if you go for the lunchtime specials.

North East

01 ADANA

91 Green Lanes, N16
071 704 6404/6399

Station Canonbury BR

Bus 73, 141, 171, 236

In the heart of London's Turkish suburb is this very lively family-style restaurant. Save yourself the agony of choosing and start with mezze, which comes in generous portions of taramasalata, hummus, imam bayildi, feta, cacik. The cabinet in front of the open kitchen displays a wonderful selection of kebabs – lamb, quail, sheep's testicles, kidneys. In the background

Open Sun–Sat 1200–2400

Credit Cards All

Price Range ££

Type Turkish

BAMBAYA

1 Park Road, N8
081 348 5609

Station Finsbury Park
underground and BR + bus

Bus 14a, 41, W2, W7

Open Tues–Sat 1830–2300
Sun 1830–2230

Credit Cards Access, Amex,
Visa

Price Range ££

Type Afro-Caribbean

FLORIANS

4 Topsfield Parade,
Tottenham Lane, N8
081 348 8348

Station Finsbury Park
underground and BR + bus

Bus 14a, 41, W2, W7

Open Sun–Sat 1200–2300
(closed daily 1600–1700 and
2230 on Sunday)

Credit Cards Access, Visa

Price Range £–£££

Type Italian

MARMARA

19 Green Lanes, N16
071 226 1866

are chefs a'grilling and doner kebab a'swirling. The aubergine kebab stuffed with spicy meat is great. The house special – sulu yemekler, is a traditional Turkish dish which changes daily. Drink raki if you're up to it – the wine list leaves a lot to be desired. The friendly waiter does a masterly cabaret act of peeling an orange and a good time is had by all.

Crouch End may not be the centre of the universe, but it has a fair spread of cuisines (see also Florians, below, and Wisteria Tea Rooms, pages 139–40). This restaurant presents the cooking of Africa, the Caribbean and black America in a prettily tiled ex-butcher's shop, with charming, if somewhat too laid-back service. The food is delicious – spicing perhaps geared more to north-east London than tropical tastes. Especially enjoyed was the plantain stuffed with spinach with its slightly sweet, almost toffee-like texture. A first course of 'stamp and go', saltfish cakes with a fruity sauce and a coconut and spinach soup were excellent. Mainly fish and vegetarian, portions are good. The menu generally is rather limited – especially the sweets, but there are always exotic fruit and homemade ice cream. Licensed.

Painted brick walls, paper cloths and lots of happy people eating real Italian home cooking – this popular local restaurant has gained a great following in the relatively short space of time since it opened. The menu includes a risotto of the day plus other perennial Italian favourites – calf's liver (served with grilled peppers), a daily pasta dish and specials like soft-shelled crabs served on a bed of wilted spinach. Desserts include the inevitable but always delicious tiramisu or divine poached pears stuffed with almonds and mascarpone. Wines are, naturally, all Italian and fairly reasonable. Service is friendly but a little slow when under pressure. Though not cheap, it is good value – but for something really well priced, try the daily changing two-course menu in their wine bar, which is served all day.

If you turn up at opening time (0930) you can have a plate of soup – and what soup it is – but the main food is available from about 1130 and they close 'when the food runs out', so plan to get there early. Don't go

Station Canonbury BR

Bus 73, 141, 171, 236

Open Sun–Sat 0900–2130

Credit Cards None

Price Range £

Type Turkish

here if you want soignéed elegance – it is a workman's caff, but the food is terrific. The proprietor, Hakan, is a charming ex-hairdresser, who told us they made village food and 'Never judge a restaurant by its looks.' He's not wrong. Soup might be lentil or lamb's tongue with garlic vinegar and chilli – both packed with flavour, served with huge chunks of fresh bread. Choose from four or five trays of hot food – there's no menu – whatever is cooked is on show. Stuffed courgettes, aubergine kebab, lamb and beans. It is all hearty peasant food, very tasty and very filling. But leave room for the lightest, creamiest most delicious rice pudding imaginable – school dinners were never like this. Green Lanes lacks the charm of the Bosporus, but it's a whole lot cheaper than a package tour.

SIMA TANDOORI

239 Mile End Road, E1
071 790 6766

Station Stepney Green underground

Bus 25, N97

Open Sun–Sat 1200–1430 and 1800–2400

Credit Cards All

Price Range £–££

Type Indian

Fresh blue tablecloths inside are a bit at odds with the gilded figures outside this East End restaurant, where the service is kind if rather uncomprehending. The special murg massalum is pricey, but since we weren't able to elicit what it was, it remains a mystery. A vegetable thali and a chicken dish provided a more than adequate, well-cooked and very tasty lunch – and reasonable too.

THE THAI GARDEN

249 Globe Road, E2
081 981 5748

Station Bethnal Green underground

Bus 106, D6

Open Mon–Sat 1200–1500 and 1800–2300

Credit Cards All

Price Range £–££

Type Thai

Fresh and simply furnished, this vegetarian and seafood restaurant serves beautiful food – a feast for the eye and palate. Very reasonable set lunch and evening menus and the *à la carte* has a wide choice of prawn, pomfret, squid and other fish, as well as interesting, often very spicy, vegetarian dishes.

South West

BUZKASH AFGHAN RESTAURANT

4 Chelverton Road, SW15
081 788 0599

Station Putney BR

Bus 39, 74, 85, 93, 265

Open Mon–Thur 1200–1500
and 1800–2300
Fri–Sat 1200–1500 and 1800–
2330
Sun 1800–2300

Credit Cards All

Price Range ££

Type Afghan

CHUTNEY MARY

535 King's Road, SW10
071 351 3113

Station Sloane Square/Fulham
Broadway underground + bus

Bus 11, 22

Open Mon–Sat 1230–1430
and 1900–2330
Sun 1230–1530 and 1900–
2200

Credit Cards All

Price Range ££–£££

Type Anglo-Indian

RIVA

169 Church Road, Barnes,
SW13
081 748 0434

Afghan artefacts – jewellery, rugs – make you feel you are sitting in a tent in this friendly restaurant. The best lassi ever – with spices, mint and slivers of cucumber. The food is 'cautiously' spiced and very tasty. Set lunch is ample and the Western touches – an amuse gueule of pakora 'all the way from Wimbledon' and a lick of sorbet are fun. Starters include pasta stuffed with leek and served with minced lamb and yoghurt; prawns in a pancake; aubergine purée. Main courses of chicken, fish or lamb come with vegetables or rice. The desserts are great: homemade ice cream with pistachios, firnee – ground rice cooked with milk, almonds and pistachios (very light) – or fruit salad. The *à la carte* menu is long, and if you don't know your way round the waiters will charmingly guide you.

Also Caravan Serai, 50 Paddington Street, W1, 071 935 1208

Billed as the 'world's first Anglo-Indian restaurant', the food is slightly different from the usual Indian fare, with some distinctly English items like bread and butter pudding – a winner, oozing with nuts and sporting a spicy crust. The two- or three-course set lunch is very good value. Portions are generous, food well cooked, attractive and not greasy, which is a common problem with some Indian dishes. The room is very pretty, service considerate. The entrance bar serves little or big bites to accompany drinks if you don't want the full works downstairs. Sunday buffet, though reasonably priced, is not so interesting. Private parties by arrangement.

Fashionably scruffy, the menu is original and is augmented with special dishes from time to time. The grilled vegetables are nicely charred and dressed with good oil, mint and chillies – a successful and unusual combination. Other interesting dishes include roasted red snapper in onion and orange vinegar with raisins

Bus 9

Open Sun–Sat 1200–1430 and 1900–2300 (but closed Sat lunch)

Credit Cards Visa only

Price Range ££

Type Italian

and pimento, a rabbit stew with lentils, skate, a black risotto and baccala manecato. The small wine list includes a vast selection of grappa. Rapidly becoming one of London's gastronomic treats.

South East

LA COUPEE

17 Half Moon Lane, Herne Hill, SE24
081 737 1556

Station Herne Hill BR

Bus 3, 37, 40, 68, 196

Open Tues–Fri 1200–1430
Tues–Sat 1830–2400

Credit Cards Access, Visa

Price Range £–££

Type Bistro

To save you racking your brain for the meaning of La Coupée, it's a mountain road in the Channel Islands. There are well-priced set menus at both lunch and in the evening, the latter are flexible and allow you to choose from the *à la carte* if you fancy a special dish there. On the autumn menu was wild boar, and the smoked-trout starter served with scrambled eggs and oyster mushrooms included some ceps freshly gathered from near-by Brockwell Park. Good homemade soup, plenty of vegetables and desserts including a warm fig tart served with clotted cream were all notable. Service is relaxed and friendly and the attractive upstairs room, blissfully music free, gives you the feeling of being in a private dining room. On occasional Sundays they have regional dinners or wine tastings, lunches and events of food and wine interest.

MANDALAY

100 Greenwich South Street, SE1
081 691 0443

Station Greenwich BR

Bus 1, 180

Open Tues–Sat 1900–2230
Sun 1230–1530

Credit Cards All

Price Range £–££

Type Burmese

There are, apparently, only eight Burmese restaurants in the whole world outside Burma so the advice of the chatty proprietor, Gerald, is most welcome to guide you through the intricacies of his country's cuisine. The menu is well designed and instructive and, usefully, suggests complete meals which combine soup and rice and main dish with vegetables. There is a fair selection of vegetarian dishes. The set menu for Sunday lunch is a good way to sample a number of different dishes, such as oh'n mo hkawk swe, a traditional breakfast dish of egg noodles, chicken broth, coconut, onions, crispy noodles and chicken – well spiced and likely to give you a great start to the day. A tomato consommé comes with the main courses, along with fried cabbage and rice (plain or coconut). Desserts are limited – a semolina cake or mango ice cream. Well worth a journey to south-east London if you can't make it to south-east Asia.

PIZZERIA CASTELLO

20 Walworth Road, SE1 6SP
071 703 2556

Station Elephant and Castle underground

Bus 12, 35, 40, 45, 68, 171, 176

Open Mon–Fri 1200–1430
Mon–Sat 1730–2300

Credit Cards Access, Visa

Price Range £

Type Italian pizzeria

Just by the Elephant and Castle (hence Castello), south London friends have been keeping this one quiet for years. It is within a few minutes' drive of the South Bank theatres and concert halls, so perfect for a post-entertainment pizza or pasta. Be careful if you start with the garlic bread – actually pizza dough oozing with butter and lashings of garlic – it might fill you up before you get to the purpose of your visit. The pizzas are all freshly baked with thick, fluffy bases and very generous toppings, including all the old favourites – Napoletana, margherita, etc, plus a vegetariana (mushrooms, peppers, artichokes, mozzarella, tomatoes and corn) and the house special, a Castellana. Desserts (if you have space) are standard Italian specialities – as is the wine list. The friendly Italian waiters provide speedy and cheerful service, even under the tremendous pressure of Saturday-night hordes. Definitely book if you want a post-theatre pizza. There's a wine bar downstairs which offers (threatens?) music every night.

Street London

There's not a lot to boast about in London's markets today. Despite the long history of street produce markets (Hackney's Hoxton Street market has been on the same site since medieval times), we still don't have anything to compare with the glories of, say, Florence, Toronto, Seattle or Barcelona, let alone Paris, when it comes to selling produce from a barrow.

Berwick Street is definitely the best we have to offer, but even there the choice is limited. The ethnic markets are interesting, but the quality can be dubious.

We detail a few street markets that we have found worth visiting. The following list contains additional recommendations from friends, but don't forget, you need your wits about you to find a bargain: East Street Market, SE17; Kingston Market, Kingston, Surrey; North End Road, SW6; Portobello Road, W11; Tachbrook Street, SW1; Tooting Market, SW17.

Central

BERWICK STREET MARKET

Berwick Street, W1

Station Tottenham Court Road/Oxford Circus/Piccadilly Circus underground

Bus 3, 6, 7, 8, 9, 13, 14, 15, 25

Open Mon–Sat 0900–1700 inc Good Friday and Bank Holiday Mondays

One of London's liveliest street markets with high-quality produce and a good choice of unusual fruit and vegetables. There are often tremendous bargains to be had, shouted out by the stallholders with operatic voice projection. One stall, which is laid out like a geometric pattern – a feast for the eye – has wild mushrooms like chanterelles and pieds de mouton in season. Through a short passage you come to Rupert Street, where there are just a few stalls with especially fine salads and vegetables – pricier than the Berwick Street merchants but worth it for something special, and they might find a particular item for you if necessary. Although officially open at 0900, nothing much happens in Berwick Street before about 1100.

Berwick Street Market

North West

INVERNESS STREET

Camden Town, NW1

Station Camden Town underground

Bus 24, 27, 68, 74, 134, 168

Open Mon–Sat 0900–1700

Mainly fruit and vegetables, but there are other stalls with poultry, cheese, eggs, etc. The quality tends to vary quite a lot from stall to stall so it is worth spending a little time perambulating and inspecting before you buy. Not surprisingly the more reliable merchants always seem to have long queues, especially at weekends when the market has many more stalls. As in so many markets, they are not averse to passing off rubbish and prices are not always remarkably low, but it is certainly an important part of Camden Town life.

SHEPHERD'S BUSH MARKET

Shepherd's Bush, W12

Station Shepherd's Bush/ Goldhawk Road underground

Bus 94, 237

Open Mon–Sat 0900–1700 (half-day closing Thur)

This market stretches from Goldhawk Road to Uxbridge Road and provides a great diversity of stalls and shops. There are a few halal butchers, at least one good fishmonger, shops selling cookware and household goods at reasonable prices. Plus quite a number of fruit and vegetable stalls, many selling food of Caribbean origin as well as Indian and Pakistani. Quality varies but you may find some unusual items. See Moon Foods (page 64) for good ethnic supplies in the middle of this market.

North East

CHAPEL MARKET

Chapel Street, N1

Station Angel underground

Bus 4, 19, 43, 153, 263a, 279

Open Wed–Sat 0800–1830
Tues and Sun 0800–1230

A market full of surprises – from fairly standard fruit and vegetables to the odd stall with a very good selection of salads and another with a variety of mushrooms. You could find fresh herbs and many items not found in ordinary street markets. Definitely worth a look.

RIDLEY ROAD

Ridley Road, E8

Station Dalston Kingsland BR

Bus 22a, 56, 67, 149

Open Mon–Sat 0900–1700 (approx)

A real hotch-potch of a market with food and fashion all jumbled up together. A lot of Afro-Caribbean greengroceries and meat, a smoked salmon stall, fish, and the wonderful bagel shop and Turkish Food Centre (see pages 20 and 67). It looks fairly grotty, but in amongst the mess there's some good food to be found. Round the corner in Winchester Place is a small stall selling tropical produce – aloe vera, soursops, and fresh cactus – indispensable for Mexican cooking. Further along Kingsland Road there's a Turkish baker and a deli.

South West

BRIXTON MARKET

In and around Electric Avenue, Popes Road, Brixton Station Road

Station Brixton underground and BR

Bus 2b, 3a, 12, 45, 59, 109, 133, 159, 250

Open Mon–Sat (inc Good Friday) 0900–1730
Wed 0900–1300

The market rambles around a few streets and to the uninitiated presents some pretty alarming-looking goods. But if you are after West Indian fruit, vegetables like sweet potatoes, yams and unusual peppers, and meat, including violent-coloured pigs' trotters, entrails and scraggy poultry, then this is the place for you. All the Afro-Caribbean favourites are to be found in one or other of the shops and stalls in the area.

See also Robinson's in Granville Arcade, page 69.

South East

DEPTFORD HIGH STREET

Deptford High Street, SE8

Station Deptford BR

Deptford High Street may not be the most beautiful street in London, though the eighteenth-century parish church of St Paul (by Thomas Archer) is worth a visit. For a taste of tropical climes visit the market all along the street, where there are a number of

Bus 1, 188

Open Wed and Sat 0830–
1530

shops and stalls selling West Indian and West African food (for which see Eunice Tropical Food Shop, page 69). If you are looking for coco yams, sweet yams, Brazilian yams or Guyana yams this is the place for you. You might also find bread from a West Indian bakery (all the way from Birmingham), Caribbean drinks or mango or soursop, a tiny pea-like vegetable called sasumba, or a huge jelly nut, dainty bananas or giant plantains and fresh hot peppers. It isn't all exotica in this street though, and there are plenty of ordinary fruit and vegetable stalls.

LEWISHAM MARKET

Lewisham High Street
(outside Lewisham Centre)

Station Lewisham BR

Bus 36b, 47, 54, 122, 181, 208

Open Tues–Sat 0900–1630

In front of the Lewisham Centre, this is not a very large market, but worth knowing if you are in the area and looking for good, well-priced fruit, vegetables and fish. One stall sells Cypriot produce with fresh olives, honey and baby aubergines, and others have West Indian vegetables. There are some great bargains to be had, especially at weekends, and the stall holders are particularly friendly – unlike some other London street markets.

❧ *Capital Caterers* ❧

Everyone loves a party, but not everyone relishes the work it involves. Calling in a caterer to make your celebration go with a swing can be a smart move. Luckily for us, our friends like to party so we've sampled some of the best the catering sorority has to offer. Our favourites, nearly all one-woman bands, are here. For a wider overview we have found *The Perrier London Party Guide* (Nicholson, 1990) to be an excellent vade-mecum for party giving.

Many firms listed offer a catering service in addition to their main business. The following entries from other sections may be of interest: Bagatelle Boutique; Burchell's of Old Isleworth; Careys; Coffee Shak; Culinary Arts; A. Ellinas; Finns; Fulham's Pie and Mash; Giacobazzi; Ivano; Joe & Mary; A. A. King; The Narrow Gauge (Shop); The Orangery; The Pie Man Food Company Limited; Rosslyn Hill Delicatessen; La Touraine; Le Traiteur Français; Westside Caterers.

CLARE'S FARE

96 Archway Street, Barnes, SW13
081 878 4755 (24-hour answerphone)

Cordon Bleu (see page 188) trained Clare Cave started her business twenty-four years ago and has since spent her holidays working in the kitchens of many top chefs, including Raymond Blanc. She has numerous longstanding and loyal clients, including the Duke of Westminster (and some even grander, though her lips are sealed). Her highly trained staff have been with her for years and she can find you a classy venue or a prettily decorated marquee, plus a band, flowers, special effects, anything your heart desires. But the food is the thing Clare is famous for. She will tailor a menu to suit you (vegetarian dishes a speciality). Presentation is guaranteed to please — whether it is a small lunch or dinner (at home or in the boardroom), cocktails for 400, a dance for 500 or a sit-down meal for 150.

RUTH DENNIS CATERING

96 Mortlake Road, Kew
081 876 3830

A personal cook/caterer, Ruth works from home and can help with any type of function and any kind of food (within reason). She excels at small celebrations – dinners, buffets, cocktails and weddings, with a long list of clients who return regularly for her consistently good food.

NATHALIE GRAY

69 Oakhill Road, SW15
081 874 5089

Established for over twenty years, Nathalie works mainly on her own so caters relatively small parties – cocktails for up to 150, dinners up to eighty, plus city lunches. She specialises in Latin American and Peruvian food (she was brought up in Peru), but she will also cook English, Spanish and French food – and anything else too. Among her regular clients are Latin American embassies, associations, banks, etc.

CELIA KEYWORTH

071 267 8872

Celia has a devoted following for her distinctive style and imaginative menus. She's popular with London foodies who know she can pull out all the stops and make a stunning party. Hers is not run-of-the-mill food – Middle Eastern is a speciality and she'll also do Mexican, Italian or whatever theme you wish, all presented on interesting china or in baskets. She has private and corporate clients with varying requirements – buffets, weddings, cocktails – from fifty to 500, but no dinner parties.

NEWINGTONS

081 802 8810

A caterer who cares about her customers is the best description of Sarah Pierce. Her bubbling personality and utter professionalism inspire confidence in her many clients, for whom she will cook intimate dinner parties, business lunches, extravagant wedding feasts or cocktail parties. She loves all those fiddly little items which most of us can't be doing with – as Shirley Conran said, 'Life's too short to stuff a mushroom.' Happily Sarah is on hand to do that for us.

MELANIE PINI

47 Downshire Hill, NW3
071 435 5477

More of a private chef than a caterer. Melanie cooks everything from a lunch for two up to a dinner for 250 or cocktails for 1,000. The food is traditionally French, but sushi is also a speciality. There's great emphasis on presentation. Well-fed clients include Gonzalez Byass, Krug and the Rothschilds.

SARAH RAMSBOTTOM

10 Edith Grove, SW10
071 352 1975

Sarah is the caterer who caters for cookery writers' book-launch parties – so she must be good if she can please professional eaters out and critics. She is a one-woman band (no marquees), so she won't do anything too large – up to 200 for cocktails, 100 for a buffet. She describes her food as a 'broad spectrum' – she can really do anything you wish. Prices are realistic (though not cheap) – 'popular' to quote a satisfied client. She'll travel anywhere within reason (flew to Rome for a wedding) and claims never to have cooked a vol-au-vent in her life. An intuitive cook, professional pride won't let her turn out the standard British party food.

SHAW FOOD

3 Hereford Road, W2
071 229 5079

The two arms of Veronica Shaw's business are Veronica's restaurant and Shaw Food, her catering company. Old and authentic British recipes are what she is best known for (she catered for a big thrash at Hampton Court to celebrate Henry VIII) and she is also very concerned with healthy eating and has a large vegetarian section on her menu. Dishes in the restaurant are marked for low fat, high fibre, etc. She will provide food for a small wedding party or a grand buffet.

❧ Classy Classes ❧

Learning about food, cookery and wine falls into two categories – professional courses and those for the interested amateur. The former are rather thin on the ground whilst there is a better choice in the latter, particularly when it comes to wine.

It is always worth looking at *Floodlight* to see what your local evening institute has by way of cookery classes; many of them now have wine appreciation courses too.

The following entries from other sections may also be of interest for the courses they run in addition to their main business: The Barnes Wine Shop; Celebration Cake Craft; Jeroboams; La Reserve; La Vigneronne.

Central

CHRISTIE, MANSON & WOODS

8 King Street, St James's, SW1
85 Old Brompton Road, SW1
071 839 9060 and 071 581 7611
fax 071 839 7869

Station Green Park/Piccadilly Circus/South Kensington underground

Bus 9, 14, 22, 38

Open Mon–Fri 0900–1730

The name of Christie's is famous in the world of wine for its auctions of fine wines, which are held at the King Street address for high-class wines and at Old Brompton Road for more everyday wines. There's an opportunity to taste before every sale at 1600 (sale at 1700). The firm also runs highly regarded courses on wine. The general wine course (six evening sessions over six weeks) is held two or three times a year. Their master classes, which are held three or four times a year would be just one evening on, say, 'Château Latour'. Phone for details.

LE CORDON BLEU

114 Marylebone Lane, W1
071 935 3503
fax 071 935 7621

Station Bond Street
underground

Bus 2a, 2b, 13, 18, 27, 38,
74, 113, 159

Founded in 1933 by Rosemary Hume, a graduate of Le Cordon Bleu Paris, the London Cordon Bleu has taught generations how to cook Beef Wellington and hazelnut meringue gâteau. Now under co-ownership with the Paris school, it has undergone a major refurbishment (there's even air-conditioning), with four professionally equipped kitchens (and special baking/ boulangerie and pastry kitchens) and two demonstration rooms, heralding a move away from the domestic cookers of yesteryear. They will be offering a variety of courses and aim to teach career cooks as well as interested amateurs. Students can gain work experience in hotel/restaurant kitchens or transfer to the school in Paris. The good news is Sarah Nops is still Principal.

LEITH'S SCHOOL OF FOOD AND WINE

21 St Alban's Grove, W8
071 229 0177

Station Kensington High
Street underground

Bus 10, 27, 28, 31, 49

Leith's courses are amazingly wide ranging and there is something to please almost everyone seeking first-class training in all aspects of food and wine. The three-term diploma course can be taken as a whole or as beginners, intermediate and advanced. This is serious stuff – with demo and lecture and practical class every day for up to eleven weeks, plus homework. Participants are offered careers advice, along with pâtisserie, Middle Eastern cooking, restaurant cooking, butchery and many other useful skills. Students go into restaurants or freelance catering. The courses are eligible for career development loans. There are one- to four-week holiday courses (for interested amateurs) and also one-week special courses (e.g. low fat or Italian cooking). Some evening classes are 'hands on'; Saturday mornings are demonstrations. Wine-tasting classes and restaurant management are just a couple more courses at this enterprising organisation.

KEN LO'S MEMORIES OF CHINA COOKERY SCHOOL

14 Eccleston Street, SW1
071 730 4276/7734

Station Victoria underground
and BR

Bus 11, 239, C1

This is the only Chinese cookery school in Europe and, amazingly, septuagenarian Ken Lo, the maestro Chinese chef, is still teaching, along with chef But, the top chef at Ken's Memories of China restaurant, Deh-Ta Hsiung, Terry Tan (Thai cooking), Madam Fei (demonstrating her famous Peking duck) and others. There are demonstration classes and the evening ones include a sumptuous meal afterwards. Occasionally 'Dishes from Sarawak' are taught. Sarawak is part of Malaysia, the food is a mixture of Chinese, Malay, Nonya and Indian cuisines. All these classes are very good value (especially those with dinner).

*Deb-Ta Hsiung in Ken
Lo's kitchen*

SOTHEBY'S WINE DEPARTMENT

Unit 5, Albion Wharf,
Hester Road, SW11
071 924 3287
fax 071 924 3110

Station for seminars Bond
Street underground

Bus 6, 7, 8, 10, 12, 13, 15,
113, 135, 159

Open Mon–Fri 0900–1700

Sotheby's wine seminars (held at their London sale-room) – a course of six evenings – don't lead to a qualification but are for fun and information. The tutored tastings, chaired by Master of Wine Serena Sutcliffe, are often run by a château owner who talks about his/her own wines in depth. Phone or write for details. As you would expect from this famous auction house, Sotheby's holds about eight wine sales a year – phone 071 924 3287 for details, with pre-sale tastings. Mainly fine and rare wines, vintage port, fine names, fine prices. You can also buy a vineyard with the help of Sotheby's.

North West

BETSY'S KITCHEN

3 St James's Gardens, W11
071 603 3907

Betsy Newell is an American who has lived in France and Italy (and is now involved, together with London-based food writer Anna del Conte, in a cookery school at her Tuscan estate). These various influences are to be found in her cookery classes in London, where she runs 'hands on' sessions in her kitchen for up to ten people on Tuesday and Thursday mornings. They cook and then eat lunch, which might be formal dinner-party food or more simple healthy family food. Phone to ask about both London and Italian courses.

GILLIAN BURR

071 586 0156

Here's a brave lady – Gillian has been teaching kosher cookery for some years in her own kitchen in St John's Wood. Among her most devoted clientele are children aged from nine up to teenagers. She also has classes for young people about to go out into the world, as well as young brides (how about the grooms, we ask?). Courses are for four sessions 'hands on', so the small groups are able to come to grips with the intricacies of making cholla (twisted bread loaves), soups and main dishes. Classes for 'grown ups' are geared towards dinner-party food, with presentation an important adjunct to the cooking. Phone for details.

COOKING AT THE CHANTRY

The Chantry, Spaniards
End, NW3
081 455 0200

Station Golders Green
underground + bus

Bus 210

Ley Zeff is a confident, generous and very hospitable cook whose students sit around her kitchen work area and watch her put together a three-course meal. Ley runs her six-week courses on Thursday mornings in her beautiful Hampstead home. You arrive for a cup of coffee at 1030 then watch, discuss, question, while the menu takes shape. Ley describes the food as 'eclectic' – Italian, French, Middle Eastern – the common thread being that everything can be prepared in advance. At one o'clock you sit down to eat the fruits of Ley's labours – and very elegant and delicious they are. For good cooks who want some inspiration, it's not cheap, but you can learn a lot and it's fun, but serious too.

CULINARY ARTS

081 883 3799

Nadine Abensur runs vegetarian cookery classes in north London with three-day 'hands-on' courses, from beginners up to chef's standards. Food is very classy – not the 'Bulgar burgers' variety. It's highly colourful, imaginative and very tasty, with a lot of Moroccan influences. She only takes eight people at a time so it is intimate and highly personal. Nadine also caters weddings and other parties big and small anywhere in London and the home counties. Phone for details.

South West

JULIE CAMERON

32 Rusholme Road, SW15
081 788 5500

Highly intensive, practical beginners' courses of one or two weeks, for a maximum of ten people which teach from complete basics to making a soufflé. There are also demonstrations for dinner-party cookery

Station East Putney
underground

Bus 37

THE FULHAM ROAD WINE TASTING COURSES

899–960 Fulham Road,
SW6
071 736 7009

Station Parsons Green/Putney
Bridge underground

Bus 14

THE GRAPE CONNECTION

17 Ham Common,
Richmond, Surrey
081 940 7576

South East

B. R. MATHEWS

12 Gypsy Hill, SE19
081 670 0788

Station Gypsy Hill BR

Bus 2, 137

Open Tues and Fri 0930–
1700
Sat 0930–1400

(which include lunch with wine) and 'Chalet girl' courses in the autumn. Julie, who has been running her school for more than seven years, also does specialist day courses – fish, sauces or whatever.

Apart from the regular wine tastings which this enterprising outfit offers in the shop, it also runs highly regarded courses in its purpose-built basement. The stated aim is to make wine fun and their team of tutors represents some of the country's best Masters of Wine and experts in their fields. 'Understanding Italy', 'What's My Wine', 'A Vinous Mousetrap' are just a few of the courses in the programme.

This enterprising company has evolved a brilliant system for making sense of wine by simplifying wine lists and wine shelves. Peter Noble has a lifetime's experience of wine and passes on his knowledge together with a talented team of experts. They preach that it's the grape and not the country that dictates our taste and their courses, in central London, aim to expand knowledge of wine through that principle.

Established for over 100 years as a bakers' sundriesman, now that bakeries are mechanised Mathews relies on its mail-order business and shop, selling everything the professional or amateur baker and cake decorator needs for cake decorating as well as making/baking. Their cake-decorating courses are very popular and highly regarded in the cake world. There is a wide range of courses, everything from beginner up to exhibition level. Prices are very reasonable too. Teacher Tombi Peck, the leading cake specialist decorator in the world, teaches three-day courses. Brenda Purton takes royal-icing day courses.

Enquire Within

Unlike newspapers in North America which produce weekly food supplements, we are ill served in this regard, apart from some excellent regular Saturday features in the quality press. Listings of food events are erratic, but perhaps our motley collection of sources of information on food and eating matters will be helpful. We are lucky to have one specialist bookshop for food books, but thanks to the interest in cookbooks, whether for reading or gifts or even using them, most of the major bookstores can put up a reasonable show. Hatchards, Dillons and Waterstone's are usually happy to help.

The following entries from other sections may also be of interest when seeking information about food or drink: Chelsea Physic Garden; Cornucopia Health Food; Japan Centre; Neal Street East; The Tea House; Wild Oats; Wholefood.

Central

DAUNT BOOKS

83 Marylebone High Street, W1
071 224 2295

Station Baker Street underground

Bus 2a, 2b, 13, 18, 27, 30, 74, 113, 159

Open Mon–Sat 0900–1930

Primarily a bookshop for travellers, there's also a select choice of cookbooks. The shelves are divided by countries, and along with the guidebooks and maps there are books to give a flavour of the literature and cuisine of each – ideal for research or planning an itinerary. Informed staff are very helpful.

DINING BY NUMBERS

Central London 0839 200051
Inner London 0839 200052

Dial one of the given numbers and you get through to this original service, which advises you on where to eat. There are five areas within each section, eleven cuisines and three price ranges and after listening to a fair amount of chat you will possibly make a

Outer London 0839 200053

choice and even have the chance to make a reservation. It's a fairly painless (but possibly expensive) way to find a restaurant.

ENTERTAINMENT

25 Bruges Place, Randolph Street, NW1
071 482 1115

Membership of this American-inspired 'leading leisure discount programme', which has been in existence for more than thirty years, entitles you to dine at a discount in hundreds of different restaurants in London ranging from short order to fine dining. There are also savings on hotels, theatres and other events, and an international network to save you money when travelling. Well worth the £50 or so for annual membership if you eat out a lot and travel a bit.

THE GUILDHALL LIBRARY

Guildhall, EC2
071 606 3030

Station Bank underground

Bus 6, 8, 9, 11, 15b, 76, 133, 149, 214, X15

Open Mon–Sat 0930–1700 (restricted on Sat)

The Guildhall library has its own collection of books related to food, some of which came from the Cooks' Company (one of the City's ancient livery companies). It also holds the André Simon collection of books on wine and food and the Masters of Wine's collection. More recently it has acquired the food and cookery books of the late Jane Grigson. The library is open to the public, but you have to order what you want to see through the catalogue, in a system similar to the British Library's. That means a short wait, rather than browsing along the shelves.

MEET 'N' EAT LIMITED (AND SOIREES)

28a Seymour Place, W1
071 629 5534
fax 071 495 0131

In spite of the advert, reading 'How many times have you wondered if all the really stimulating people have disappeared off the face of the earth? Would you like to meet a new circle of friends but don't know where to find them?' the organisers of this dinner-party club for business people insist that it is absolutely NOT a dating agency. Indeed, most members seem to go just for a good dinner with entertaining company. Annual subscription is around £52 plus VAT and events include dinner at Le Gavroche (see page 161) for £100, a lecture on stress management, £25; a Saturday cookery lesson and lunch with a three-star chef from France, £50. Restaurants, usually in central London, might be an Italian bistro one week, a Chinese banquet at the Inn of Happiness (see page 163) the next, or American Japanese (Benihana). Prices vary from £25 up and include VAT, service and several glasses of wine.

Soirées is run by the same outfit and is probably London's only restaurant club for gay men catering for business executives and professionals who want a fun evening with a good dinner and lively conversation. Dinners held in private rooms in restaurants and hotels.

MEXICOLORE

28 Warriner Gardens, SW11
071 622 9577
fax 071 498 0173

Station Battersea Park BR

Bus 44, 170

Open Phone to check

For your next Mexican fiesta, here's the place to go. This enterprising outfit provides a range of services, educational, fun, food – anything and everything to do with Mexico. They visit schools and colleges, community arts centres, etc, etc, with their music, dance, drama and can supply ready-cooked frozen Mexican meals (free delivery within ten-mile range for orders over £15). They come from La Mexicana Quality Foods run by Lourdes Nichols and you can have burritos, enchilada, refried beans, anything you fancy. Mexican cooking utensils are in there with the ponchos and piñatas – phone for details.

RESTAURANT SWITCHBOARD

081 888 8080

Open Mon–Sat 0900–2000

A free information and advisory service which has been going for over twelve years. It has updated lists for all restaurants in London cross-indexed for area, price, type. It contributes to the *Good Food Guide* and *Time Out* and relies on critics and satisfied customers for advice. This is a personal service, with information given instantly, or within twenty-four hours for more complicated requests, such as where to find dinner for up to 2,000.

SCIENCE MUSEUM

Exhibition Road, SW7
071 938 8111/8008/8080

Station South Kensington underground

Bus 9, 10, 14, 30, 52, 74, C1

Open Sun–Sat 1000–1800
Sun 1100–1800

The Food for Thought Gallery, sponsored by Sainsbury, has displays on the science of food and modern eating habits, and 'specials'. It is just as interesting for adults as children and there are excellent resource packs available for teachers. The special sets include a Sainsbury's shop from the 1920s, a 1950s coffee bar, a 1926 Lyon's Corner House (with 'Nippy') to illustrate the changes in 'eating out'. There's a smellerama which shows how human senses affect perceptions of food. Other exhibits show food in the home and in the factory, food and the body (additives and hygiene), trading, and food and society. Entry charge up to 1600 – free thereafter.

North West

BOOKS FOR COOKS

4 Blenheim Crescent, W11
071 221 1992

Station Ladbroke Grove
underground

Bus 15, 52, 52a

Open Mon–Sat 0930–1800

This is, without doubt, THE place for everyone who is addicted to buying cookery books. Amongst the 5,000 titles always in stock you can find all the most recently published books, as well as many old cookery books, and 'wants lists' are welcomed if you are searching for something particular. There is a big section of international cookbooks – from the United States, Germany, Australia, France and many other countries. An extra bonus is the enthusiasm and knowledge of Heidi Lascelles and her second-in-command, Clarissa Dickson Wright, who are always ready to advise and discuss. There is a small demonstration/test kitchen at the back of the shop where guest chefs frequently come to cook and/or launch their new books, from Elizabeth David down. Excellent, well-made coffee, cake and light lunches are always available. They have a mail order service and all purchases can be posted for you. All credit cards accepted.

North East

WOOD STREET LIBRARY

Forest Road, E17
081 521 1070

Station Walthamstow Central
underground and BR + bus
and Wood Street BR

Bus 123, 275

Open Mon–Tues 1000–2000
Fri 1000–1730 Sat 1000–1700
Closed Wed–Thur

This branch of Waltham Forest libraries holds the London libraries' collection of cookery books. It may be a long way to go, so phone first to check your journey won't be wasted.

Food on Wheels

Once upon a time it would not have been at all remarkable to have a paragraph about food which is delivered to your home. Now it is the rare enthusiasts who are prepared to bring their wares to you. We have enjoyed meeting a few of them and we hope you will too.

We have not listed all firms which deliver, though it can be assumed the larger stores offer this service. The following entries from other sections may also be of interest: Aroma; Birley's Sandwich Bars; M. J. Bradleys; Brunel; Food Parcels; Katie's of Mayfair; Markus Coffee Company; Mexicolore; Monmouth Coffee House; The Narrow Gauge (Shop); The Wren Café.

THE FRESH FISH COMPANY

100 Bayswater Road, W2
tel and fax 071 402 5414

Thoby Young is passionate about fish and declares that the best and freshest fish in Britain comes from Cornwall, where the waters are the cleanest. As he puts it poetically, 'The small fishing boats are the past of our fishing industry, but also the future.' His business is to bring that fish to your doorstep, at the drop of a phone call. He sells no frozen, farmed or imported products, only what he can buy in Cornwall. It's a service which is market oriented so he can't quote prices until the day as that depends on what's available. A fixed-price delivery charge for small orders makes it well worth while splitting a delivery amongst a few friends. Phone him to discuss his piscatorial pursuits and to find out about the ever-expanding range of fine foods he can deliver through his Fresh Food Catalogue. Payment by Visa or Access.

GIDEON'S

081 346 5652

Early each morning Gideon is to be found at Covent Garden market choosing organic fruit and vegetables – 'Nothing old or tatty.' He only buys enough for the day's orders, ensuring freshness, no waste and exceptional standards. When he started his delivery service he had his hatchback car and his enthusiasm for fresh produce. Now he has eight employees and four vans – which says as much for his entrepreneurial skills as it does for the growth of interest in organic foods. He makes up boxes of whatever produce is best that day, so his customers never know exactly what they will receive. He delivers from north London to Parsons Green in the south and Hackney in the east, and plans to expand further afield.

RICHARD HART

081 876 3955

What's that old line about buying something from a used car salesman? Richard Hart has been delivering fresh coffee (beans and ground) all around central London for more than fifteen years, but his other business is dealing in used cars. Many of his clients are business firms (to whom he gives a free coffee machine) and he has recently created a new blend, Directors, which he felt was useful for offices where people may have differing tastes. He carries an extensive range of fine coffees – Italian continental roast (made from top-quality arabica beans), Kenya AA and peaberry, Colombian, mocha, blue mountain blend and others. His is a very personal service – he'll supply machines, filters, descalers and will even pop in and repair your machine.

SARA JAYNE

071 228 9068

Sara Jayne's truffles are handmade, only with the best possible ingredients – Devon cream and the finest French couverture – which explains the price. But connoisseurs of the truffle are happy to indulge their passions. There are ten varieties, including calvados, cognac, clementine, crème de menthe, crushed almonds, and fudge. Sara will do her best to deliver to you – or you can find them at Les Spécialités St Quentin and Careys (see pages 118 and 121). Phone to discuss delivery.

THE NARROW GAUGE

PO Box 34, SW15 2UB
tel and fax 081 877 1234

Kate Catleugh conceived the idea of gourmet low-calorie meals and took it to the appropriate medical boffins for their opinions. Given a stamp of approval for their nutritional content, she went ahead with her development chef to create a comprehensive range of dishes which can constitute a complete diet programme. These meals can be delivered daily on a regular two-week cycle to your home or office and provide a painless and delicious way of following a calorie-controlled regime – no temptations since you can opt out of cooking and shopping for the duration. It's a lot cheaper than going to a health farm and you can carry on your life as normal. These dishes are also available at The Narrow Gauge shop in the City (see page 133–4) and at selected Europa supermarkets (phone The Narrow Gauge for details).

NATURAL FOODS LIMITED

081 539 1034

The answer to an organic shopper's prayer – a huge range of organic foods delivered to your door – all over Greater London. Fruit and vegetables, all organically produced, mostly organic meat, all organic cheese, organic bread baked daily – everything you'd find in a good shop, without the bother of lugging it home. They're constantly expanding their range – everyone wants fresh fish so that should be swimming your way soon. No minimum order but a small charge, irrespective of size. The catalogue is user friendly.

PAT PIGGOTT

0472 884683

Three times each week Pat Piggott does a punishing twenty-four-hour day, starting at the fish market in Grimsby. After preparing his van and packing it with the day's stock, he drives four hours to north London and starts his rounds, finishing in the late evening. He then drives home to Grimsby. If you are fortunate enough to live in his catchment area – Highgate, Hampstead, Hendon, Finchley or St John's Wood, you could telephone him and ask him to call by with his mobile fish shop. He'll have on board the freshest fish – whatever the North Sea has yielded the night before. Prices are competitive and he's very helpful. If you need a whole lot of anything for a party he'll organise that for you, and his delivery time can be fairly flexible.

RUFIES

15 Clapham High Street, SW4
071 720 0633

Station Clapham North underground and Clapham High Street BR

Bus 45a, 88, 155, 355, N87

Open Sun–Sat 1200–0200

Indian food to take away, or they'll deliver locally for a minimum order of £5, with a dozen or more main courses (including mutton masala on Fridays) and vegetarian or non-vegetarian lunch-boxes. This is a well-kept shop with appetising food.

☙ *Ethnic London* ❧

London has always been a trading port with a long tradition of receiving visitors from around the globe. Those who stayed have added to the tapestry that is London and have made it an exotic melting pot in so many ways, not least gastronomically.

Almost no aspect of our book is untouched by some ethnic influence and is, we are in no doubt, the richer for it. As they are scattered throughout the book we have brought them all together here for quick cross-reference.

Perambulating round London we have observed how ethnic markets and shops often provide good value and choice, and it is hard to escape the fact that the majority of the restaurants we list serve ethnic food, which is no surprise since value for money is one of our prime criteria. Soho used to be predominantly Franco/Italian, but Chinatown is now a well-defined quarter there. Green Lanes in Haringey starts at Newington Green as mainly Turkish and becomes more Greek as it goes along. The more you look the more you see and frequent visitors can distinguish the differences as well as the similarities.

Ealing is a great mix of Poles, Greeks, Iranians, Armenians – all reflected in the variety of food shops and restaurants in this sprawling suburb. Due north is Ealing Road, Wembley, which on a sunny Saturday could as well be Bombay with its gorgeous saree shops, the smell of the spices and displays of exotic fruit and vegetables, which seem more fitting here than in a chilly supermarket.

Huguenots, Jews and Bangladeshis have all found shelter in the area around Brick Lane. What was once a church for the resident silk weavers and then a synagogue is now a mosque. In the shops the pickled herring barrels have been replaced by halal meat counters and samosas are now sold instead of latkes.

West Africans can find a taste of home in Deptford market and West Indians will travel across town to Brixton for saltfish, colourful and curious cuts of meat, mangoes and much besides.

At Henley's Corner in north-west London there's a delightful cross-cultural link, with Uncle Ian's deli diner rubbing shoulders with a Japanese mini-market and more Japanese shops are concentrated in Brewer Street. Edgware Road is the summer home to many from the Middle East, coming to life at night, with its pavement cafés and hubble-bubble pipes. The writer Penelope Lively's description of London is so apt: 'thousands of mirages – Caribbean islands and Indian villages and shimmering intense snatches of Turkey or Greece or Poland. The place is not just itself, it is a reflection of the rest of the globe.'

Afghan
Buzkash Afghan Restaurant

Afro-Caribbean
Bambaya
Brixton Market
Brixtonian
Cecil's Bakery
Deptford High Street
Lewisham Market
Margaret's
Moon Foods
Ridley Road Market
Robinson's
Shepherd's Bush Market

Austrian
Austrian Sausage Centre

Chinese
Chinatown Fish and Meat Market
Golden Chopsticks
Inn of Happiness
Joy King Lau
Ken Lo's Memories of China Cookery
   School
Loon Fung Supermarket
Matahari
Moon Foods
Neal Street East
New World
Wing Yip

French
Bagatelle Boutique
Boucherie Lamartine
Cannelle

Four Seasons, The, Inn on the Park
Gavroche, Le
Gourmet Gascon, Le
Hippocampe, L'
Magno's Brasserie
Maison Bouquillon
Specialités St Quentin, Les
Tante Claire, La
Tarte Julie
Terrace Garden, Le Meridien, Piccadilly
   Hotel
Traiteur Français, Le
Villandry

Greek
A & C Co
Adamou
Andrea's
Au Gourmet Grec
Ellinas, A,
Lewisham Market
Michli, Andreas, & Son
Milia, Chris
Moon Foods
Olympic Bakers Pâtisserie
Paul's

Hungarian
Louis Pâtisserie

Indian
Ambala
Brixton Market
Chutney Mary
Chutneys
Deepak Cash & Carry Grocers
Everfresh Limited
Fudgo

Majjo's Food
Nature's Delight
Popat Store
Rani
Rufies
Sima Tandoori
Superfresh Limited
V. B. & Sons
Vijay Indian Restaurant
Viniron

Iranian
Joe & Mary
Westside Caterers

Italian
Angelucci Coffee Merchants
Arts Theatre Café
Barretta, Philip
Camisa, I., & Son
Carluccio's
Ciaccio
Coffee Gallery, The
Da Giuliano
Delicatessen Shop, The
Delicatessen Piacenza
Di Lieto
Fabrizi
Florians
Fratelli
Fratelli Camisa
Gallo Nero
Gazzano, G., and Son Limited
Giacobazzi
Institute of Contemporary Arts
Lina Stores
Luigi's Delicatessen
Luigi's Euroteca
Olga Stores
Pizzeria Castello
Riva
Salumeria, La
Salumeria Estense
Terroni, L.
Versilia Restaurant

Japanese
Hamine
Ikkyu
Japan Centre
Matahari
Neal Street East
Simpson (Piccadilly) Ltd
Wing Yip
Yoshino

Jewish
Amazing Grapes
Beigal Bake, The
Burr, Gillian
Carmelli Bakeries
Corney, J. A., Limited
Daniel's Bagel Bakery
Hendon Bagel Bakery
Panzer Delicatessen Limited
Platters
Ridley Hot Bagel Bakery
Rogg, J.
Stoller, Sam, & Son
Uncle Ian's

Latin American
Nathalie Gray

Mexican
Mexicolore

Middle Eastern
Green Valley, The
Moon Foods
Ranoush
Al Sultan

North American
Harrods (West Side Express)
Kenny's
Panzer Delicatessen Limited
Savoy, The (American Cocktail Bar)

Polish
Belsize Village Delicatessen
Daquise
Gourmet Grec, Au
Grove Gallery, The
Parade Delicatessen

Ealing Road, Wembley

Portuguese
A & C Co
Belsize Village Delicatessen
Lisboa Delicatessen
Lisboa Pâtisserie
Mimma

South-East Asian
Mandalay
Matahari
Moon Foods
Tawana Oriental Supermarket

Southern African
Emory St Marcus
Grahams Butchers

Spanish
Garcia, R., & Sons
Maison Bouquillon
Meson Don Felipe
Rebatos
Remos, Los

Thai
Bedlington Café
Churchill Arms, The
Talad Thai
Tawana Oriental Supermarket
Thai Garden
Thai Garden, The

Tunisian
Adam's Café

Turkish
01 Adana
Aziz Baba Deli Pastahanesi
Camlik
Marmara
Ridley Road Market
Turkish Food Centre
Yasar Halim

West African
Charlie's West African Food Shop
Deptford High Street
Eunice Tropical Food Shop

Index